MONETARY CONDITIONS FOR ECONOMIC RECOVERY

FINANCIAL AND MONETARY POLICY STUDIES

volume 11

MONETARY CONDITIONS FOR ECONOMIC RECOVERY

For a list of the volumes in this series see final page of the volume.

MONETARY CONDITIONS FOR ECONOMIC RECOVERY

Edited by

C. van Ewijk and J.J. Klant
University of Amsterdam

1985 **MARTINUS NIJHOFF PUBLISHERS**
a member of the KLUWER ACADEMIC PUBLISHERS GROUP
DORDRECHT / BOSTON / LANCASTER

Distributors

for the United States and Canada: Kluwer Academic Publishers, 190 Old Derby Street, Hingham, MA 02043, USA
for the UK and Ireland: Kluwer Academic Publishers, MTP Press Limited, Falcon House, Queen Square, Lancaster LA1 1RN, UK
for all other countries: Kluwer Academic Publishers Group, Distribution Center, P.O. Box 322, 3300 AH Dordrecht, The Netherlands

Library of Congress Cataloging in Publication Data

ISBN 90-247-3219-0 (this volume)
ISBN 90-247-2605-0 (series)

PRINTED IN THE NETHERLANDS

CONTENTS

Preface   VII

List of contributors   IX

Opening Address by
W.F. Duisenberg   1

Introduction by
C. van Ewijk   7

PART I   NATIONAL MONETARY POLICIES

1. What role for monetary policy today?
   A.Lamfalussy   21

2. US monetary policy in recent years: an overview.
   S.H. Axilrod   39

3. Monetary control: the British experience.
   C.A.E. Goodhart   59

4. Monetary control: the German experience.
   H. Schlesinger   85

5. Monetary control: the Dutch experience.
   M.M.G. Fase   95

PART II   INTERNATIONAL MONETARY COORDINATION

6. International monetary policy to promote economic recovery.
   W.H. Buiter   129

7. European monetary cooperation and financial stability.
   P. de Grauwe   161

8. The optimal exchange rate system and its significance for
   economic recovery.
   H. Jager   187

9. Policies and responsibilities of the International Monetary Fund:
   back to basics
   T. de Vries   221

PART III   MONETARY CONDITIONS FOR ECONOMIC RECOVERY

10. Lessons of the monetarist experiment.

    N. Kaldor   243

11. The significance of recent experience with monetary policy
    in shaping future economic policy.

    P. Korteweg   263

12. Monetary conditions for economic recovery:
    the Dutch perspective.

    G.A. Kessler   279

13. Monetary conditions for economic recovery:
    the international perspective.

    E. van Lennep   313

PREFACE

An international symposium on Monetary Conditions for Economic Recovery was organised in Amsterdam from 14-16 November 1984 by the Department of Macroeconomics, Faculty of Economics of the University of Amsterdam, to honour its distinguished member, Professor G.A. Kessler, who had recently retired from his Chair of Monetary Economics. Experts on monetary theory and monetary policy from various parts of the world took part in the discussions on both the theoretical and practical aspects of the theme. The papers have been collected in this volume.

Our debts in organizing the symposium and preparing this volume for publication are many. The symposium was financed through the support of a number of sponsors whose names have been listed on the next page. The Netherlands Bank accommodated the conference sessions. The organizing Committee owes much to the successful efforts of its members Jean Morreau, Casper van Ewijk and Annette Deckers. We are grateful to the President of the Netherlands Bank for his introductory speech on the work of Professor Kessler, which is included in this volume. Wouter Zant assisted in editing the volume for publication. Most of all we indebted to the participants for their contributions and their cooperation in revising their manuscripts. They profited from the comments of the invited discussants: J.A.H. de Beaufort Wijnholds, E.J. Bomhoff, E. den Dunnen, H. de Haan, S.K. Kuipers, Th. Peeters, J.L. Schneider, J.C. Siebrand, P. Stek, J.J. Sijben, H.J. Witteveen and all the other guests who took part in the discussions.

University of Amsterdam   J.J. Klant

June 1985   Chairman Organizing Committee

SPONSORS

Faculty of Economics, University of Amsterdam

Netherlands Organization for the Advancement of Pure Research (ZWO)

De Nederlandsche Bank N.V.

Algemene Bank Nederland N.V.

Amsterdam - Rotterdam Bank N.V.

Amsterdamse Effectenbeurs (Vereniging voor de Effectenhandel)

Bank der Bondsspaarbanken N.V.

Bank Mees & Hope N.V.

Banque Paribas Nederland N.V.

Banque de Suez Nederland N.V.

Investering Maatschappij Nederland Financial Services B.V.

Kas-Associatie N.V.

Koninklijke Luchtvaart Maatschappij N.V.

F. van Lanschot Bankiers N.V.

Nationale Investeringsbank N.V.

Nationale-Nederlanden N.V.

Nederlandsche Middenstandsbank N.V.

Philips International B.V.

Pierson, Heldring & Pierson N.V.

Postgiro - Rijkspostspaarbank

Rabobank Nederland

Shell Nederland B.V.

Staal Stichting 1966

LIST OF CONTRIBUTORS

Editors

C. van Ewijk, Lecturer in Economics, University of Amsterdam;

J.J. Klant, Emeritus Professor of Economics, University of Amsterdam.

Authors

S.H. Axilrod, Staff Director for Monetary and Financial Policy, Board of Governors of the Federal Reserve System;

W.H. Buiter, Professor of Economics, London School of Economics;

W.F. Duisenberg, President of De Nederlandsche Bank;

M.M.G. Fase, Assistent Deputy Director, De Nederlandsche Bank and Extraordinary Professor of Economics, Erasmus University Rotterdam;

C.A.E. Goodhart, Chief Adviser, Bank of England;

P. de Grauwe, Professor of Economics, Catholic University of Louvain;

H. Jager, Professor of Economics, University of Amsterdam;

N. Kaldor, Emeritus Professor of Economics, King's College Cambridge;

P. Korteweg, Treasurer General, Ministry of Finance, The Netherlands;

A. Lamfalussy, Assistent General Manager and Economic Adviser, Bank for International Settlements;

E. van Lennep, Former Secretary-General, Organisation for Economic Cooperation and Development (OECD);

H. Schlesinger, Vice-President, Deutsche Bundesbank;

T. de Vries, Alternate Executive Director, International Monetary Fund and Visiting Professor, John Hopkins University;

OPENING ADDRESS
in honour of Professor G.A. Kessler

W.F. Duisenberg

We are gathered here today in honour of Professor Kessler, whose official academic carreer is coming to an end. Although, as many present are aware, this does not mean that he feels the time has come to discontinue his activities in the economic field, today's conference provides a perfect opportunity to say a few words about his work, at least his published work. I will attempt to set out the mainstreams of his thinking, without adhering to their chronological sequence or going into too much detail.

Those who wish to find out more about Kessler's scientific work, will soon discover that his extensive monograph on monetary equilibrium and balance-of-payments equilibrium, which appeared in 1958, is a must. For generations of students, including myself, this book was compulsory reading.

The organization of the book into three parts gives an indication not only of its contents, but also and especially, of Kessler's penchant for systematics: his predilection to start with basic truths. The first part of the book is about monetary equilibrium in a closed economy, the second deals with the concept of balance-of-payments equilibrium, and the third gives a synthesis of the two preceding parts under the heading of monetary equilibrium and balance-of-payments equilibrium in an open economy.

I find it is well-nigh impossible to do justice to the profusion of theories contained in this book. That is why I have made a small selection of ideas which crop up regularly in Kessler's later work. In the first place a vital rôle is played in Kessler's thinking by a disturbance of the circular flow in the economy and its monetary guises. (Today, over 25 years later, Kessler seems to have lost none of this ardour for equilibrium in the circular flow of the economy). This is a sequel to the ideas of professor J.G. Koopmans on neutral money or monetary equilibrium. In the wake of Koopmans and the then President of the Netherlands Bank, Dr. Holtrop, Kessler based his theories on the simple truth that, for the economy as a whole, the algebraic total of money creation, dishoarding, liquidity destruction and hoarding comes out at nil. This is an *ex post* tautology (or equation balance) which comes to life only in an *ex ante* context. In this view, a monetary disturbance arises when this *ex post* equality is obtained by means of induced "residual item financing". This definition can be applied only when it becomes clear which inflationary or deflationary financing is spontaneous and which is induced. This may subsequently help to localize and neutralize or prevent the monetary impulses which "cause" the disturbance.

The question whether inflationary or deflationary financing is a reaction or an impulse, crops up frequently in Kessler's work. Impulses occur when there are deviations from "normal" behaviour, while there is – in Kessler's opinion – normal behaviour when the flows of liquidity – or in other words the circular flow – is not interrupted. Thus a monetary interpretation is attempted of the main economic phenomena in the real sector of the economy. With this theory Kessler ventures on the slippery domain of causality, a topic which was given much attention in the seventies by economists who were interested in the question whether "money matters" (e.g. Federal Reserve Bank of St. Louis; discussion on Granger-Sims causuality and endogeneity). Kessler has always clearly stated his views on this matter. Where Keynes and his early post-war disciples laid emphasis on budgetary policy as an equilibrating force, Kessler in his book stresses the requirement of monetary equilibrium and the importance of monetary policy as a means to achieve economic equilibrium where full employment is achieved as nearly as possible. These ideas were later integrated in the mainstream of economic thinking[1].

(1) An illustration provides the work of two dyed-in-the-wool Keynesians such as A. Blinder and R. Solow, who co-authored an article "Does Fiscal Policy Matter?", published in the Journal of Public Economics (1973), pp. 319-337.

Many of the problems broached by Kessler in his book were later studied extensively and in great detail in the literature. A subject that has (sofar) been insufficiently discussed in the literature is the way different methods of public financing affect the money and capital markets, and their impact on interest rate movements and monetary stability. Kessler was right when he asserted that such problems can be brought to light only by means of monetary assessment and that monetary theory has a much greater rôle to play in this context than Keynes, or rather Keynes' disciples, assumed.

Several of Kessler's original views can be found again in his later work as for example in his introduction to "Money in an open economy" (1972), which contains the selected writings by Dr. Holtrop. His paper on monetary indicators (1974), and to a lesser extent, the monograph published by the University of Amsterdam in 1983 on the conditions for economic recovery, which deals with employment in a stagnating economy, also contain elements of his earlier thinking.

A remarkable feature of much of Kessler's work is his neglect of measurement or quantification of the economic relations described. This is surprising because even at the time of writing his major book, such was not unknown, as illustrated by e.g. Tobin's work on the demand for money and on economic growth and monetary expansion[1]. In support of his qualitative approach, Kessler puts forward the argument that it is (well-nigh) impossible to model expectations, a theme which is, incidentally, very modern. However, the assertion that Kessler preferred qualitative analysis must immdiately be followed by the remark that, on occasion, he liked to use macroeconomic statistics to support or illustrate his case. He also encouraged economists of a younger generation - especially in the past decade - to examine economic relationships econometrically, at the same time warning them not to become prisoners of their own products.

A personal highlight in Kessler's career as an economic scientist was undoubtedly his inaugural address delivered at the University of

(1) See J. Tobin (1956), "The interest-elasticity of transactions demand for cash", *Review of Economics and Statistics*; J. Tobin (1955): "A dynamic aggregative model", *Journal of Political Economy*.

Amsterdam in 1963. This discourse on money and society included Kessler's views on the so-called Radcliffe report "On the working of the monetary system". In my opinion, part of his comment is still valid today because it concerns the age-old problem of how to choose the best monetary aggregate. In his address, Kessler said that the Radcliffe committee had expanded British monetary thought, but that, in doing so, it had lost sight of the essence of monetary phenomena. It had consequently arrived at wrong and – from the point of view of policy – ineffective conclusions. In Kessler's opinion, there is a fundamental difference between wealth in the form of near money and wealth in the form of other financial assets. This means that the moneary field and the financial sphere do not coincide fully. Monetary policy can and, indeed, must confine itself to influencing the creation and availability of monetary liquidity. Together with budgetary policy, it forms part of the normal instruments to maintain domestic and external equilibrium.

Kessler did also theoretical work outside the monetary field. I have in mind particularly his analytical work on the distinction between the market sector and the budget sector, which has had great intellectual influence, especially among policy makers. Initially this influence made itself felt notably through policy papers but later Kessler also brought his work into the academic forum. This is well illustrated by a short article in the Dutch professional weekly "Economisch Statistische Berichten" in 1979, two extensive papers presented to the meetings of the Dutch Economic Association (Vereniging voor de Staathuishoudkunde) in 1979 and 1981, and the monograph published in 1983 by the University of Amsterdam, which I referred to before. His views on this matter also came to the fore through the report in 1978 of the Committee of Economic Experts of the Social and Economic Council of which Kessler was an ex officio member, the recommendations of the Social and Economic Council on the growth and size of the public sector, also in 1978, and the Bank's Annual Reports.

Kessler's analysis centres on the idea that the financing of public expenditure could jeopardize the continuity of income earned in the market sector. This is the case when income earners in the market sector shift the burden of taxation and social insurance contributions to capital income earned in the market sector. It must be remembered that in contrast with the situation in the budget sector, the maintenance of continuity in the market sector is dependent on positive operating results. Kessler has never failed to point out that an increase in public spending should have consequences for the disposable income of workers in the market sector, if a (further) shrinking of financial strenght is to be prevented. Kessler did not confine himself to giving a qualitative analysis of this major problem, but tried to illustrate the interaction between the budget and market sectors with the aid of empirical data. This prompted him to rearrange the available statistical data. In recent years Kessler gave a great deal of attention to this matter, doing much innovating work.

I have highlighted only a few of the scientific activities which Kessler performed while he was a director of the Bank (until 1981) and during his University professorship. Time restrictions prevent me from going into topics such as the dimension analysis which formed the subject matter of an article in De Economist in 1963. Neither have I discussed Kessler's work on exchange rates and employment, his publi- cations on international lending or his teaching work as a professor at the Faculty of Economics of the University of Amsterdam. I would like to mention, however, that, as far as I have been able to glean, Kessler published only three book reviews, the last of which appeared over 30 years ago. Apparently he prefers writing on his own research to writing on research of others. We know Kessler to be a man with a passion for analytical economics, who, when necessary, tried to derive policy guidelines from his analyses. For that he deserves to be highly praised; I believe this conference, which is entirely in this spirit, to be a fitting tribute.

INTRODUCTION

C. van Ewijk

Fifteen years ago it is unlikely that the subject of this volume would have provoked serious controversy among leading central bankers. Confronted with the present high unemployment figures and moderate inflation rates most economists would have soon agreed that European economies need to be actively reflated. Today these same figures, however, appear to provide the grounds for precisely the opposite policies. This 180 degree turn in economic thinking, noticed by *Schlesinger*, marks the supersession of the Keynesian cum Phillips-curve consensus of the late 1960s by the pragmatic monetarist consensus of the early eighties. In practice this entails that counter-cyclical stabilisation has been abandoned and replaced by structural anti-inflation policies based on rules for monetary growth.

The major innovation in the implementation of monetary policy has been the adoption of monetary targeting. Although in some countries targets had already been published for a longer period, it has only been since the second half of the seventies that targets have become the centre-piece of monetary policy. Germany adopted targeting in 1975; the Federal Reserve Board changed its policy after the historical press conference on October 6, 1979, when its Chairman, Mr. Volcker, announced a new system of monetary control. This new policy aimed at the stringent guidance of money growth, particularly M1, within pre-announced monetary target ranges. Some months later the United Kingdom followed by adopting the "Medium Term Financial Strategy", according to which growth of £M3 was to be gradually and steadily reduced over a four-year period.

Yet, pragmatic monetarism appears to have lost some of its attraction since then. It may be observed that most papers contained in this volume stress the need for flexible and "judgemental" policies. Obviously, instead of tying monetary policy to rigid rules it would be preferable to provide the monetary autorities with more room to manoeuvre once again in order to be able to respond better to the varying circumstances. This change in attitude is explained both by the success of the new policy, and also by its lack of success. On the one hand the succesful reduction in inflation took away much of the fuel for strong counter-inflation policies, while on the other hand problems with the implementation of monetary targeting proved considerably greater and more tedious than was suggested and hoped for by its proponents. Finally, although the new policy was certainly effective in reducing inflation, growing doubts emerged as to whether it also contributed to the wider goal of achieving a stable price climate. The exaggerate movements in (real) interest rates and exchange rates pointed to the contrary.

These factors have led to a significant relaxation of the rigour with which monetary targets are pursued. In 1982 both the US and the UK abandoned their stringent money control regimes and moved towards more judgemental policies. As a corollary monetary policy has lost much of its apparent clarity. Since at present control is no longer focussed on one single target (M1 or £M3) but on a range of targets for different monetary aggregates, it has become impossible to make a straightforward assessment of the stance of monetary policy. It is often even difficult to discern the objectives of monetary policy . As *Axilrod* points out for the US, present monetary policies are based on a mix of considerations concerning monetary as well as real developments rather than on the control of inflation alone.

This state of things is reflected in the papers presented at the conference on Monetary Conditions for Economic Recovery which are included in this volume. The main theme of the papers dealing with national monetary policies (*Part I*) concerns, of course, the appraisal of what *Kaldor* calls the "monetarist experiment" of 1979-82. Was it indeed a "terrible failure" as Kaldor suggests? And what conclusions can be drawn from it for the rôle of monetary targeting in present monetary policy? The papers in *Part II* are concerned with the international aspects of monetary policy. *Part III* contains four lectures discussing the lessons that can be drawn from recent experiences both for theory and for the shaping of future monetary policy. By way of introduction a brief survey of the main themes and conclusions of this conference will now be provided.

SHOCK-THERAPY

The pragmatic monetarist consensus which emerged in 1979-80 formed in many respects a response to the developments in the previous decade. After the first oil crisis policy had not succeeded in bringing down inflation to an acceptable rate. Most central bankers felt that monetary policy had been much too accommodating then. In addition the size of international financial markets had increased immensely and so also had "fluidity" as a result of which speculative capital flows - and thus expectations on future policy - were exerting an ever greater influence on the monetary transmission mechanism.

In this environment monetarist policy rules gained considerable attractiveness. By tying monetary policy to clear and credible targets for money growth it was argued that inflation could be brought down effectively and without great social cost. Moreover, when money growth was controlled in a firm and steady manner, it was thought that this would also contribute to the emergence of orderly markets and thus a stable price climate in general.

It should, however, be doubted whether these theoretical considerations were really decisive in turning the balance in favour of monetary targeting. Both *Axilrod* for the United States and *Schlesinger* for Germany stress that political and psychological factors were as least as important. *Schlesinger* states that besides its rôle in breaking the "inflation psychology" and resisting the vicious spiral of depreciation and inflation, targeting was very important in overcoming the resistance within the Bundesbank against the necessary adjustments, especially in the interest rate.

In the United States the primary motive for the policy change in 1979 was the fundamental distrust in the Fed's policy that had emerged due to the high inflation, the weak dollar and the fact that till then targets had practically never been achieved. Consequent to this lack of credibility, conventional measures to support the dollar, such as raising the discount rate or tightening the reserve requirements, had become ineffective in restoring confidence in the dollar and the Fed's policy. In order really to convince the public of the Fed's new intentions, it was therefore necessary to announce and introduce a new, more direct system of money control. *Axilrod* points out that the psychological effect of this change was in fact more important than its implications for the controllability of money supply. In discussions he underlined this by pointing out that achievement of the target was in practice far more important than the actual height of the target.

Although this economic shock-therapy was certainly effective in reducing inflation, strong doubts nevertheless emerged on the merits of the new policies, especially in those countries where monetary targeting had been applied most rigidly and mechanically. Despite the new methods of control it proved very difficult to keep money growth within the target ranges. Moreover, the efforts to control money stock turned out to have a strong destabilising spill-over to interest rates and exchange rates. From the papers on domestic monetary policies it can be made up that these problems were related to the instability of money demand on the one hand and to the increasing difficulty of controling money supply on the other hand.

MONEY-DEMAND SHIFTS
It is well-known that monetary targeting hinges on the two fol-lowing conditions:
a) monetary authorities have effective control of money supply;
b) there exists a stable relationship between money stock and aggregate demand.

Another way of stating the second condition is that demand for money should be a stable function of aggregate demand. Neither condition has proved to be without difficulties in practice.

As regards money demand both *Axilrod* for the US and *Goodhart* for the UK report recurring unforeseen shifts in the demand for money curve which confronted monetary policy with great problems. With the benefit of hindsight *Axilrod* concludes that in 1975-76 an unrecognised downward shift caused monetary policy to be considerably more expan-sive than it was at that time thought and meant to be. In 1982 the Fed was confronted with a sharp *upward* shift in demand for money (M1) which threatened to make monetary policy far more restrictive than the figures for money growth revealed. This upward shift eventually forced the Fed to abandon its stringent targeting regime and accomodate the ensuing increase in money demand.

For a large part this instability of money demand can be attributed to the speed of institutional change, especially deregulation, and the rapid introduction of financial innovations. In the US many new accounts have been introduced offering a money-market related interest rate and thus circumventing regulation. The so-called negotiable-order-of-withdrawal (NOW) accounts which were introduced around 1979 already encompassed some 30 per cent of M1 in 1984. For the UK *Goodhart* points to the rôle of changes in the system of monetary control in causing shifts of demand for £M3. When in 1980 exchange controls and the "corset" were abandoned money growth jumped as high as 18.7 per cent despite the intended restrictive stance of monetary policy.

As Schumpeter stressed, innovations do not come in a steady pace from heaven, but are induced by the economic circumstances. In the present case it is evident that those innovations should for a large part be attributed to *Goodhart's Law*, which states that the economic relations of a certain variable change as authorities adopt it as an objective variable of their policy. This is because measures aiming at control of this variable will inevitably change the behaviour of banks and the public, inducing circumvention and disintermediation. Experiences with the control of M1 in the US and £M3 in the UK appear to corroborate this law.

In Germany and the Netherlands the above-mentionend problems with innovations and circumvention seem to worry monetary authorities less. *Schlesinger* for Germany and *Fase* for the Netherlands hardly even mention the problem. The main reason for this seems to be the different institutional structure of the financial sector in continental Europe. In Germany and the Netherlands this sector is dominated by a few large banks which operate under the close supervision of the central banks. Owing to this "officially encouraged cartelisation" (*Lamfalussy*) innovations and institutional change seem to be introduced at a much more gradual and controled pace.

CONTROL OF MONEY SUPPLY

The second category of problems are related to the fact, stressed with great fervour by *Kaldor*, that in the present system the stock of money is essentially an endogenous variable. This implies that money stock is in first instance determined by the public and that central banks can only exert an indirect influence, i.e. by making it more attractive or less attractive for the public to hold its wealth in money form. *Goodhart* observes several developments which have made it increasingly difficult to influence this behaviour of the public in a reliable manner.

The traditional method of controlling money stock is through varying the rate of interest. Since, however, at present most components of money stock (even of M1) offer market-related interest rates, the interest elasticity of money demand is sharply reduced. According to *Goodhart* it is often found to be insignificant now in empirical studies. In the short run even a reversed relationship may be often observed, i.e. a rise in the money market rate leading to an *increase* in money stock. This is due to the fact that interest rates on "money" deposits (e.g. time-deposits) are more directly linked to the money-market rate than the rates on competing non-money assets (e.g. saving deposits).

In general it can be concluded that demand for money depends not so much on the level of interest rates but rather on their structure, i.e. the spread between interest on monetary and non-monetary assets and between deposit and lending rates of banks (the cost of intermediation). In recent years this has become increasingly relevant because of the fluidity of financial markets and the improved liability management of the private sector.

Another consequence of the financial innovations is that they tend to blurr the distinction between money and non-monetary assets. Since most transaction balances presently offer market-related interest rates and most assets with longer maturity can easily be transferred into transaction balances, it has become practically impossible to find a clear and sensible criterium to delimit monetary from non-monetary assets. Since any criterium is necessarily arbitrary, the money statistic is always liable to interpretation problems, especially when frequent shifts occur between assets just on both sides of the "money" boundary. In the event the very concept of money as distinguished from 'other' financial assets may even lose its significance at all.

One attempt to deal with these problems is to construct a so-called *Divisia Aggregate*. In this index for "money", different weights are assigned to the components of money corresponding to their degree of liquidity. *Fase* discusses the merits of such a Divisia-aggregate for the Netherlands on the basis of empirical results for the so-called Törn-quist-Theil index, which assigns weights to the components of money according to their interest-rate differential with long-maturity private loans. According to *Fase* this index may be a good alternative for the M2 concept traditionally applied by The Netherlands Bank, as it could make better allowance for innovations and gradual changes in the financial system.

With regard to the method of money control most authors observe a tendency towards deregulation, especially in the Anglo-Saxon world. Even the United Kingdom with its traditional preference for direct controls seems definitely to have opted for less dirigist methods, although it is not yet clear what method. In 1980 monetary base control was put forward as an alternative, but difficulties in introducing this system were so great that it was abandoned later. *Goodhart* points out that the principal instrument used recently is debt policy of the public sector. In an effort to compensate excessive banklending the authorities have sold long debt in exchange for short debt (treasury bills and commercial bills), on a large scale, to such an extent that it has even created the so called 'bill-mountain' problem. The monetary impact of this policy is that long interest rates are pushed up relative to short interest rates, thereby inducing a shift from (short) monetary assets towards (long) non-monetary assets.

As was mentioned before monetary control in Germany and the Netherlands is less affected by the worries of deregulation and innovation. Nonetheless it can be observed that the Netherlands Bank has also suspended its direct credit control scheme despite the sharply rising liquidity ratio (M2/NNP). On the other hand, however, *Kessler* still stresses the need for an extra, direct instrument for controlling money creation as in open economies the interest rate variable is fully subordinated to external (i.e. exchange rate) policy. Such an extra instrument is in his view a pre-requisite for being able to pursue an independent domestic monetary policy. It will be evident that this call for direct control will get more support in the cartelised financial system of continental Europe than in the Anglo-Saxon world where deregulation is fully under way.

INTERNATIONAL ASPECTS

The rapid integration of international financial markets presents, according to *Lamfalussy*, one of the greatest challenges to policy makers in recent times. Owing to this integration most monetary problems have become global rather than national in nature. This raises many questions with regard to international coordination of monetary policy, optimal exchange rate regimes and the control of international lending. These are the main themes of the papers included in Part II of this volume. The problem of coordination is in the first instance tackled by *Buiter* on the theoretical level and then by *De Grauwe* on the more practical level of the experience with the European Monetary System (EMS).

Buiter deals with the necessity of international coordination of monetary (and fiscal) policies with reference to the case of disinflation. Starting from a simple two-country, rational-expectations model he shows that disinflation by purely monetary means will inevitably involve social costs in terms of output and employment losses, except under the very restrictive assumption of a "classical wonderland" where all markets clear and prices are perfectly flexible. For a more realistic world with price- and inflation-slugishness *Buiter* shows that social cost can only be avoided if an appropriate mix of monetary, tax and public spending policies is chosen. Besides credible reductions in money growth to ensure structural elimination of inflation, the authorities should also adopt a program with tax cuts or an incomes policy to break core inflation, flexible public spending to maintain aggregate demand equilibrium, and finally a once and for all increase in money supply in order to accomodate the fall in velocity, ensuing from on the reduction of anticipated inflation.

As *Buiter* points out such optimal policies require genius or good luck. In practice there will in general be a lack of both of these factors. A major recent attempt at international monetary coordination is the European Monetary System. To what extent this system has been successful is analysed by *De Grauwe*, who compares the experiences of EMS countries with those of some non-EMS countries. On the whole his conclusions are rather negative. Although the EMS seems to have been successful in stabilising nominal exchange rates in the short run, *De Grauwe* doubts whether this is also true for the longer term movements in exchange rates. Further *De Grauwe* finds no evidence that EMS countries were anymore successful in resisting the upward pressures on interest rates from the US. With regard to growth and investment the small EMS countries performed even worse than small non-EMS countries. This raises serious doubts about the merits of the EMS, and *De Grauwe* therefore concludes that programs for more monetary coordination should be better put on the "back burner".

From a quite different point of departure, *Jager* comes to a conclusion much akin to *De Grauwe*'s on the importance of exchange rate regimes. *Jager* analyses the question of the preferable exchange rate regime by applying optimal control techniques to an empirical model of the Dutch economy. Four regimes are taken into consideration, viz. a) pegging the guilder to the D-mark, b) freely floating exchange rates, c) managed floating and d) a crawling peg. Although this last regime turns out to perform best in all respects, the differences between this regime and the other regimes considered are surprisingly small. This suggests that if all other policy instruments are appropriately set, the choice of the exchange rate regime will have only a minor additional effect on economic welfare.

De Vries deals with the problem of international monetary coordination from yet a different viewpoint, viz. the rôle of the International Monetary Fund. His main concern is the increased rôle of uncontrolled international capital flows, which threaten to destabilise exchange rate movements. For many developing countries they have contributed even more serious problems in the form of immense debts, which in their turn threaten the stability of the western financial system. The basic cause of these disruptions is, according to *De Vries*, to be found in the lack of control of international capital transfers. In his view the process of liberalisation of international capital markets has gone too far, and as a remedy he pleads for restoring the rôle of the IMF in direct surveillance over international lending. This would be more effective than international harmonisation of national monetary policies and far better than leaving it to competition between borrowers and lenders.

MONETARY POLICY SINCE 1982

As mentioned above the "new" policies introduced in 1979 were undoubtedly effective in bringing down inflation. In the US inflation fell from 15.1 per cent in the first half-year of 1980 to only 1.4 per cent in the first half-year of 1982. In England inflation dropped from 19.4 to 3.9 per cent in this same period. That these countries were not unique in this success appears from the figures for the OECD as a whole which show a decline of 14.4 to 4.3 per cent. This did not imply, however, that these policies were also succesful in achieving the wider objective of a stable price climate. On the contrary, many indications point to seriously disturbed prices: interest rates were abnormally high, espe-cially in real terms; exchange rates seemed far from their (real) equi-librium values, and expectations of future prices seemed disturbed as well.

Moreover, doubts remain about the lasting nature of the fall in inflation. Several authors believe that inflation is only low because of the severe recession ensuing from the restrictive policies. According to *Lamfalussy*, the battle against inflation has been won, but whether the war is won is very uncertain. In a similar argument *Van Lennep* warns that in comparison with previous business cycles the recent decline in inflation is by no means extraordinary. *Buiter* is even more pessimistic and argues that it is important to start now with the development of sensible anti-inflation policy packages for after the "next inflationary outburst".

This uncertain situation is reflected in today's monetary policy. Since the stringent regimes of money control were abandoned in 1982, central banks have followed a much more flexible and judgemental course. Targets were shifted somewhat to the background and more attention was again paid to interest rate and exchange rate develop-ments. Thus after first having tied their policies - and hence market-expectations - to rigid targets for one particular money aggregate, it was now necessary to de-emphasize those targets in order to restore room to manoeuvre for more discretionary policies. Only in Germany has the system of monetary control appeared to have changed little, but, as can be inferred from *Schlesinger*'s paper, the targeting policy of the Bundesbank has contained a reasonable degree of flexibility from the outset.

With regard to the rôle of monetary policy in economic stabilisation opinions seem to diverge. Most central bankers appear to agree with *Kessler*'s statement that the rôle of monetary policy is very limited and is of a conditioning rather than of a causative nature. Consequently monetary policy should be primarily directed at the structural control of inflation. This is underlined by *Van Lennep* who stresses that monetary policy alone cannot solve all problems currently facing OECD countries. In this connection the announcement of targets is thought to be a useful device despite all the difficulties ensuing from it. Both *Lamfalussy* and *Goodhart* argue that a pre-commitment is necessary in order to avoid "randomization" of monetary policy. *Axilrod* and *Schlesinger* regard monetary targets as still the best guard against shifts in the demand for goods and services, even more so as recently the money demand function seems to have become more stable again.

Although these policy principles sound firm and in full accordance with the pragmatic monetarist consensus, they leave many unresolved questions, in practice, notably - as pointed out by *Lamfalussy* - with regard to the right stance of monetary policy in the present situation of large-scale unemployment and the unsatisfactory growth of demand in Europe. For example, should or should not monetary authorities have accommodated the recent strong growth of money demand? According to *Van Lennep* they should not, for otherwise the old fault of too expansive policies during the early stages of recovery would be repeated. On the other hand *Axilrod* and *Korteweg* argue that the strong money growth was rightly accommodated because it was due to a structural shift in money demand. This illustrates that present thinking on monetary policy, which stresses flexible and judgemental policies, leaves considerable room for discretionary policy by the central banks. One might even ask what is really left of the pragmatic monetarist consensus and what actually distinguishes present policy from prudential Keynesian policies. According to *Kaldor* monetarism, in Britain at least, is already "vieux jeu". In his view the failure of the "monetarist experiment" corroborates the basic conclusions of the Radcliffe Committee in 1959, that it is impossible to hold grip of the money stock in the present system and that thus the regulation of interest rates is the real "centrepiece of monetary action".

CONCLUSION

As will be evident from this brief survey the conference did not yield uniform and clear-cut conclusions concerning to monetary policy to be pursued in the future. Nevertheless, for the centres at which policy is actually made, the central banks, it would appear that pragmatic monetarism, although weakened and sometimes difficult to distinguish from conservative Keynesianism, still emerges as the dominant view.

Despite *Buiter*'s warning at the conference that the Keynesian child should not be thrown away with the monetarist bathwater, most central bankers prove very reluctant to put some of the burden of cyclical stabilisation on monetary policy. In their view lasting reduction of inflation by a consistent monetary policy is still the most important *monetary condition for economic recovery.*

PART I

NATIONAL MONETARY POLICIES

1. WHAT ROLE FOR MONETARY POLICY TODAY?

A. Lamfalussy

1. INTRODUCTION

The conference organisers have given me the challenging assignment of presenting, by way of introduction to this conference, a paper on the rôle of monetary policy in a "disequilibrium situation". I have taken the liberty of interpreting this as a suggestion that I reflect on the rôle of monetary policy in today's world. I do this not simply because, in a narrow technical sense, we permanently live in a situation of disequilibrium - the "state of tranquillity" of economic theory is a theoretical construction which may, or may not, help us to understand what is happening in the real world but which never corresponds to an actual situation. More important, to my mind, is the fact that the signs of disequilibrium in more meaningful terms are more numerous and more disturbing today than they have been for some time.

Let me mention some of the most obvious manifestations or causes of imbalance in the world economic situation:
- the continued coexistence of unemployment and inflation;
- high real interest rates, with their possible adverse implications for capital formation;
- major shifts in the international division of labour and, consequently, in domestic industrial structures;
- massive capital inflows into the world's wealthiest country;
- major departures from purchasing power parity and the wild gyrations of the dollar in the foreign exchange markets;
- the international debt situation;
- signs of domestic financial fragility;
- and, last but not least, the potential impact of innovation and deregulation of financial markets.

How should practitioners of monetary policy respond to such a situation? On a strategic level, should they pursue a policy of monetary

Monetary Conditions for Economic Recovery, ed. by C. van Ewijk and J.J. Klant

targeting, on the assumption that this is their best, and in fact only, possible contribution towards markets? From the tactical standpoint, should they adjust their policy stance and/or their operational control techniques? Finally, in a longer-term perspective, and in terms of financial regulation and change, what is the optimum financial structure towards which they might wish to strive?

2. THE 1979-80 CONSENSUS VIEW ON THE ROLE OF MONETARY POLICY

Let me begin by trying to put these questions into some historical perspective. Once upon a time - around 1979-80 - a remarkable consensus emerged among the policy-makers of the western industrial countries on the use of monetary policy in the fight against inflation. The main components of this consensus might be summed up in the following three propositions:

a) among the major policy objectives, priority should be given to the fight against inflation;

b) by taking a restrictive stance, monetary policy should play a crucial rôle in achieving this objective;

c) restrictive monetary policy should be implemented by exercising firm control over the growth of the money supply which, in turn, should lead to, or coincide with, the re-emergence of positive real interest rates.

It is worth reminding ourselves that this consensus did not imply a genuine conversion to the creed of "pure" monetarism; it could more appropriately be called (as it was by the Governor of the Bank of England) "practical" monetarism. Qualifying the monetarism practised by central bankers at that time as "practical" was well-founded for two sets of reasons.

First, on the theoretical level. While clearly acknowledging that money (and even the money supply) mattered a great deal indeed when fighting inflation, practical monetarists did not share without substantial qualification any of the basic premises underlying monetarist reasoning, namely:

a) that in the medium term money is "neutral" with regard to the level of real economic activity;

b) that the private economy is basically stable;

c) that the demand for money is a stable function of a few variables, primarily income and interest rates;

d) that there is a predictable functional relationship between the targeted money supply figure and the stock of high-powered money; and

e) that, on the assumption that authorities adhered strictly to publicly announced money supply targets, rational expectations would drastically reduce the inevitable social costs associated with disinflation.

On a more practical level central bankers never failed, even during this period of happy consensus, to express their concern about several possible developments. Firstly, they warned us that a policy mix combining expansionary fiscal policy with restrictive monetary policy could drive interest rates to excessive levels – an assertion that, quite clearly, does not fit into the monetarist frame of thought. Secondly, they insisted on the need for moderation in wage settlements, arguing that without such moderation the deceleration in the growth of nominal expenditure would lead to rising and lasting unemployment. Thirdly, in particular in the United States, they voiced their concern that financial innovations might blunt the efficiency of monetary control techniques. Fourthly, more a European concern, the idea of excluding interest rates from the range of intermediate or even operating targets prompted fears that the implementation of a restrictive monetary policy might lead to undesirable exchange rate developments.

However, despite these practical concerns and the misgivings about the theoretical foundations of monetarism, there was still a firmly held belief that restrictive monetary policies, implying a gradual reduction in the rate of growth of monetary aggregates and positive real interest rates, should play a decisive rôle in fighting inflation.

It is against the background of this "historical consensus" that I should like to examine some of the problems that the monetary authorities of the western industrial countries are facing today. I propose to touch upon three sets of problems: the question of the appropriateness of the current stance of monetary policies in those countries – mainly in Europe – in which inflationary pressures have diminished considerably but where, at the same time, unemployment is high and still rising; the problems relating to the current level of real interest rates within the framework of increasing international integration of financial markets; and the problems arising for monetary control and the stability of financial institutions from the tide of innovation and from deregulation.

3. MONETARY POLICY AT A TIME OF DECLINING INFLATION RATES AND STUBBORN UNEMPLOYMENT

The best starting-point is to ask ourselves whether the major shift towards restrictive policies that occurred in 1979-80 has achieved its objective and, if so, at what cost and whether this achievement is likely to be of a lasting nature.

There can be no doubt that the last four years have witnessed a substantial decline in inflation rates. The rate of increase of consumer prices in the G-10 countries as a group peaked some time during the winter of 1980-81 at close to 12 per cent. It is now running at something below 5 per cent. And it may be noted that the extent of the decline was fairly similar in all the G-10 countries, although it was naturally somewhat smaller in those whose currencies depreciated in effective terms. There is, therefore, strong evidence that the monetary policy objective has been achieved. What is perhaps even more encouraging is that during the whole period there was only one year - 1982 - in which the group's combined GNP actually declined. Small positive rates of growth were recorded in both 1980 and 1981; after the setback in 1982 recovery began in 1983 and is now proceeding at a relatively fast pace. From 1980 to 1984 the group's GNP expanded in real terms by about 9 per cent.

Admittedly, this positive but relatively modest expansion was unable to prevent a considerable increase in unemployment, which rose from about 6 per cent of the labour force in 1980 to a peak of 8.5 per cent in 1983. It then started declining, but only as a result of favourable developments in North America. In Europe, on the other hand, the unemployment rate continued to worsen. Moreover, all forecasts point to still higher unemployment, even under relatively optimistic assumptions about Europe's future growth.

If one adds to this the gradually deteriorating structural pattern of unemployment - the fact that the unemployed remain out of work for longer and longer periods, the heavy concentration of unemployment among the young, major regional differences - it is easy to understand why, with inflation apparently more or less under control, many are beginning to wonder whether it is still right to give first priority in economic policy to the fight against inflation. Would it not be justified to relax the stance of monetary policies in Europe, thus abandoning their medium-term perspective, in order to accelerate the pace of recovery, particularly in those countries in which the fiscal policy stance is itself relatively restrictive?

Several reasons can be advanced for answering this question in the negative. Firstly, on the assumption of a further deceleration in price/wage inflation, these policies already allow for a reasonable potential rate of economic growth. Moreover, doubts remain as to the lasting nature of the success achieved in the fight against inflation. A battle, or even several battles, may have been won, but not the war. Current rates of inflation would have been considered alarmingly high in a number of countries during the golden 1960s. Who can be confident enough to say that inflationary expectations have been eradicated? One does not need to be a pure monetarist to fear that a visible relaxation of monetary policies might revive them - in other words, that the recent favourable shift of the Phillips curve might prove to be short-lived. Monetary-policy-induced demand stimulation would then be equally short-lived and current inflation rates could rise without any lasting improvement in the labour market.

Secondly, even if this argument could be cast aside - i.e. even if it was possible to accelerate economic recovery through active demand management - the recent OECD study on unemployment suggests that a substantial part of European unemployment is not of the Keynesian variety. That part cannot be cured by faster growth of nominal demand; the solution lies in active micro-economic policies, the main ingredients of which are education, increased labour mobility, the dropping of minimum wage requirements for young entrants into the labour market, and so forth. Some might object that the current US experience, in which fast growth goes hand in hand with an unexpectedly speedy

drop in unemployment, warns us not to overstate the case for "structural" unemployment. I have some doubts about the relevance of the US
example in this particular instance. The comparison of unemployment
figures across the Atlantic is a notoriously risky exercise from a statistical point of view. Moreover, a large part of the impressive employment performance of the US economy can be explained by the
transfer of labour from the internationally traded goods sector to the
sector of non-tradables mainly services. This may be possible, though
not necessarily advisable, route for a country with an overvalued
exchange rate and a weak balance-of-payments constraint. But to what
extent could European countries afford to follow this model for ab-
sorbing unemployment?

This leads me to exchange rate considerations, which present a
third reason for giving a negative answer to the question I have just
raised. The "decoupling" of European (specifically DM) interest rates
from those of the United States has, to some extent, been successful –
but at the cost of accepting a decline in exchange rates. This has so
far been a tolerable cost. Booming exports at the expense of the US
economy have given a helping hand to a modest revival of domestic
demand. At the same time, the weakness of dollar-denominated commodity prices has partially offset the cost-push inflationary impact of the
fall in the effective exchange rates of the European currencies. But
such a trade-off has its limits: unless there is a marked shift in exchange rate expectations against the dollar a renewed widening of the
interest rate differential could well put the European currencies under
unacceptable external inflationary pressure.

So far, so good. I am ready to defend this line of reasoning
against any relaxation of monetary policies with a fair degree of conviction. But how does this view stand up against the obvious need to
consider monetary policy options in a wider framework? And by "wider"
I mean both geographically, looking at the western industrial world (or
perhaps even the world) as a whole, and taking account of fiscal policy
stances as well.

4.   THE LEVEL OF REAL INTEREST RATES IN A FINANCIALLY INTE-
      GRATED WESTERN WORLD

The need for a geographically enlarged horizon seems to me overwhelming in view of the extensive integration of financial markets in the
western industrial world. This integration is one of the most striking
facts of recent economic history and presents a considerable challenge
to policy-makers, perhaps the greatest that they have faced for some
time. It also presents an intellectual challenge to economists, who are
desperately trying to catch up with the changing international scene:
witness, for example, the turmoil into which the theory of exchange
rate determination has been thrown in the wake of the large and en-
during movements in the dollar's real effective exchange rate.

Measuring financial integration is no easy matter and the significance of individual indicators is open to debate. Helpfully, all of them
point towards greater integration. The volume of capital flows has
increased considerably – a recent spectacular example is provided by
the large-scale capital imports into the United States. There has been a
dramatic growth in turnover on the foreign exchange markets, not to
mention the more recent expansion of trading in foreign currency and
interest rate futures. Banks' balance sheets have become more and more
internationally oriented, whether looked at in terms of cross-border
claims and liabilities, of assets and liabilities denominated in foreign
currencies, of profits originating from international transactions, or of
reliance on international interbank funding. The large banks' liquidity
management is integrated on a worldwide basis; and these banks offer
similar services to corporate treasurers. The technology of communi-
cations is developing at a rapid pace. Financial innovations are
spreading more and more quickly from one country to another: look at
the speed with which currency and interest rate swaps have become
common practice in international banking.

More significantly, all current studies of which I am aware confirm
that interest parity is almost instantaneously observed in the Euromarkets, even in periods of swift interest rate fluctuations. Finally,
and even more significantly, interest rate variations in the United
States have had an appreciable impact on interest rates elsewhere. As I
have noted, exchange rate developments have limited this influence but

have not offset it completely. In other words, a transmission mechanism
is operating between domestic financial markets even in a system of
fairly generalised floating – just as there is a cyclical transmission
mechanism through the flow of goods and services despite the existence
of the same floating system.

As a result of this advanced integration of financial markets, it
has become difficult – perhaps even meaningless – to assess the stance
of the monetary policy or monetary/fiscal policy mix of any large country without looking at the group of industrial countries as a whole. Let
me try to approach some of our "global" problems by hanging them on a
common peg, namely that of real interest rates. Are these interest rates
too high today? If so, why? Because of the US policy mix or for other
reasons? Answers to these questions, it seems to me, follow four schools
of thought – and I apologise for this inevitably arbitrary classification.
May I also add that these schools of thought do not necessarily lead to
mutually exclusive conclusions but can, in fact, be regarded as complementary.

Firstly, there are the agnostics, who themselves fall into two
categories. There are those who express doubts about the feasibility of
measuring the level of real interest rates and, therefore, of forming
meaningful views about the appropriateness of their current levels. A
minor (and probably not insurmountable) practical problem underlying
such doubts relates to the complexity of fiscal systems, which makes it
difficult to compare the after-tax interest burdens of individual market
participants, in particular when they belong to different countries. A
more fundamental reason for doubt lies in the difficulty of measuring
inflationary expectations, which may well (indeed, are likely to) differ
from actual inflation rates. Since survey data are of rather doubtful
quality many economists refuse to pass judgement on the current level
of real interest rates. While I have some sympathy for such secpticism,
I nevertheless cannot help but feel that when observed inflation rates
have been declining for some time, with nominal interest rates remaining
unchanged and in some instances even rising, something is likely to
have happened to the level of real interest rates, and this "something"
was surely not a decline. In the same way, I do not deny that tax
advantages reduce in many cases the burden of high interest charges –

except when a business corporation has no taxable income.

Other agnostics agree to measure real interest rates in an ex post sense, but point out that while real interest rates are currently higher than in the 1970s (when they were in fact negative), they are not much, if at all, higher than in the 1960s. The anomaly to be explained is why real rates were so low ten years ago, not why they are so high today. This is, partly at least, a valid observation, but it misses the point that the level of real interest rates cannot be judged by historical standards exclusively, but has also to be set against the current trend in real growth. An economy growing trendwise at the rate of 2-3 per cent cannot support real interest rates of 5 or 6 per cent for more than a very short period – if there is no decline in the interest rate, growth will come to a grinding halt.

Secondly, there are those who do not question that real interest rates (again defined as the nominal rates minus actual inflation rates) are high by any standards, but ascribe this fact to the incorporation into current interest rates of one or two kinds of premia. There would be, in this view, an inflationary premium due to the persistence of inflationary expectations which should be attributed either to the long historical experience of inflation, or to the lack of credibility attached to the monetary authorities' commitment to fight inflation (itself a result of these authorities' inability to keep the growth of money supply on a gradually decelerating, stable, course) or simply to the deficit spending of the fiscal authorities. There would also be a premium to cover the increased uncertainty derived from the high volatility of interest rates. For some observers, the culprit again is the lack of stability in the rate of growth of the money supply. For my part, I would be ready to acknowledge the existence of both these premia, although I do not believe that they tell the whole story; nor do I believe that they should be explained exclusively in terms of observed money supply behaviour.

A third set of answers is given by those who argue, much in the classical tradition, that the level of real interest rates is governed by the "real" economy, i.e. by the rate of return on real assets, and not by monetary factors. Monetary policy is therefore unable to influence it, except perhaps in the very short run.

Applying this reasoning to current circumstances produces the following line of argument. Let us acknowledge that real interest rates in the United States are at present quite high by historical standards; let us further admit that this triggers massive capital flows into the United States which, in turn, keep the dollar at its present high level and at the same time bear some of the responsibility for also keeping real interest rates in Europe and Japan at levels that are somewhat higher than in the past, although less so than in the United States. The point is then made that this state of affairs has not much to do with respective monetary and fiscal policy stances, but is due to the marked increase in the rate of return on real assets in the United States, reflecting the much better response of the US economy to the challenge of the current economic environment. Europeans have them- selves to blame rather than the US policy mix; the solution for Europe lies in improving the performance of its real economy, specifically in implementing policies that would lead to higher real rates of return on capital.

Anyone who has been brought up in the classical tradition is bound to feel some sympathy for this view. Whatever my sympathy, I nonetheless have some doubts. I am prepared to acknowledge that the rapid pace of the US recovery, despite what seem to be rather high real interest rates, lends plausibility to the argument; I can also imagine that many market participants outside the United States actually believe that prospective real returns are higher in the United States than elsewhere – to say this is almost tautological. However, the fast pace of the US recovery can also be explained in terms of the most conventional IS/LM diagram – as a matter of fact, the problem that neo-Keynesians encountered a few years ago was exactly the reverse: why was it that the take-off of the US economy occurred with such a delay? Moreover, one knows perfectly well that tax rebates on investment have helped to make capital quite cheap for US businesses: I would hardly call these tax concessions a "real" adjustment, however, justified they may have been from a policy point of view. Last but not least, market sentiment is no proof that real returns are, or will be, in fact high. The ability of financial markets to adequately forecast future earnings is, to say the least, doubtful. As Prof. Tobin would say, their "funda- mental-valuation efficiency" is questionable. Nor am I aware of empirical evidence showing that, in any systematic way, rates of return on real assets have increased much more sharply in the United States than in either Europe or Japan, or are today at a higher level. This, admittedly, does not preclude their out-performing European ones in the future, but to believe this I would need more evidence than current market behaviour.

This leads me to the fourth school of thought, which puts the responsibility for high real interest rates squarely on the shoulders of US policy-makers. Real interest rates are high in the United States, and also relatively high elsewhere, because of a US policy mix that combines an expansionary fiscal stance with restrictive monetary policy. An appropriate change in the mix would lead to a lower real rate in the United States and, indirectly, both to a lower dollar on the exchange markets and to lower real rates in the rest of the western industrial world.

But what would this "appropriate" change be? Broadly speaking, two contrasting answers are given to this question, with shades of opinion between them.

On one view - what one might call the "mainstream" view - the change should imply a tightening of the US fiscal stance, preferably by cutting expenditure but if necessary by raising taxes, while keeping US monetary policy on its present course, i.e. continuing the gradual reduction of money supply growth rates. By helping to lower nominal and real interest rates in the United States, such a policy would also contribute to lowering them in western Europe and Japan, and would at the same time bring exchange rates into better balance.

The second view questions the wisdom of tightening US fiscal policy without a corresponding fiscal stimulus elsewhere and advocates a concomitant relaxation of the US monetary policy stance, possibly with some tightening in Japan and Europe. It is argued that the fiscal policy of the western industrial world taken as a whole is not expansionary, since the positive fiscal impulse emanating from the United States is, to a large extent, offset by the restrictive fiscal stance of the other major western countries. The OECD has provided some statistical basis for this view, suggesting at least a partial offsetting of the US expansionary impulse by contractionary fiscal impulses in some other countries. On this view, therefore, the explanation for the high level of world real interest rates must lie in generally tight monetary policies, or perhaps in high real rates of return, but certainly not in excessively stimulatory fiscal policies in the western world as a whole. The conclusion drawn is that, other things being equal, a tightening of the US fiscal stance would lead to a worldwide economic slowdown. Hence the suggestion that the adoption of a tighter US fiscal policy should be accompanied by fiscal expansion elsewhere, while monetary policy should be relaxed in the United States and left unchanged (or perhaps somewhat tightened) in the rest of the world. Incidentally, the second part of this proposition would also be endorsed by some international monetarists, who explain the strength of the dollar directly in terms of an excessively tight US monetary policy set against an insufficiently tight one in Europe and Japan.

It will come as no surprise to you that my own conclusions incline towards what I have called the "mainstream" view, although I must admit to an uncomfortable feeling that this view does not take full account of the international interdependence, financial and real, of the western world. For the sake of stimulating discussion, let me try to make clear the three reasons which nevertheless prompt me to support it.

The first is that I regard the rapidly developing imbalance in the US external position, which, rightly or wrongly, I link to a large extent to the US fiscal policy stance, as a potential threat to international financial stability. A part of this imbalance was, and still is, welcome - otherwise the US economy could not have acted as the world locomotive, a rôle that the United States alone was, and is, able to perform. But the sharply deteriorating US international investment position - at an annual rate of $100 billion - combined with the crucial rôle of external financial flows in the financing of US domestic sectors, are unsustainable. At almost any time they could, in the event of a sudden shift in international portfolio preferences against the dollar, raise the spectre of financial shocks whose effects on both the United States and the rest of the world could quickly erode the currently beneficial "real" impact of US growth on the world economy. This is not, of course, a forecast, just a reminder of a possible secenario combining recession and high interest rates in the United States that policy-makers would be well advised not to rule out.

Secondly, we should not forget a principal lesson of the late 1970s, namely the importance of keeping inflation in the United States well under control not only for the sake of the US economy but also for that of the world as a whole. Hence my inclination to view any relaxation of the US monetary policy as a dangerous exercise.

Thirdly, I do not believe that either Europe or Japan has the same degree of freedom from external constraints as the United States. Even that of the United States is not complete; that of Japan and Europe is very limited indeed. There is no symmetry in the world economy. In other words, any relaxation of some importance of fiscal policies in Europe - quite apart from the fact that any such proposal is a non-starter since no major European government at present in power would be prepared to consider it - would carry with it major dangers for external balance, as the Germans well know from the experience of 1980-81 and the French from that of 1982-83, not to mention the dire consequences of further postponing the expenditure cuts needed to correct the over-extended position of the public sector. That this need for budgetary consolidation may exert a somewhat deflationary influence on the world economy must be accepted as a fact of life. The trouble is, of course, that for the two reasons just mentioned any such influence can be compensated from the US side only up to a point - hence the difficult balancing-act of welcoming some fiscal and external imbalance in the United States, but not too much.

5.   FINANCIAL INNOVATIONS AND DEREGULATION

Let me turn finally to a third area of concern for monetary policy-makers: the implications of financial innovations and of deregulation for the conduct of monetary policy.

Two general observations - or suggestions for discussion - to begin with. The first is a plea for more extensive and more systematic analysis and information. As regards analysis, I find it disturbing that we seem to know so little about the driving forces behind financial innovations and why they seem to occur more extensively in some countries than in others. The list of factors contributing to innovations is of course reasonably well-known: high and variable inflation rates; efforts to circumvent regulations or to reduce the burden of taxation – or, on the contrary, making use of opportunities offered by deregulation; the desire to limit risks associated with greater uncertainty (e.g. interest or exchange rate volatility); competitive pressure to meet customers' needs; the emergence of new technology. But do we really understand why some or all of these influences have led to such a sudden speeding-up of the process of innovation in recent years and why have they done so especially (or only apparently so?) in the United States?

It is at this point that factual information, or rather the lack of it, becomes important. As I already pointed out a few years ago, it is remarkable to observe that public discussion of innovation and deregulation is so much centred on the Anglo-Saxon world. What is the state of affairs in these respects elsewhere – in particular in some of the major continental European countries? It is true that as a result of historical developments (such as the traditional interconnection between securities business, underwriting and commercial banking) the continental European practice of universal banking had led to a de facto state of deregulation well before developments currently observed in the United States or the United Kingdom? Or, on the contrary, is privately managed but officially encouraged financial cartelisation the real European way of life? Can it not be said that retail banking technology as applied to payment systems is far more advanced in some European countries than either in the United Kingdom or in the United States? More generally, in what respects is Europe financially more, or less, "backward" than the Anglo-Saxon countries? And why?

My second observation calls for an equally ambitious programme of research in the field of normative financial economics. In his 1984 Fred Hirsch memorial lecture, Prof. Tobin offered us four criteria of efficiency of the financial system, while confessing to "an uneasy Physiocratic suspicion" that a global cost-benefit analysis would not necessarily come down in favour of complete financial deregulation. The heart of the matter, to my mind, is that, since we have never experienced completely free financial markets, no convincing empirical testing is possible. And I stress the word "completely": to observe what may

actually happen during a period of transition from more to less regulation, or vice versa, can provide misleading information on the merits,
or demerits, of a fully deregulated financial world. In general terms,
lopsidedness in regulations can lead to situations which are difficult to
assess. In a well-known recent case a bank that was free to compete
for its assets, but not for its liabilities, got itself into trouble. Was
there too much regulation on one side of the balance sheet or too little
on the other? Or was it just an isolated case of mismanagement? And so
it is left to pure theory to tell us whether the observed inefficiencies of
financial markets (on any of Tobin's four criteria) are due to regulation
or other types of government interference or are an integral part of the
functioning of even completely free financial markets. Any such theor-
ising is bound to be influenced by social or political philosophy or
simply by personal bias and prejudices.

However that may be, in the present world of rapid innovation and
progressive deregulation monetary policy-makers face two major problem
areas. One relates to the implementation of monetary control in its
broadest sense, i.e. not only the choice of the appropriate control
targets or intermediate policy objectives, but also the modus operandi of
the transmission mechanism from monetary variables – aggregates or
interest rates – to prices and real output. The identification of operational or intermediate targets may be seriously disturbed by the process of financial innovation and the blurring of institutional boundaries
resulting from deregulation. As to the transmission mechanism, it is
bound to be affected by the generalisation of floating interest rates and
by the spreading use of financial futures. But how? An answer to this
question is needed not simply to provide central bankers with intellectual or moral comfort, or to establish rules of accountability, but also
to preserve the usability of monetary policy as the main macro-economic
policy instrument. At a time when the practical or fundamental limitations of fiscal policy have become so obvious, loss of effectiveness of
monetary policy would surely have to be counted as a social cost to be
set against the benefits of deregulation in any global cost-benefit
analysis.

The same applies to the second area of problems generated by
innovation and deregulation, which might be grouped under the heading

of the stability of the financial system. The question here is not the theoretical one of whether financial crises are or are not part and parcel of a completely free financial system. This is an interesting question but one that has little practical relevance. We do not, and shall not in the foreseeable future, live in a financial system completely free of government interference or of "distortions" of other kinds. What I have in mind is the very practical question of how central banks are supposed to discharge their duty to preserve the stability of financial markets, i.e. to prevent and/or to manage crises, in an environment characterised by an ongoing process of deregulation and innovation – with the emphasis on the word process. To act as lenders of last resort or as supervisors at such a time of transition in financial markets is not an easy business.

And their task is being dauntingly complicated by the concurrence of two other developments. The first is the process of worldwide financial integration I mentioned earlier in connection with the appropriate stance of the policy mix. The fact that innovation is taking place in such an environment renders much more arduous the task of bank management, auditors and supervisors alike. Let me just name one example: the assessment of the risks implied by such off-balance sheet items as financial futures contracts, which in some cases substitute for international interbank funding. The second development brings me back to where this paper has started: the process of disinflation, but this time seen from the prudential angle. Not unexpectedly, high real interest rates, slower growth and disinflationary price developments have produced casualties among bank customers, domestically and internationally, not to mention banks themselves; and the casualties have in some cases been multiplied by large and unexpected exchange rate movements, changes in energy prices and shifts in the international division of labour. Such casualties are continuing to occur even today, in the midst of a recovery, which clearly shows that the process of adjustment is still very much under way. I doubt that we have seen the end of the story, especially since cyclical upswings do not last for ever.

6. CONCLUDING OBSERVATIONS

By way of conclusion let me try to pull together the threads running somewhat loosely through my argument into a few propositions – which is perhaps also a way of confessing to having a few preconceived ideas, such as a basic disbelief in most of the premises of monetarist theory (but not in all of its policy conclusions).

The first is that one should not expect too much of monetary policy. Given the widespread disenchantment with incomes policy and the inflexible orientation of fiscal policy on both sides of the Atlantic, there is a danger that monetary policy may be required to perform more than it can deliver. Central bankers have always tried to avoid falling into this trap, and their natural instinct of survival has been right. Restrictive monetary policy can lead to noticeable results in the fight against inflation. But, when the labour market is rigid, the social cost will be high and lasting unemployment; and when a public-sector deficit pulls the policy mix in the opposite direction interest rates may become stuck at a dangerously high level. At least, when restrictive monetary policy is applied with sufficient vigour, inflation will decelerate. But it is hard to see monetary policy of any kind leading to a sustainable, well-balance, non-inflationary recovery without the help of other policies. There is no monetary policy trick that can undo the potentially disruptive influence of a strongly expansionary US budgetary policy (or, for that matter, of a structural budget deficit anywhere else); nor can European monetary policy be expected to speed up real capital formation and lastingly alleviate unemployment without a shift in income distribution in favour of profits, greater mobility in the labour market and improved entrepreneurial performance.

By emphasising these limits to monetary policy I do not mean to underrate its indispensable contribution to the fight against inflation, a task that seems to me to be still unfinished. It can make this contribution both directly, by restraining spending, and indirectly, by helping to defuse inflationary expectations. This second objective is best served, to my mind, through the implementation of a medium-term targeting policy, the targets being either monetary aggregates or the exchange rate tied to the currency of a large non-inflationary country or to a basket of currencies in which non-inflationary countries have a large share. Either of these targets will make plain the monetary authorities' commitment to the cause of eradicating inflation. In this way central banks can provide market participants with at least one element of stability in an otherwise highly uncertain environment. But even here some modesty is in order. The implementation of either of these targeting techniques may well create instability of another kind - in particular in the context of a wrong policy mix - of which the prime example is, of course, interest rate misalignment or volatility. There will be no general financial stability simply by sticking to monetary targets.

Last but not least, I should like to stress the importance of carrying out monetary targeting in a medium-term perspective. As I have already mentioned, the financial systems in many western industrial countries are, to varying degrees, caught up in three interconnected evolutionary precesses: one of innovation and deregulation; one of growing internationalisation; and, lastly, one of disinflation. And as a result of advanced international financial integration, even those countries where innovation is less buoyant and/or where the end of the disinflationary process is (perhaps) in sight, cannot isolate themselves from the rest. I am not aware of a historical precedent that could serve as a satisfactory guide for the short-term conduct of monetary policy in these circumstances. Nor do I know of any credible theoretical contribution that could enlighten monetary policy practitioners in carrying out their day-to-day business in such a fluid environment - and this is just another way of saying that I regard the monetarist recipe of disregarding the practicalities of a rapidly changing world not as a credible advice. To navigate in these uncharted waters, central bankers will have to apply a great deal of pragmatic flexibility which, occasionally will have to temper the strict adherence to targets. They will run into criticism both from academics and politicians, but this is just a professional risk to take. Applying rules in our world without discretionary judgment is a pipedream bordering on irresponsibility.

2. U.S. MONETARY POLICY IN RECENT YEARS: AN OVERVIEW

S.H. Axilrod[*]

1. INTRODUCTION

U.S. monetary policy in recent years, in terms of its basic thrust, has aimed at curbing inflation and setting the stage for sustainable economic growth. In the process, the shorter-term policy stance and the day-to-day operating procedures have been complicated by, and have had to be adapted to, a variety of powerful exogenous forces. Among the more important from the mid-1970s through the early 1980s have been large oil price increases, a credit control program, deregulation of and innovations in banking and deposit markets, emergence of a large structural budget deficit, a large current account deficit in the balance of payments accompanied by what many believe to be an overvalued dollar on exchange markets, and strongly embedded inflationary expectations.

Not all exogenous forces are purely exogenous. Rising inflationary expectations in the late 1970s were in part the product of earlier monetary policies (as well as other events) as they affected attitudes toward the future, but once embedded they were exogenous to and influenced current policies - as in October 1979. The present deficit in the current account and high foreign exchange value of the dollar also could be viewed in part as endogenous to policies being pursued, or at least to the mix of fiscal and monetary policies; however, the deficit and the exchange rate have also been exogenous to policy in the degree that they have reflected shifts in preferences toward dollar assets, for any given interest differential, on the part of foreigners and U.S. residents who normally had invested abroad.

* The views expressed in this paper are not necessarily those of the Board of Governors of the Federal Reserve System.

This paper analyzes how monetary policy has evolved over the recent period in response to the exogenous forces facing it, forces that have also shaped the responses of financial and goods markets to the stance of policy. The review starts around the mid-1970s, to set in relief the more recent period beginning in late 1979, when there was a significant shift in monetary strategy – a shift that was designed not only to provide greater assurance that actual inflation would be curbed but also to reduce inflationary expectations with less of a lag, given past price behavior, than might otherwise occur. A relatively prompt abatement of expectations might be accomplished if the public's belief in the credibility of monetary policy's will to achieve price stability over time were greatly enhanced. If that were to lead to quicker wage, price, and interest rate adjustments for any given money supply target, the adjustment process to a noninflationary environment would be eased. In one sense, monetary strategy in recent years can be viewed as a continuing struggle to attain and maintain credibility in face of continuing shocks and disturbances in money, credit, and goods markets.

2. U.S. MONETARY POLICY IN RECENT YEARS

2.1. The period before October 1979

The change in operating procedures announced by Chairman Volcker at an unusual Saturday press conference on October 6, 1979 was, at the time and more so in retrospect, a watershed event. It signalled a shift to greater emphasis on reserve aggregates in carrying out monetary policy and, by implication, greater concern with achieving goals for monetary aggregates (especially M1) and less concern with interest rates. The shift had its historical basis partly in experience over the several previous years following the first oil shock in late 1973 and early 1974.

That shock contributed to a sharp rise in the U.S. consumer price index of more than 12 per cent from the end of 1973 to the end of 1974, following an almost 9 per cent rise over the preceding year. Such price increases had generally been in the 1 to 2 per cent area in the last half of the 1950s and first half of the 1960s. Subsequently, there had been a step-up to price increases in the 3 to 6 per cent range for the years from 1966 to 1972.

I would tend to attribute some part (a third to a half) of the faster price increases of '73 and '74 to the oil and other commodity price shocks of the time, abstracting from the impact of the phase-out of price controls during the period. Money growth had accelerated earlier in that decade, producing with some lag (of a year or two) upward pressures on the aggregate price level. But with M1 growth averaging around 7.5 per cent annually in 1971 and 1972, the degree of acceleration did not seem sufficient in itself to produce price increases as large as we saw in the aftermath of the first oil shock (see Blinder (1982)).

However much one might apportion, on technical econometric grounds, the price increases after the oil shock to the shock itself or to monetary policy, the price increases appear to have led to a rise of inflationary expectations. Despite the ensuing recession, consumer prices rose by 7 per cent over 1975 (when they probably still reflected some of the direct impact of import price increases) and expanded in a 5 to 7 per cent range during the next two years of recovery. Thus, after the initial response to the oil price shock, inflation did not revert to its earlier range, but was somewhat higher – even during recession and the early stages of recovery – reflecting, as well as providing an impetus to, higher inflationary expectations.

The tendency for inflationary expectations to worsen was but-tressed in 1978 when price increases accelerated further and the dollar deteriorated markedly on exchange markets. Efforts by monetary policy to curb these adverse developments involved conventional approaches of the period. In late 1978, for instance, a package was announced that encompassed a one percentage point increase in the discount rate, a supplementary reserve requirement of 2 per cent on large time deposits (the deposit instrument most readily employed by banks at their own initiative to finance growing credit demands), a tightening of conditions in the money market through more restrained open market operations, and, together with the U.S. Treasury (and with the cooperation of foreign official institutions), mobilization of a large amount of dollars to help support the currency on exchange markets.

In the event, this package had little success in stemming inflationary pressures and attitudes. That can probably be attributed in part to the overhanging effect of the monetary policy pursued over the preceding several years, as well as to behavior of monetary aggregates during much of 1979.

In 1977 and 1978, M1 growth had accelerated to slightly over an 8 per cent per annum pace, after growing by an average of 5.5 per cent per year over the previous two years. Not only did this acceleration itself appear to signal that policy was becoming more expansionary, but also the credibility of policy was being eroded by the consistency with which actual M1 growth came in above adopted target ranges in a strong economy. This psychological effect was made even worse in the circumstances of the time by the fact that new one-year target ranges were adopted quarterly, with the most recent quarter serving as a base (so that there were four one-year target periods ending in each quarter of a year) and with no apparent effort to make up for the preceding overshoots. This became known as "base drift". The erosion of credibility because the targets were missed and because the process of target setting also led to a perception that they were perhaps not serious constraints fueled inflationary expectations.

In addition, it appears that, with the benefit of handsight, the actual growth of M1 in 1975 and 1976 was much more expansive than the relatively low growth rates - rates that were within targets adopted for those years[1] - suggested. There were a series of financial market innovations in that period spurred by relatively high market interest rates which greatly increased the opportunity cost of holding non-interest bearing demand deposits[2] and led cash managers to seek other outlets for highly liquid funds. Depositors shifted funds out of demand deposits to other newly emerging highly substitutable instruments at

---

(1) The first "year" for which M1 targets were announced was the period from March 1975 to March 1976. Subsequently, there were one-year targets based on each quarter of the year. Starting with the QIV '78 to QIV '79 year, monetary targets have pertained only to calendar years.
(2) While demand deposits by law earn no explicit interest, there are implicit positive returns, more sizable for large businesses than for consumers and small businesses.

banks and other depository institutions – savings accounts that became available mainly to smaller businesses, accounts with telephone and pre-authorized transfers, etc. Demand deposit holders probably also shifted funds into market instruments in the process of re-evaluating their whole approach to cash management. It is probable that the change in approach to cash management in that period reduced the desire to hold M1, given actual income and interest rates, by on the order of 3 to 4 percentage points in each of the two years (see Porter, Simpson, and Mauskopf (1979)). This meant that 5.5 per cent a year of M1 growth should, in terms of its economic effect, be construed as more on the order of 8 to 10 per cent – quite expansionary and well above target.

Growth of M1 failed to slow over the first three quarters of 1979. At the same time, prices were placed under additional upward pressure by the second oil shock in the early part of the year. Over-all price increases moved into the double digit area. That had also occurred in 1974, but in the earlier period there had been less of a build-up in inflationary expectations and less of an erosion in the credibility of the Federal Reserve's will and capacity to control the situation.

2.2. From October 1979 to the fall of 1982

The conditions facing monetary policy in the fall of 1979 were in some respects similar to those in the fall of 1978. Inflation was worsening, as signalled not only in the domestic markets but also by a sharp drop in the dollar's value on exchange markets. However, by the fall of 1979 it had become even clearer that the cumulative lessening of confidence in monetary policy had contributed additionally to a substantial worsening of inflationary expectations.

Thus, the policy announced on October 6, 1979 contained a new approach to implementation of open market operations in addition to the more conventional one percentage point rise in the discount rate and an additional reserve requirement applicable to increases in large time deposits and certain other managed liabilities. An important objective of the new approach was to help convince the public that the Federal Reserve would in practice achieve its monetary targets – was indeed changing its fundamental operating procedures to do so – and thereby increase the credibility of monetary policy and facilitate the transition to a noninflationary environment.

This new approach has been amply described and evaluated elsewhere (see Axilrod and Lindsey (1981); Axilrod (1981); Axilrod (1982); For a more critical assesment see Brunner and Melzer (1983)). Its essence was to secure direct control of aggregate bank reserves – for operational purposes, nonborrowed reserves – and let interest rates vary as a product of the interaction between the nonborrowed reserve path and the emerging demand for reserves. It was believed that this would increase the odds that money growth, particularly M1 (the aggregate most closely related to the reserve base), would in fact be controlled within target ranges, given a relatively predictable relationship between the supply of reserves and the supply of money over a reasonable length of time. Previous efforts to control money growth used money market conditions – typified in much of the 1970s by the federal funds rate (the rate charged on overnight loans of reserve funds among banks) – as the guide for open market operations. Such efforts had foundered partly on policy-makers' innate caution in adjusting any policy instrument and partly, and more fundamentally, on the difficulty in predicting the relationship between market interest rates and money growth, a difficulty that was compounded by uncertainties being introduced by inflationary expectations about the interpretation and significance of nominal market rates.

The change in policy procedure, in addition to whatever merits it may have had on its own as a more effective means of controlling money, was an effort to counteract the build-up of inflationary expectations that was a major obstacle to an orderly reduction of inflation. As noted earlier, those expectations may have been partly the result of earlier monetary policies. They were also the product of two successive oil price shocks. One impact was to shift the Phillips curve upward, leading to a higher rate of inflation given the natural unemployment rate. The policy adaptation in that context represented an effort to improve the trade-off between unemployment and the rate of inflation by itself leading to a shift in attitudes in labor and product markets that would bring the curve back down.

In undertaking that change, it was clearly understood that the desirability as a policy target of M1, or other monetary aggregates, depended on its having a reasonably stable or predictable relationship to the ultimate objectives of policy - sustained economic growth with general price stability. Thus, M1 would be less desirable as a policy target, or certainly as a relatively rigid one, the more the uncertainty about public preferences for it, given income and interest rates, as had been the case in the mid-1970s. However, evidence from econometric models suggested that the large-scale demand shifts of that period had not been repeated (or reversed) in later years of the decade.

Still, innovations and regulatory changes affecting the public's disposition to hold M1, as well as other monetary assets, were in process that had to be taken into account in setting target ranges and that also necessitated a redefinition of M1 and other aggregates. Interest-bearing accounts against which checks could be written (termed NOW accounts), offered by both banks and thrift institutions, were introduced first in New England and then in a few other states. M1 was redefined in 1980 to include such accounts, and certain other definitional changes affecting it and the broader aggregates were also made at the time (see Federal Reserve Bulletin (February 1980), 97-114). Later, NOW accounts were introduced on a nationwide basis at the beginning of 1981. The annual growth ranges for M1 set from 1979 through 1981 attempted to make allowance for shifts in funds that would take place in the course of the year in response to the introduction of new accounts. Effects of the shifts were confined almost entirely to M1, since shifts among various deposit instruments were offsetting in the higher order aggregates.

Tying policy operations more closely to the behavior of M1 to reduce inflationary pressures and inflationary expectations heightened the need to assess on an ongoing basis whether, or to what extent, institutional change was affecting public's attitudes toward and use of the aggregate in relation to estimates made when the targets were set. This assessment was made more complicated by the increased instability of M1, month-by-month and quarter-by-quarter, as compared with earlier periods. A question naturally arises about whether that short-run instability was itself the product of the particular operating procedure used.

That seems doubtful in the conditions of the time. Much of the variation was associated with the credit control program introduced in the spring of 1980 and rescinded several months later. The program as such was mild, but the psychological impact on the public was strong - leading to a sharp rundown in debt, the money supply, and interest rates after inception followed by a ballooning of all three after re-scission. Beyond that, the financial innovations, variations in credit demands, and general uncertainties about the future engendered as an almost inevitable by-product of the fight against inflation and questions about its ultimate success were associated with large variations in attitudes toward financial assets and concomitantly money. Given these conditions, it would seem as if money variations were the product mostly of short-run demand disturbances; thus, if money growth some-how could have been stabilized from month to month, the probable result would have been even greater interest rate volatility (see Tinsley (1981)).

2.3. The shift in policy approach in late 1982

The policy adopted in October 1979 was successful in reducing the rate of inflation - with the rate of increase in consumer prices dropping rapidly from about 12.5 per cent in 1980 to about 4 per cent in 1982. M1 growth fell to 7.5 per cent in 1980, 5 per cent in 1981, and about 6 per cent (annual rate) over the first three quarters of 1982 - after growing at a little more than an 8 per cent annual rate in the 2-3/4 years prior to October 1979.

The cost of the reduction in inflation was a substantial recession with relatively high levels of unemployment. In that sense, the new operating procedure for monetary policy had not led to a very large, virtually miraculous downward shift of the Phillips curve lowering the inflation rate sharply for any given unemployment rate. Still, so far as can be judged from qualitative information, the willingness to stick to the new procedure through a very difficult and volatile period greatly increased the Federal Reserve's credibility in fighting inflation. Thus, it seems likely that the approach itself did, as time went on, have at least some beneficial impact on attitudes in labor and product markets and on the position of the Phillips curve.

Some "casual" empirical evidence that is at least not inconsistent may be found in recent wage and price data. Through the first year and a half of an exceptionally rapid economic recovery accompanied by a sharp drop in the unemployment rate, consumer prices have increased relatively moderately - remaining around 4 per cent at an annual rate. True, prices typically do not tend to accelerate noticeably until later in an expansion. But wage settlements have thus far been unusually modest given the reduction in the unemployment rate.

Moreover, the policy shift in late 1982 - when the new operating procedure was abandoned as M1 was de-emphasized, followed by a very rapid surge of MI growth - did not tend to exacerbate inflationary expectations. Even though M1 expanded at near an 11.5 per cent rate from mid-1982 to mid-1983, long-term interest rates declined sharply over the period, and the dollar actually appreciated somewhat on exchange markets. Thus, it might be concluded that the credibility obtained during the period of a rather strict reserve aggregate-M1 oriented operating procedure was at least in some part responsible for enabling the Federal Reserve to accommodate to a sharp reacceleration of M1 growth without igniting inflationary expectations. Of course, the weakness of the economy at the time was another and very important factor keeping inflation expectations from reviving.

3.   DE-EMPHASIS OF M1

The precipitating event for the de-emphasis of M1 was the maturity of a very large volume ($31 billion) of all-savers certificates in October 1982, and uncertainty about how M1 might be affected in the process of the public's reinvesting those funds in other instruments[1]. In addition, movements of funds into and out of M1 were also going to be affected in uncertain amounts by regulatory changes scheduled within a couple of months permitting the introduction of money market type

(1) The certificates,which bore a very favorable yield and originally a one-year maturity , had been authorized by law a year earlier as part of a special effort to channel funds into agricultural and housing loans. The large volume issued in the first month matured in October 1982, and most holders did not have the option of reinvesting in the certificates.

accounts at banks and thrift institutions. But the more sustained de-emphasis of M1 as a guide to policy implementation was connected basically with the apparent change in preference by the public that was becoming observable for holding liquid assets in the form of M1. There was evidence of increased demand for M1, given income and interest rates, leading to historically atypical, sharp declines in the velocity of M1 or smaller than usual increases at the same time as M1 growth was moving above target ranges in the latter part of 1982 and through much of 1983.

While it was uncertain how long such a shift in preference would last, it seemed at least in part related to the change in structure of deposits that had taken place in the previous years and in the role played by the new assets in M1 in the public's portfolio choices. In particular, NOW accounts had grown by that time to nearly $100 billion, or almost 30 per cent of the deposits in M1, and these accounts - whose turnover on average was low relative to demand deposits - served both as a repository for longer-term savings and a means of payment. As interest rates declined in reflection of weakening credit demands and abatement of inflationary expectations, the public increased the amount of funds it was willing to place in NOW accounts, just as it was also increasing the amount of funds flowing into ordinary savings accounts. As market interest rates declined the opportunity cost of holding money in interest-bearing NOW accounts dropped relatively more rapidly than in the case of demand deposits that bore no explicit interest. Thus, incentives for holding M1-type assets had shifted favorably.

Even without the change in the structure of M1 caused by the introduction of NOW accounts, one might well have expected a decrease in M1 velocity as interest rates dropped sharply. And the drop relative to a prior trend might have been expected to be permanent in the degree that it reflected a downward adjustment of inflationary expectations (with increased demand for money relative to goods) and an associated sustained lower level of market interest rates (with increased demand for money relative to other financial assets).

It has been much debated whether the observed reduction in velocity reflected:

- a movement along an existing money demand curve as interest rates

dropped;
- a shift in the existing demand curve;
- the emergence of a new demand curve with a different interest-elasticity and implying a different long-run trend in velocity;
- or simply aberrant behavior related to special, non recurrent circumstances of the time such as uncertainties affecting financial and other markets that may have heightened precautionary demands for highly liquid assets (see Axilrod (1983); Simpson (1984); Brayton, Farr and Porter (May 1983)).

It is probably even now still too soon to be certain of the explanation, or the relative importance of various explanations. But in view of all the unusual circumstances and institutional changes through the early 1980s, it seems unlikely that monetary policy was dealing simply with a movement of money in relation to income implied by a pre-existing demand curve. Of course, even if it had been, and if that curve implied a sufficiently large interest-elasticity of money demand, it would still be the case that rapid money growth would have needed to have been encouraged.

That conclusion would be drawn on the assumption that the demand for goods and services at any given level of interest rates had fallen exogenously (as was quite likely given the reduction of inflationary expectations), so that an especially large actual money growth was required both to encourage economic expansion and to satisfy the demands of money holders. In other words, given a downward shift in the demands for goods and services, the velocity of money would tend to drop for any given money supply; the choice for policy is whether the drop would be more reflected in rising money or lower income.

Since the latter part of 1983, the income velocity of M1 has been rising at a pace not far from earlier cyclical experience. This has contributed to some restoration of confidence in that aggregate as a guide, though it has not been restored to the same role as before late 1982. It is still too soon to be sure about the underlying trend, not to mention the cyclical behavior, of its velocity, given the changed composition of the aggregate as well as the new deposits and fund outlets (such as money market deposit accounts and money market funds) in other, higher-order aggregates that also serve as both a means of payments and a store of liquidity.

Many would take the view that the trend increase of M1 velocity has been lowered on the thought that, with deregulation of deposit rate ceilings, the pace of technological innovation may diminish. Also, with deposits in M1 more affected by savings motives, the elasticity of demand with respect to income may be higher than previously. But the intensifying competition for financial and payments services and the still evolving deposit markets leave considerable room for doubt about any such conclusion with respect to M1, and have also complicated, and made more uncertain, the interpretation of the other monetary aggregates.

In all of these circumstances, while the aggregates remain as important guides to policy operations, and policy objectives are presented in terms of money and credit aggregates, ongoing money supply behavior has needed to be interpreted, more so than usual, in light of surrounding economic and financial conditions. The implementation of policy has thus necessarily become more judgmental than it was in the late 1979- late 1982 period. The result is that changes in pressures on bank reserve positions do not more or less automatically respond to variations in money demand as they affect the demand for reserves relative to a fixed nonborrowed reserve path. Rather, the reserve path is more frequently adjusted on a week-to-week basis to accommodate to short-run money behavior, with the degree of reserve pressure embodied in the path - indexed by the amount of borrowing allowed for at the discount window - judgmentally set, in light of incoming information, as thought consistent with desired money and credit growth over a longer period.

Partly in view of the uncertainties that came to affect the monetary aggregates because of institutional change, the Federal Reserve also introduced a broad credit aggregate - the debt (whether incurred in domestic markets or abroad) of domestic nonfinancial sectors - for monitoring purposes and began stipulating annual growth ranges for that aggregate as well as for measures of the money supply. A debt aggregate is less affected by shifts in preferences for differing financial assets, and provides a basis for assessing the interaction of credit and money demands in relation to the underlying policy objective sustained economic growth and reasonable price stability.

4.   THE IMPACT OF FISCAL POLICY

The credit variable and its components have proved to be especially useful in evaluating the impact of fiscal policy on credit markets and in relation to monetary policy. Fiscal policy, as measured by
growing high employment deficits (accompanied by even larger actual
deficits), has been a major element in shaping the rapid recovery and
expansion following the 1981-1982 recession. In 1983, U.S. Government
debt expanded by 21.5 per cent, whereas it had risen by almost 8.5
per cent on average in the first year of five previous recoveries. At
the same time, private debt rose by around 8 per cent, close to its
pace in the first year of earlier recoveries. Spurred evidently by the
rise in federal borrowing, total debt rose by almost 11 per cent last
year, about 3 percentage points more than the average of earlier recoveries, while nominal GNP grew about the same as its average in the
comparable earlier periods.

By the second year after a cyclical low in economic activity,
federal debt expansion normally slows sharply to about a 4 percent
rate. In the first half of 1984, however, federal debt expansion, while
slowing somewhat from the year before, continued at a very rapid 15
per cent annual rate. At the same time, private debt expansion accelerated to about an 11 per cent annual rate (abstracting from growth of
merger-related debt issues), about the same as in comparable periods of
earlier recoveries. The sustained strength of federal debt expansion
brought total debt growth in the first half of this year to a little less
than a 12 per cent annual rate (again abstracting from merger-related
debt) - above the range for the year anticipated by the Federal Reserve
in setting its money and credit ranges and also nearly 4 percentage
points more than in the second year of earlier expansions.

With fiscal policy remaining quite stimulative into the second year
of expansion, and with the market concerned that deficits would remain
large even as economic growth continues, nominal and presumably real
interest rates have remained relatively high. Indeed, market rates rose
into the summer of 1984. However, after mid-year, through early fall,
first long-term and later short-term interest rates declined somewhat,
retracing a part of their rise earlier in the year.

The behavior of interest rates during the current year was consistent with growth of M1 and M2 within target ranges. The money demand function, which had behaved atypically during the recession and very early in the recovery, seemed in late 1983 and thus far in 1984 to be more consistent with historical expectations. Thus, the rise of interest rates in the first part of 1984 can be viewed more as the result of strong credit demands stemming from an upward shift in the demand for goods and services, impelled in part by the continued federal deficit. Subsequent declines of rates probably reflected moderation, or expected moderation, of private credit demands, and demand for money as economic growth slowed over the summer and as indications of upward price pressures remained limited. In addition, there was some lessening of tension in the financial system as Latin American debt negotiations were in process of resolution and problems with certain large depository institutions were contained.

5.   BALANCE OF PAYMENTS AND DOLLAR EXCHANGE RATE

The strength of demands for goods so far this year has not been reflected in additional upward price pressures, or in conventional signs of anticipated upward price pressures, such as intentions to accumulate inventories well ahead of sales. While this good price performance partly reflects the still relatively sizable amount of unused labor and plant resources, it may also reflect the increased conviction that monetary policy will in fact restrain inflation and work toward price stability. But the ability of U.S. demands for goods and services to increase unusually rapidly in the first eighteen months of recovery without signs of further price pressure also needs to be considered in relation to the relatively high value of the dollar on exchange markets and the sharp turn toward deficit in the U.S. current account of the balance of payments – a deficit that reached $42 billion in 1983 and may be estimated close to $90 billion at an annual rate in the first half of 1984 (with trade deficits that are some $15 tot $20 billion deeper).

The deficits have permitted expansion of spending by domestic sectors without concomitant pressure on U.S. productive capacity and resources. Over the first six quarters of recovery, real GNP rose by 7.25 per cent (annual rate) while real spending increased by 8.75 per cent (annual rate). As an aspect of that, private investment and the

Federal deficit were financed to a greater extent than normal by net inflows of foreign saving. Such inflows amounted to almost 12.5 per cent of the sum of net private investment and the federal deficit in 1983 and rose to 20 percent in the first half of 1984.

More remarkable than these arithmetic relationships to GNP and its components, the current account deficits have not been accompanied by any significant tendency for the dollar to decline in value on exchange markets. Indeed, quite the opposite, and from the end of 1982 through September 1984 the dollar rose by about 22 per cent on a multilateral trade-weighted basis. Foreigners have been quite willing to finance U.S. consumption in excess of output and private investment and a budgetary deficit in excess of domestic saving. The question naturally arises whether this should be construed as an event exogenous to policy, or should be viewed as the product of policies in place.

It is probably some of both. As a response to policies, it would seem to be less related to monetary policy alone than to the mix between fiscal and monetary policies – a mix that has worked, through shifts noted above in the demand for goods and services induced by fiscal policy, to keep interest rates higher than they otherwise would be. As an event exogenous to policy, it reflects the shift of international investment preferences toward the United States, for any given interest differential, caused by political disturbances abroad, reduced confidence in countries burdened with debt crises, and a positive change in attitude toward the U.S. as confidence in its economy revived (signalled first, perhaps, by the huge stock market rally in the second half of 1982).

Particularly to the extent that dollar exchange rates have remained high for exogenous reasons, one might view the current account deficit as capital-account determined rather than vice-versa. In that sense, the growing demand for goods and services could be accommodated in part by "artificially" low-priced imports, taking pressure off domestic resources and keeping the level of domestic prices lower than it would otherwise be. Once the exogenous shift in investment preferences toward the dollar is completed, and particularly if it begins being reversed, there is the risk that domestic prices will adjust upwards – although any such rise could be moderated to the extent that domestic demands are reduced commensurately (by, for example, more fiscal restraint) or foreigners more than usually absorb a reduction in home currency profits. However that eventually works out, the unusually large current account deficit and relatively high exchange rate make it difficult to be certain that progress toward price stability has been as great as the published price series might suggest.

6. CONCLUDING OBSERVATIONS

This broad review of monetary policy in the U.S. during recent years suggests a number of general observations, as well as observations more specific to current conditions.

a) Monetary policy has been confronted both by shifts in the demand for goods and services, given interest rates, and in the demand for money, given interest rates and income. Downward shifts in the demand for goods and services seemed evident from the psychological impact associated with initiation of the credit control program in early 1980 and during the recession of 1982 when inflationary expectations began to wane; upward shifts appeared as the credit control program was lifted and more recently in the wake of the turn to a quite expansionary fiscal policy. The shifts related to the psychological impact of the credit control program were very short-run in nature, disturbances of no more than a quarter or so. The impacts of other shifts noted took place over a more sustained period. Meanwhile, through much of the period since the mid-1970s there were widespread institutional and regulatory changes introducing new instruments to serve as money or money substitutes, or affecting the implicit or explicit price of old instruments, that led to shifts in the demand for money relative to historical experience.

b) It is by now very conventional wisdom that a money supply target for monetary policy will produce better policy in the face of shifts in the demand for goods and services than it will in face of shifts in the demand for money. It does not necessarily follow that a money supply target, or guide, should be abandoned when there are shifts in the demand for money. So long as shifts in demand for goods and services are with us - and I suspect that they are, except for occasions, the dominant type of shift - there is obvious value to a money supply guide, but one that necessarily entails certain judgmental adjustments to allow for, among other things, shifts in money demand.

c) Shifts in money demand may be most easily and clearly allowed for in advance in monetary targets when a known regulatory change is to take place, such as payment of interest on demand deposits (to which the introduction of NOW accounts was tantamount), with fairly predictable one-time effects. When institutional change is taking place from internally generated market process, as in 1975-76, it is extremely difficult to know what will happen in advance, requiring adjustments on an ongoing basis as best that may be estimated. Or after the initial adjustment to a regulatory change, like the introduction of NOW accounts nationwide, has been accomplished, it may also be some time before one can be reasonably certain in advance how the public will respond in varying economic circumstance given the changes in the composition of money assets and presumably also in the motives and sensitivity to changing market conditions of money holders.

d) The advantage of retaining money guides is that they provide protection against the everpresent, unanticipated shocks to demand for goods and services and provide the public with a sense that there is a discipline on the central bank, even though uncertainties about money demand tend to argue for a more judgmental approach to policy implementation, including a willingness to adjust targets in light of evolving circumstances. For instance, one might argue that money growth targets should have been lowered in 1975-76, just as the M1 target was effectively raised in 1982-83. The ability of a central bank to adjust or miss monetary targets without impairing its credibility in fighting inflation depends on the underlying conviction in the marketplace that the central bank has the will to encourage price stability. That obviously depends on surrounding circumstances, actual price behavior, and the whole historical background that goes into determining a central bank's "image". In the late 1970s, money target misses, and evidence of accelerating prices, eroded the market's confidence in the Federal Reserve's will. That has not happened thus far in the 1980s, reflecting, one might judge, the credibility gained by the policy approach of late 1979 to the fall 1982 and the continuing moderate behavior of prices after that policy approach was dropped and followed by a more judgmental one (but still based on money targets). Moreover, money growth in 1984, as measured by M1 and M2, has been well within target ranges.

e) While the credibility of monetary policy has increased in recent years, there is probably some way to go before the public is fully convinced that policy is aimed at and will achieve price stability over some reasonable period of time. Considerable progress has been made in curbing inflation, but there can be doubt about the exact extent of progress to date in part because of the still relatively strong dollar exchange rate in face of persisting large current account deficits and in part because the more intense upward price pressures normally are later in an expansion. Future prospects for curbing inflation further are also subject to doubt because the lack of progress so far in reducing planned federal deficits raises questions in the minds of market participants about the will of the government generally.

f) Nominal market interest rates that have been high relative to the observed comparatively low increase in the average level of prices as the current economic expansion has continued may be taken as an indication that inflationary expectations, though lower than in the early 1980s, remain well above zero. However, interest rates appear to have been high in real as well as nominal terms, reflecting in part the exogenous upward shift in the demands for goods and services engendered by the continuing stimulative fiscal policy.

g) In contrast to the behavior of interest rates in credit markets, price and wage behavior in labor and product markets do not seem to suggest particularly strong inflationary expectations. Unless one takes the view that the real rate of return on investment goods over time will be exceptionally high, the question arises as to why borrowers have been willing to pay prevailing high nominal and real market interest rates. Business borrowers would do so to finance longer-term capital outlays either if they expect inflation to accelerate or if they expect market rates to decline. In the latter respect, while the present yield curve does not suggest future rate declines, corporate financing has been concentrated in the short-term market or in floating rate obligations, an approach consistent with expectations, or hopes, that current capital outlays can be refinanced later at lower market rates. There is an obvious potential for problems if there are expectational differences

about inflation between real and financial markets - or between expectations in both markets and intentions on the part of monetary
policymakers. A conflict in expectations between real and financial
markets cannot be long sustained, resolvable either as expectations in
financial markets improve or as they worsen in real markets. An improvement of inflationary expectations in financial markets could take
the form of shifts out of money-type assets into intermediate- or
longer-term securities, with consequent downward impacts on interest
rates on such securities, as well as on short-term interest rates as
reserves were provided to maintain money growth. A worsening of
expectations in real markets would be manifested in upward price pressures needed, among other reasons, to generate the income for servicing
high interest rate debt (as it became more feared that existing debt
would not turn out to be refundable at lower rates). Assuming U.S.
monetary policy is in fact on a course toward reasonable price stability
over time, an early improvement in financial market expectations represents the smoother process of adjustment - an improvement that
would be greatly promoted by a turn toward a less expansionary fiscal
policy.

REFERENCES

Axilrod, S.H. (1981), "New Monetary Control Procedure: Findings and
Evaluation from a Federal Reserve Study", *Federal Reserve Bulletin*, Vol. 67 (April), 277-290.

Axilrod, S.H. (1982), "Monetary Policy, Money Supply, and the Federal
Reserve's Operating Procedures", *Federal Reserve Bulletin*, Vol.68
(January), 13-24.

Axilrod, S.H. (1983), "Issues in Monetary Targeting and Velocity", in
Federal Reserve Bank of San Francisco, *Monetary Targeting and
Velocity*, Proceedings of a Conference (December), 4-13.

Axilrod, S.H. and Lindsey, D.E., (1981), "Federal Reserve System
Implementation of Monetary Policy: Analytical Foundations of the
New Approach", *American Economic Review, Papers and Proceed-
ings*, (May), 246-252.

Blinder, A.S. (1982), "The Anatomy of Double Digit Inflation in the
1970s", in Hall, R.E. (ed.), *Inflation: Causes and Effects*,
Chicago.

Brayton, F. Farr, T. and Porter, R. (1983), "Alternative Money Demand Specifications and Recent Growth in M1", (Board of Governors of the Federal Reserve System, Division of Research and Statistics, May).

Brunner, K. and Meltzer, A.H. (1983), "Strategies and Tactics for Monetary Control", *Carnegie-Rochester Conference Series on Public Policy*, Vol. 18 (Spring).

Porter, R.D., Simpson, Th.D. and Mauskopf, E. (1979), "Financial Innovation and the Monetary Aggregates", *Brookings Papers on Economic Activity* (1), 213-229.

Simpson, Th.D. (1984), "Changes in the Financial System: Implications for Monetary Policy", *Brookings Papers on Economic Activity* (1), 249-272.

Tinsley, P.A. and others (1981), "Money Market Impacts of Alternative Operating Procedures", in Board of Governors of the Federal Reserve System, *New Monetary Control Procedures*, Federal Reserve Staff Study, Vol. 2.

3. MONETARY CONTROL - THE BRITISH EXPERIENCE

C.A.E. Goodhart[*]

1. INTRODUCTION

This paper is concerned with the evolution of monetary control during a period of structural change. It reviews the British experience from the late 1950s to the present, and considers the way in which control techniques have both influenced and been influenced by financial innovation. Structural changes appear to come in waves. In Britain, the main structural forms of financial intermediation had remained essentially unchanged and constant over the first 60 years of the twentieth century. Since then, however, the industry has undergone a major transformation with some far-reaching consequences for monetary control. The dynamic for change arose in part from increased volatility and uncertainty in world financial markets from the late 1960s, reflecting in large part the unsettled, worse inflationary experience of this period, but also responded to pressures from competition to relax some of the constraints imposed by financial regulation, as well as the rapid advance of information technology.

The paper begins by reviewing the control arrangements before the pressures for change began to gather momentum. The principal statement of policy at this time was the report of the Radcliffe enquiry in 1959. (Committee on the Working of the Monetary System, The Radcliffe Report, August 1959, Cmnd. 827). Section 1 considers the main precepts of the Radcliffe Report and the pressures for change in control arrangements which followed in 1971 and the problems which quick-

[*] The preparation of this paper has owed much to the help of Mr. C.B. Wright. Nevertheless, the opinions and arguments presented are solely those of the author himself, and should not be attributed to any other person or institution.

ly emerged. The third section deals more fully with the relationship
between structural change and monetary control after 1971. In particular, it is concerned with the implications for monetary control of the
banks' adoption of liability management. Section 4 then considers an
alternative control system, monetary base control, which was actively
discussed in 1979. Finally, the paper considers some of the current
issues confronting the monetary authorities.

2.   THE POST RADCLIFFE ENVIRONMENT

The post-war commitment to full employment under fixed exchange
rates caused successive governments throughout the 1950s and 1960s to
direct policy toward the achievement of sustained economic growth,
subject to the constraints imposed by the balance of payments. The
broad strategy of counter-cyclical demand management through fiscal
policy was balanced by an essentially permissive role for monetary
policy, generally in the form of secondary supporting measures. Radcliffe saw this role as one of influencing "liquidity" - a very broad and
unquantifiable concept - through adjusting the general level of interest
rates, supported at times of particular pressure by a range of direct
restrictions on credit, principally in the areas of instalment finance and
bank lending. Interest rates, however, were judged to command only a
very modest and uncertain influence on real expenditure, and came to
be seen more as an instrument directed toward international capital
flows in support of the exchange rate [1]. The extension of capital
mobility after 1958 and the subsequent growth of the market for euro-
dollars, led the Bank increasingly into this aspect of policy.

Interest rates were therefore normally set with reference to the
broad aims of economic policy, particularly the achievement of external
objectives. They were not, by and large, adjusted specifically to influence bank lending or the growth of the monetary aggregates, nor
was there much sustained attempt to achieve these latter ends by placing

(1) An important exception was the strong link seen between interest
rates and housebuilding. See, for example, "The Operation of Monetary
Policy Since the Radcliffe Report", Bank of England, Quarterly Bulletin
(BEQB), December 1969, page 454.

pressure directly on banks' cash or liquidity ratios[1]. The high levels of government debt in bank portfolios after the war, and the desire to maintain interest rates reasonably stable at appropriate levels, would have rendered credit control by this means very uncertain in its effect, and, with the authorities looking with one eye to recurring and worsening pressures on sterling, and with the other to the need to roll over maturing debt, credit control came to depend more and more upon direct and specific restrictions particularly during the 1960s. Furthermore, the experience of the 1930s, and the legacy of Keynes' own strongly-held views, led many of those in authority to aim to maintain interest rates as low (and as stable) as could be consistent with holding onto the external parity.

While this approach was conceptually simple, the authorities became increasingly concerned with the disadvantages of direct controls, the problems of administering what was essentially a voluntary agreement with the banks, and the longer-term distortions which the presence of restrictions was encouraging. At one extreme, new forms of financial company were taking advantage of the very specific coverage of the controls (see, for example, "Competition, Innovation and Regulation in British Banking", BEQB, September 1983, page 364). At the other extreme, the cartel arrangements operated by the London Clearing Banks were receiving critical public scrutiny [2].

Parallel to these developments, academic and market opinion in the late 1960s was opening the way to a renewed discussion of monetary control techniques Research at the Bank and elsewhere (see, for example, "The Importance of Money", BEQB, June 1979; and Fischer (1968)) had identified apparently stable relationships between both broad

---

(1) Ibid, page 454. The cash and liquid asset ratios were also thought to fulfil a prudential role, although the latter was seen as exerting some leverage on monetary expansion, particularly when supported by calls for special deposits.
(2) This was exemplified in two public discussions of bank behaviour, the first concerning pricing policy and the second concerning a proposed merger between three London Clearing Banks:
(i)   National Board for Prices and Incomes Report, No. 34, "Bank Charges", 1967;
(ii) Monopolies Commission (HMSO), 1968.

and narrow definitions of the money supply, interest rates and money income. Interest rates, it seemed, could provide a reasonably predictable control over credit expansion by influencing the stock of money which the non-bank private sector planned to hold, and hence contain or promote the growth of bank liabilities.

Changes in the stock of broad money, e.g. M3, moreover, have their asset counterparts in the growth of bank lending to the private sector, the public sector's borrowing requirement, net of debt sales to the non-bank private sector, and external monetary flows. (For the derivation of the asset counterpart identity to M3 see "Domestic Credit Expansion", BEQB, September 1969, page 368). The ability to identify, examine and assess changes in the stock of broad money in terms of these asset counterparts has several advantages, notably in encouraging a coherence between different policy instruments. (On this, as on many other points raised in this paper, readers could also usefully refer to the paper by J.S. Fforde, "Setting monetary objectives", BEQB, June 1983). These components may be thought of as the contributions to monetary growth of credit policy, fiscal policy, debt management and external policy. This analysis reaffirmed the particular importance given to influencing the volume of bank lending to the private sector, but also underlined the emerging concern with broader monetary growth. In 1969, the authorities (a term which comprehends both the Bank and the Treasury, under the overall guidance of the Chancellor of the Exchequer), (prompted by the IMF who ascribed the apparent failure of the British balance of payments to recover after the 1967 devaluation to an excessively-accommodating monetary policy), adopted the concept of Domestic Credit Expansion (DCE; see "Domestic Credit Expansion", BEQB, September 1969) – monetary growth net of any change in money balances directly resulting from an external monetary flow – and stated their intention to achieve a satisfactory rate of DCE. Both DCE and the other measures of money supply were to be used as indicators; yet, for a further two years, direct controls on bank lending remained in force, and continued to be the principal means of restraint.

In 1971, however, with an improving balance of payments offering scope for shifting the balance of attention back to domestic concerns, and with a relatively sluggish economy providing an advantageous occasion both for ending direct controls and for the adoption of greater interest rate flexibility, the Bank introduced a radical change in its monetary control arrangements. Competition and Credit Control, as it came to be known, confirmed the Bank's commitment to the broader monetary aggregates as the main indicator, but now placed interest rates as the central pivot through which monetary control was to be achieved. The new arrangements dismantled the existing direct controls on lending and replaced the cash and liquid assets ratios applying to the deposit banks, by a single ratio of specified reserve assets to sterling deposit liabilities to be maintained by all banks. Discussing the new arrangements in a speech in Munich prior to their introduction, the then Governor summarised our intentions. "What we are adopting is a new approach to credit control designed to permit the price mechanism to function efficiently in the allocation of credit, and to free the banks from rigidities and restraints which have, for far too long, inhibited them from efficiently fulfilling their intermediary role in the financial system" (see "Key issues in Monetary and Credit Policy", BEQB, June 1971).

3.   COMPETITION AND CREDIT CONTROL[1]

The removal of ceiling controls was unquestionably an important fillip for the banks. Reintermediation began almost immediately with lending to those sectors most affected by direct controls, notably lending to persons, rising strongly throughout 1971 and 1973. The government was simultaneously promoting expansionary fiscal measures and reacted to pressures on the exchange rate by floating sterling. At the same time, an innovative departure in banking practice – active bidding for deposits in wholesale money markets (see section 4.) – was providing funds to accommodate the rise in lending. Taken together, these three factors, reintermediation, fiscal expansion, and the intro-duction of liability management, created the conditions for rapid monet-ary expansion. In the two years to the end of 1973, M3 grew at an average annual rate of some 28% against an equivalent rate of just 8% throughout the preceding 8 years (table 1).

(1) See "Competition and Credit Control", BEQB, June 1971, for an ex-planation of the detailed changes introduced in 1971.

TABLE 1

Monetary growth after the introduction of CCC

End- year % changes at an annual rate	1963-71	1971-73
£ Bank lending to private sector	.	42.8
Of which: Persons	.	55.9
M1	5.3	9.5
M3	7.5	27.7
House prices	8.2	28.2

Such comparisons were naturally raising acute concern within the Bank and generating a good deal of criticism outside. A rapid acceleration in the growth of house prices throughout 1972 (chart 1), an associated rise in the commercial property market, and the over-rapid growth of many deposit-taking institutions beyond the reach of the then existing supervision arrangements, added to the impression of unruly markets. The new arrangements were quite clearly improving the competitive environment but had so far left unanswered the question of credit control. This was to have been achieved through the influence of interest rates on banks' sterling business. Higher lending rates would reduce demand, while higher rates available on public sector debt relative to administered bank deposit rates would lead to a transfer of deposits away from banks. In practice, however, loan demand was not noticeably or quickly responsive to higher interest rates. Indeed it proved much stronger than had been expected. The banks obtained the funds to on-lend by bidding for wholesale deposits. This, in turn, paved the way for a serious monetary distortion which had not been foreseen when the new arrangements were introduced. The stickiness of administered bank lending rates was an acknowledged feature of the monetary system. Prior to the dismantling of lending ceilings, it had no serious implications for monetary control, and, even after their removal, might not, without the availability of wholesale funds, have given rise to any serious difficulties. The rapid growth of a highly competitive market in wholesale lending to the banks meant, however, that the interest spread between bank lending rates and wholesale money market rates was to take on a new operational significance. As money market rates rose, the spread with bank lending rates was squeezed, at times

CHART 1

UK House Prices

£   Logarithmic scale

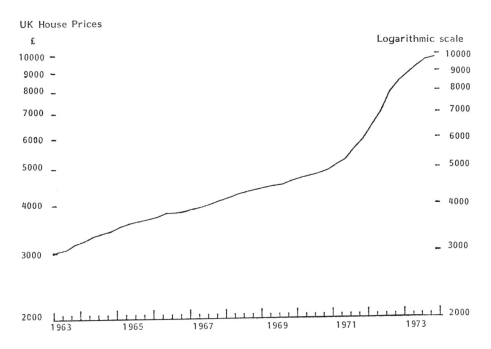

actually becoming perverse. The smaller the interest spread, i.e. the lower the price of intermediation, the greater would be the demand for liquidity. Bank customers may be encouraged to extend their liquidity using borrowed funds. In 1972 and 1973, many large customers ex-tended their borrowing from the banks only to redeposit the funds through the wholesale market. "Round-tripping", as it became known, had the effect of inflating both sides of the banks' books and con-stituted a highly unstable element in the growth of M3.

The resolute pursuit of an increasingly restrictive interest rate policy would, no doubt, have eventually broken into the spiral but the level to which rates would have been forced was by no means clear. With interest rates already at a politically unpopular level, the auth-orities chose rather the revert to a ceiling control, although of a kind which was quite unlike those previously employed. The Supplementary Special Deposit Scheme (SSD Scheme), introduced in December 1973, restricted liability management by imposing a steeply rising marginal cost on the growth of interest bearing sterling deposits. In restricting banks' liabilities rather than their assets as previous controls had done, it also reflected the change in target indicator from bank lending to the money supply[1]. The SSD scheme, "the corset" as it was more commonly known, was followed by a return to more acceptable monetary growth, although coinciding as it did with the collapse of the property market, the associated crisis which resulted for many secondary banks, and the onset of economic recession, it is difficult to establish cause and effect. M3 grew at an annual rate of just over 10% over the next three years, compared with an equivalent growth of 20% for nominal GDP. The slower growth of real output during the second half of the 1970s was a constraining factor; yet monetary pressures built up again in 1976, largely as a result of external flows, and the corset was reactivated as part of a package of measures intended to restrict domestic credit.

The 1974 and 1976-77 uses of the corset, which together added up to about two years of direct control, began again a process of disintermediation, which was eventually to lead to its abandonment following a third period from 1978-80. One of the best documented examples, the commercial bill leak, involved the banks bringing together potential borrowers and lenders and issuing funds through the acceptance of a bill which the bank guaranteed and sold on as a near substitute for a certificate of deposit. This type of operation grew rapidly throughout 1974 and 1976-77, but appeared in the banks' books only as a contingent liability and so was not measured in the growth of the money supply. The bill leak reopened during the third and final use of the corset from 1978 to 1980, but was compounded on this occasion by the lifting of exchange controls in 1979 which allowed banks to channel business through their offshore subsidiaries. The experience suggests that direct controls can only be effective over a relatively short time horizon, and when exchange controls are in operation. They need to be modified regularly, for over-reliance on even the most successful of schemes will quickly lead to control being circumvented.

(1) A full account of the operation of the scheme is given in "The Supplementary Special Deposit Scheme", BEQB, March 1982.

CHART 2

Year on year growth in money and bank lending

Per cent

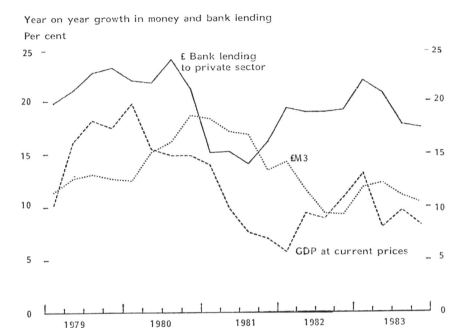

£ Bank lending to private sector

£M3

GDP at current prices

1979   1980   1981   1982   1983

The fact that the corset ceilings were circumvented through the above-mentioned channels is interesting for it demonstrates, and illustrates, a difference between UK experience and that of several other European countries. In particular, the provisions of the scheme explicitly *excluded* deposits with a maturity of more than two years from banks' eligible liabilities, and therefore from the constraints of the scheme. Within the terms of the controls, banks were therefore free to finance additional lending by attracting funds into less liquid forms of savings instruments, deposits or short term bonds. This type of non-monetary financing is common in France, the Federal Republic of Germany, Switzerland, and the Netherlands, but has so far failed to develop in the UK, despite the encouragement for its development provided by the "corset". It is interesting to ask: why not? One possible explanation is that a medium term savings instrument of this kind would have to compete with a wide range of existing instruments in the UK's financial markets, whereas there are fewer competing assets in most other European countries. This argument is not, however, entirely convincing, and the question must remain an open one.

TABLE 2

Monetary growth and corporate finance

Year end annual growth rate	1979	1980	1981	1982	1983
£M3[1]	12.7	18.7	13.5	9.3	10.4
£ bank lending to private sector	23.2	21.1	16.2	19.2	17.5
£ bank lending to industrial and commercial companies (ICCs)	15.6	19.0	2.5	3.3	7.3

ICCs sources of funds as a percentage of total sources

Internally generated	75.2	64.2	63.9	61.7	74.1
Bank lending	12.3	22.1	18.5	23.4	5.8

(1) Since 1977, greater emphasis has been placed upon an alternative definition of M3, £M3, which excludes residents' holdings of foreign currency deposits with UK banks. The change reflected the growing proportion of foreign currency deposits in M3, resulting in part from their higher sterling valuation following exchange rate depreciation, but also, particularly since the abolition of exchange control in 1979, reflecting a genuine growth in such holdings. Foreign currency deposits included within M3 are principally retained by companies to finance their overseas operations and currency trading. Changes in such deposits are consequently more likely to reflect developments in international rather than domestic markets. See "DCE and the Money Supply - A Statistical Note",BEQB, March 1977.

The removal of exchange controls and the subsequent withdrawal of the SSD scheme were accompanied by a further change of emphasis in monetary control arrangements. Targets for monetary growth had been announced publicly since 1976, but (with official intervention in the foreign exchange market limited to smoothing operations after 1979) the focus of government policy was directed even more closely to the achievements of a, publicly-announced, target path for the monetary aggregates: thus the attainment of a target path for £M3 formed the centre-piece of the Government's Medium Term Financial Strategy (MTFS), unveiled in March 1980. The lifting of controls was nonetheless marked by higher bank lending and monetary growth (see chart 2 and table 2). This was, in part, the result of reintermediation, but also resulted from high corporate borrowing in 1980 and the rising needs of the public sector as the economy moved sharply into recession.

In the absence of direct credit controls, the authorities sought to influence bank lending to the private sector by varying interest rates. Econometric results for the UK unanimously indicate, however, a rather weak (short-term) and generally imprecise link between interest rates and the demand for loans. (See Green, (1984)). Accordingly, in view of the difficulties, at least in the short run, of influencing bank lending to the *private* sector, the authorities have sought to influence bank lending to the *public* sector in their pursuit of broad money targets, and have continued to pay close attention to the way in which the public sector's borrowing needs are financed, i.e. the extent to which they lead to monetary growth. Nevertheless, with bank lending to the private sector now representing such an overwhelming proportion of banks' sterling assets, it is difficult to maintain an appropriate restraint on monetary growth unless the cost of credit, and other influences, are such as to keep the growth of such private sector lending within reasonable bounds.

By financing public sector borrowing outside the banking sector, i.e. by selling public sector debt to the non-bank private sector (in practice longer-term public sector debt – Treasury bills being held mainly by the banks and discount houses), the authorities themselves operate in a manner analogous to European banks encouraging a transfer of funds from liquid (monetary) to less liquid (non-monetary) deposits. To reconcile high bank lending with the monetary targets, the authorities have resorted to heavy funding, even at times overfunding their borrowing requirement, i.e. they have sold debt in excess of their borrowing needs[1] (table 3). This puts pressure on the liquidity of the banks, to meet which banks initially became net sellers of public sector debt, but eventually they ran down their proportionate holdings to the acceptable minimum. To relax the resulting liquidity squeeze, the authorities have been prepared to purchase bills – first Treasury bills, and then, when the amount of Treasury bills outstanding had reached its minimum acceptable level – bank commercial bills. The net result is

(1) This technique has been more effective with floating exchange rates because of the tendency, seen with fixed or managed rates, for external flows to the public sector to work against the contractionary effect of higher debt sales.

TABLE 3

Counterparts to changes in money stock (£ billions)

	1979/80	1980/81	1981/82	1982/83	1983/84[1]
PSBR	10.0	12.7	8.6	8.9	9.7
– Debt sales to non-bank private sector	9.2	10.8	11.3	8.3	12.5
+ £ lending to UK private sector	9.3	9.2	14.9	14.4	15.1
+ External and foreign currency counterparts	-2.4	0.7	-0.8	-2.8	0.1
– Net non-deposit liabilities	1.2	1.5	1.7	2.4	4.8
= Change in £M3	6.5	10.3	9.7	9.8	7.6

(1) The fiscal year in the UK is measured from April 1 to March 31. Monetary targets are phased to coincide broadly with this period, and are curently set over 14 banking months (a banking month ends on the third Wednesday of each month (except in banking December)), the targets running from mid-February to mid-April of the following year.

that the public sector is borrowing long and lending short, in the same way as some European banks which finance bank lending on the basis of bonds or longer-term non-monetary deposits.

Several consequences follow from this refinancing operation. Firstly, banks' asset structures have shifted to give even more weight to bank lending (table 4A). Secondly, the authorities have accumulated a sizeable holding of banks' commercial paper (table 4B), sometimes called the "bill mountain". As these bills mature, the authorities have to roll them over in the market, and the question has been raised whether, and how far, this process may have lessened the flexibility of the markets to take their own view of interest rate developments independently of official operations. More speculative is the question of whether overfunding involves a cost to the authorities. The actual cost ex post will depend on the relative movement of short and long-term interest rates, but it is not clear that any particular relationship should be expected ex ante.

TABLE 4A

Changes in banks' asset structure - % of total £ domestic lending

End-years	1979	1980	1981	1982	1983
£ lending to private sector	75.1	76.0	74.9	79.8	83.7
£ lending to public sector	24.9	24.0	25.2	20.2	16.3

TABLE 4B

End-March	1980	1981	1982	1983	1984
Bank of England holding of Commercial Bills	791	2806	7046	6259	9845

4. LIABILITY MANAGEMENT AND BANK LENDING

Why has the pursuit of monetary targets apparently had such a chequered record? In order to examine this question, we need to turn again to the reforms of 1971 and to the adoption by the banks of liability management. These two events were not strictly associated, but the former undoubtedly influenced the timing of the latter and the effect of each is perhaps best understood in the context of the other.

In earlier years, the standard analysis of banking practice and of the determination of the money stock implicitly assumed an institution inviting deposits at an administered and relatively insensitive sticky rate, and onlending either to the public sector, by purchasing government securities, or to the private sector, by bank loans, with the latter again at administered sticky rates (see for the implications for monetary theory of legal and institutional restrictions on banks, Jao (1983)[1]). Banks balanced their portfolios through asset management, in the short run by purchases and sales of public sector debt. So, open market operations by the authorities would squeeze the cash base of the banks, causing them to sell longer dated debt, raising yields and placing

(1) Jao argues that restrictions implicitly underlie most models of bank behaviour and that relaxation or removal can give rise to radical change.

upward pressure on lending rates. Higher yields on marketable securities would encourage the non-bank private sector to transfer resources from bank deposits, while higher loan rates would reduce demand for loans, thereby bringing the banks back to equilibrium but with a reduced book. Total sterling deposits, and hence broad money, responded to the interest spread between bank deposit rates and rates on alternative assets, e.g. government securities. Empirical research into the demand for money using data from the 1960s is consistent with this analysis. Estimated demand functions for both narrow money, M1 and broad money, M3, consistently displayed high interest elasticities. These findings played an important part in the decision to change from control of lending through ceiling restrictions to a closer concern for the money supply through interest rate management, though, as noted earlier (see section 2.) there were also other major structural considerations.

The demand functions for M3 broke down, however, after 1971. The new institutional arrangements encouraged the banks to compete for lending business, and then to fund such additional assets by bidding for wholesale deposits by offering rates comparable with those in the money market. This allowed the banks to respond to a cash squeeze either by selling public sector debt, asset management, or by bidding for wholesale deposits, liability management. Liability management effectively broke the authorities' control over the spread between deposit rates and rates on marketable assets. Varying the general level of rates now had little impact on this spread. So long as banks had profitable lending outlets, they would bid for wholesale deposits. Not only would funds be attracted into wholesale deposits from other uses, both in the UK and abroad, as the rates on such deposits rose relative to rates elsewhere, but also if this caused a reduction in the spread between borrowing and deposit rates, i.e. in the *cost* of intermediation, there would be some incentive for an increase in such intermediation, i.e. in both borrowing and deposits, to occur (see Sprenkle and Miller, (1980)). As a consequence, the influence which the monetary authorities could exert over the size of banks' books came to depend on the interest elasticity of the demand for bank lending. This latter had not, of course, been directly observable while ceiling controls were operating,

TABLE 5

The Collapse of the Corporate Debenture Market

Average share of total ICCs' liabilities %

	1970/74	1975/79	1980/83
Bank borrowing	14.3	16.8	16.5
UK debenture and loan stock	5.8	3.1	2.0

but research had suggested that the impact was comparatively small, and was to become even smaller with the widening introduction of variable rate lending[1]. Certainly the empirical results gained in later years supported this view. The interest elasticity on the demand for M3 appeared to drop substantially after 1971, often becoming statistically insignificant (see, for example, "The Demand for Money in the United Kingdom: Experience since 1971", BEQB, September 1974, page 284). Banks behaviour appeared to become less responsive to interest rates, and also less predictable. Liability management opened greater choice to the banks in response to any attempt to influence their liquidity. Where profitable lending outlets arose, they have tended to bid for funds to finance them. The 1970s were not short of such opportunities. The company sector retreat from fixed rate debenture finance in response to high and uncertain interest rates (reflecting high and uncertain infla-tion rates) in the mid-1970s provided one ample source of new bor-rowers (see table 5). To a lesser degree, the banks' entry into mort-gage finance gave another[2]. Liability management has accommodated

(1) The impact of variable rate lending on the interest rate sensitivity of the demand for loans can be challenged on theoretical grounds. For example, borrowers facing fixed rate lending could operate in futures markets to transform the fixed rate contract on to a variable rate basis. In practice, however, transactions and other costs, together with other market imperfections, mean that this does not happen on any large scale. See Goodhart (1984), 164.
(2) Banks were not significantly involved in mortgage lending until 1982. This may reflect caution in establishing long term commitments during the period of the corset, followed by a search for new markets after company demand weakened in 1981.

the competitive pressure to expand their books, which on occasions has resulted in bouts of very rapid expansion.

There may also be a further, although, for our present purpose, secondary, consequence of liability management. That is, it may have a tendency to weaken the distinction drawn for prudential purposes between illiquidity and insolvency. Under strict asset management, a bank facing a liquidity shortage might sell public sector debt or, under distress, seek lender of last resort assistance. Lender of last resort assistance might also be sought if asset sales would force down prices and transmit weakness to other banks. Under liability management, temporary illiquidity might, however, be normally met through the wholesale market. Most lenders in this market are likely, however, to possess good market intelligence and, should the ultimate solvency of a potential borrower fall under suspicion, they will be unwilling to increase their exposure. Offering a higher yield then might act as a public signal of weakness, further reducing the bank's perceived creditworthiness. Genuine instances of temporary illiquidity, where the institution is fundamentally solvent, should normally be met as they emerge through day to day transactions in the wholesale market. Where illiquidity emerges as an observable longer run phenomenon, it may often reflect market suspicion of underlying insolvency.

Associated with these changes in banks' behaviour came a marked change in the relationship between broad and narrow money. Liability management had altered the relationship between interest rates and broad money because of the inclusion of wholesale deposits in the definition of M3. By contrast, the established relationship between narrow money and incomes and interest rates was substantially unaltered by the various changes in 1971: for in the period 1971-82 the traditional banking practice in the UK (*not* a legal requirement) of not offering interest payments on sight (demand) deposits remained largely intact. In so far as a generally higher *level* of interest rates was accompanied by a shift in *relativities*, e.g. as a result of banks' aggressively bidding for wholesale funds, which made bank deposit rates relatively *more* attractive than other outlets for funds, then the total volume of interest-bearing deposits would actually tend to rise, while M1 would still unambiguously fall. The previous strong positive correla-

CHART 3

Money supply and money income

Index 1980-100   Logarithmic scale

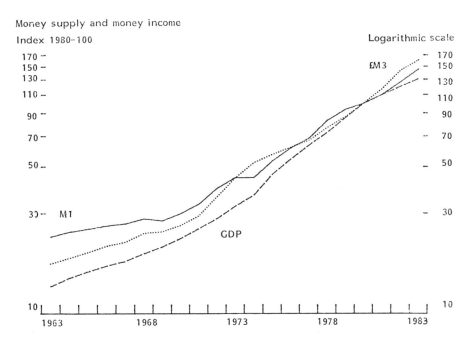

tion between M1 and M3 disappeared after 1971.

   The apparent stability of the demand for M1 after 1971 argued for less emphasis on broad money targets and for the adoption of M1 as an alternative market indicator. The authorities have, in fact, leant in this direction in recent years, although they continue to pay close attention to the development of broad monetary aggregates, notably M3. In 1982, the Chancellor's objective for monetary growth was to be judged by the performance of three indicators, including both M1 and £M3. This has been modified again in 1984, so that, for the 1984-85 financial year, the authorities have targets for two monetary indicators, £M3 and the wide monetary base, M0 (see Financial Statement and Budget Report, 1982-83), the latter serving as a measure of narrow money (see further section 6.).

   Perseverance with broad money, both now and throughout the

CHART 4

Main counterparts to the growth of £m3

£ billions

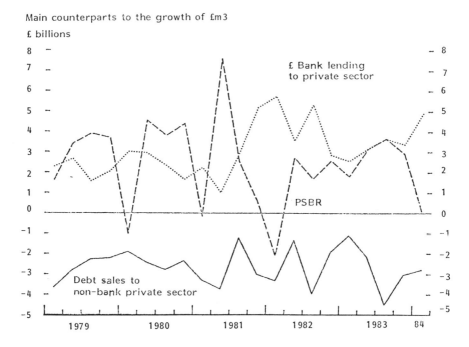

1970s, stemmed in part from the apparent association between the rapid growth of M3 in 1972-73, and the subsequent appearance of high inflation throughout 1974-75. Econometric research had demonstrated a statistically significant leading relationship from £M3 to nominal income (see Mills, (1982)), at least until 1978. Certainly the time path of broad money fitted with subsequent experience of nominal incomes and inflation during the 1970s in a way which the path of M1 did not (chart 3). The asset counterparts analysis suggests that (some) changes in broad money may be thought of as involving portfolio disequilibria resulting from fiscal policy and credit expansion. Portfolio adjustments would ultimately affect real expenditure and inflation, but would initially be reflected in £M3 and may explain its predictive content during this period (see Goodhart, (1984)).

By contrast, the apparent stability of the estimated demand function for M1 seemed, at least during these years, to offer little *predictive* guidance to future movements in nominal income. Even this relationship may be threatened, however, as structural changes and financial innovation continue to erode the distinction between money and non-monetary assets and between sight and time deposits. UK building societies now offer deposit facilities which, to varying degrees, resemble bank sight deposits. Banks in turn are introducing interest-bearing sight deposits which, for larger customers at least, provide rates close to those on time deposits. Once again, breaking down legal and institutional restrictions may lead to the failure of a previously stable demand for money equation.

Despite the breakdown of the estimated demand functions for M3 (and £M3) after 1971, this broad definition of money still possessed the analytical advantages arising from the accounting identity which links it to the level of public sector borrowing, the level of bank lending to the private sector, and to external monetary flows. While by no means wholly independent, these elements have both identifiable and potentially controllable causes, and more readily understood macro-economic consequences. The accounting framework allows the authorities to formulate and to present a coherent policy stance, for fiscal policy, debt management, lending, etc., consistently with the announced monetary target. It also gives guidance as to the appropriate focus for corrective adjustment if this target seems in danger of being missed.

This is not to say that the authorities should, or are able to, enforce strict short term control over the various counterparts of £M3. The main counterparts have been extremely volatile month to month, and even quarter to quarter (chart 4), and any attempt to "correct" such variability, if it were possible, would be at the cost of substantial swings in interest rates, forcing short term distortions back on to the real economy. Precise short run control is not strictly necessary – the relationship between the money supply and nominal income is essentially medium term – yet disturbances in the short run growth of £M3 have raised difficulties in interpreting the stance of monetary policy during recent years. The multi indicator approach to money targetry, formally adopted since 1982, should help to avoid the main dangers which the tunnel vision of strict single aggregate targetry could, in some situations, e.g. during 1980, have imposed. An alternative possibility, that was considered carefully in 1979 and 1980, was to look for new control techniques that might help to improve the trade-off between short run volatility and medium term stability. The main option then examined was to adopt some version of monetary base control.

5. MONETARY BASE CONTROL

The authorities' experience with direct controls, both during the 1960s and with the SSD scheme in the 1970s, suggested that, for any new control arrangements to be acceptable, they should not carry with them the risk of disintermediation on any significant scale. The focus of discussion was accordingly drawn away from quantitative ceilings designed to prevent market clearing, to control systems in which market forces could still be expressed through interest rates. In practice, this centred on a discussion document published jointly by the Bank and the Treasury on various forms of monetary base control (see The Green Paper, "Monetary Control", March 1980, HMSO, Cmnd. 7858).

In essence, base control relies on a ratio, customary or mandatory, between banks' deposit liabilities - the greater part of the money supply - and base money, variously defined. Control over the monetary target, say sterling M3, would then be achieved provided the authorities maintain control over base money, and the reserve ratio is fixed or moves in a predictable way. Translating this simplified model into a form which could be applied to the UK financial markets naturally raised many variants and a variety of objections and possible control problems. The two principal arguments concerned the procedure for controlling base money, and whether the ratio linking the base to the monetary target should be mandatory, or determined by the banks on voluntary grounds.

In order to achieve effective base control, the authorities would have had to consider abandoning their present lender of last resort facilities and modifying arrangements in the money market so as to give direct control over banks' balances held at the Bank. Competition for base assets would give rise to potentially volatile shifts in money market rates. A less rigid approach, described by the Green Paper as an indicator system rather than a control system envisaged the quantity of base money being determined by the market but subject to corrective adjustment in money market rates, triggered automatically by any divergence from the target path.

The argument for maintaining a mandatory reserve ratio was simply that it appeared to offer precision in the achievement of money targets. In practice, however, all of the detailed proposals which included such a ratio required some form of penalty to be charged against banks not meeting this obligation. The result would be very similar to the SSD scheme, with banks developing skills to disguise the true nature of their liabilities. Money targets would appear to be met but only through the constant ebb and flow of disintermediation and reintermediation.

In the event the authorities did not adopt base control; and the later introduction of a target for the monetary base, MO, was strictly as a narrow monetary indicator (see "Financial Statement and Budget Report", page 6, paragraph 2.09, 1984-85), at a time when the offer by a widening group of banks of interest-bearing sight deposits has been causing a structural change in the nature of the M1 aggregate[1], and while the M2 statistic, which aims to measure all retail type deposits, wherever held, was too new and untried to be relied upon as an indicator, being available only from November 1981 onwards.

In a deterministic world, the quantitative control of base money and control through interest rates are equivalent, but in a world of imperfect knowledge and imperfect markets, the effect of errors in the two control techniques may be quite different. Base money, including as it does notes and coin in circulation, is relatively insensitive to interest rate changes[2]. An unplanned or ill-judged shift in rates might accordingly cause a minor disturbance to the monetary base. By contrast, demand or supply shocks to the base could result in sizeable swings in interest rates under a system where markets are obliged to clear. Adding

(1) The growth of M1 has recently accelerated markedly (to an annualised rate of 20% over the last six months, January-June 1984) under the influence of a dramatic expansion of interest-bearing sight deposits (growing at an annual rate of 50% over these same six months).
(2) HM Treasury, "The Demand for non-interest-bearing money in the United Kingdom", Government Economic Service Working Paper no.66, February 1984. The results suggest a statistically significant interest elasticity for MO, although substantially smaller than for other narrow monetary indicators such as M1.

to this the not insignificant institutional changes that would be needed to operate base control in the UK, the authorities considered that this major change in control could not, at that time, be justified given the uncertain benefits.

6. THE CURRENT POSITION

When presenting the Medium Term Financial Strategy in 1980, the Chancellor reaffirmed the government's commitment to a coherent stance for monetary control, through the application of fiscal instruments, debt management, and interest rate policy (see "Financial Statement and Budget Report 1980-81"). Indeed the successful targeting of £M3 became the central feature of the government's counter-inflationary strategy; yet, with the lifting of exchange controls in 1979, and the abandonment of the SSD scheme in 1980, the relationship between £M3 and nominal incomes once again appeared to be undergoing change. Forcing monetary growth back into the target rage could, in those circumstances, have risked unacceptable consequences for interest rates, exchange rates and the economy more widely. High personal sector saving was being channelled through the banks to companies who in turn faced particular short-term borrowing needs as they adjusted to lower output targets. The difficulties in such circumstances of interpreting the development of £M3 was alleviated, however, by the availability of supporting information both about its asset counterparts and also its sectoral composition: this extra information proved helpful in enabling the authorities to assess developments and to guide their reactions.

Even so, £M3 on its own became an unrepresentative indicator of monetary stance in 1980 and 1981, and this led in due course, as already noted (see section 4.), to the formal use of multiple indicators, beginning in 1982. Both broad and narrow measures of money are now used to assess monetary conditions, and both are considered when deciding how to try to influence money market rates. The relationships between the monetary aggregates and interest rates appear, however, somewhat less clear-cut now than they seemed to be in previous periods, notably before the adoption of liability management and the offer of market-related interest rates on a widening range of different forms of deposit. In the short run, the growth of wholesale deposits, and on occasions of £M3 as a whole, may well be more responsive to interest relativities (which depend more on the behaviour and response of the banks themselves), than to the general level of interest rates (which the authorities can attempt to influence). In the longer term, however, the cost of credit will be a major factor in influencing credit and monetary expansion. Meanwhile, the innovation by the banks, currently in process, of offering market-related interest rates on a widening range of sight deposits, is having the effect of distorting the growth of M1, and presumably can be expected to lead to some, possibly sizeable, change in its interest elasticity when the transition period is over. For these reasons M1 was dropped from being a monetary target in the latest MTFS. The monetary base, M0, is not so immediately affected by these changes in bank behaviour, but, even in this case, the interest elasticity is quite low (relative to the past estimates of that for M1), and estimates of that elasticity have changed over time.

Yet, it is not necessarily the case that the higher the interest elasticity on a monetary aggregate, the better suited it is to serve as an indicator (or target). A high interest elasticity may lead to such a sharp change in the aggregate, with an offsetting change in velocity, as to give a misleading impression of the change in monetary stance. This occurred in 1973, for example, when accelerating inflation was accompanied by higher nominal interest rates which constrained the growth of M1 to give a possibly misleading impression of the degree of monetary restraint. Similarly, when inflation and nominal interest rates are trending downwards, the resulting incentive towards faster M1 growth may give a misleading suggestion of laxity. The adoption of the wide monetary base, M0, as a narrow monetary target, alongside £M3, earlier this year reflected this concern about the possible effects of structural changes in the banking system on M1. For a monetary indicator, as opposed to a control instrument, a low interest elasticity has a certain advantage, and on such grounds made M0 a preferable measure of money to M1. There will, of course, be problems - innovations in payments behaviour are likely to reduce reliance on notes to an unpredictable extent, and currency use is highly seasonal and may also be sensitive to activity in the "black economy", though we have yet to observe any evidence of that (see "Recent Changes in the Use of Cash", BEQB, December 1982, page 520) - yet, given the present problems with structural changes affecting M1, while M2 was new and untried, the change to M0 was advisable. It does not, however, mark any change in control technique. This latter will continue to be a mix of fiscal, funding and interest-rate management.

The introduction and implications of liability management did not, of course, begin and end with the commercial banks. A similar innovative wave of savings and payments instruments has been evident in other financial institutions, particularly in the building societies. The authorities have been conscious of the high degree of substitution between these various deposit instruments, and developed an all-encompassing broad monetary indicator, PSL2 (Private Sector Liquidity, Second Definition), which was used alongside M1 and £M3 as a target indicator both in 1982-83 and 1983-84. More recently, we have also been looking at a narrow retail deposit indicator, M2, based on a functional rather than an institutional definition. The intention has been to measure retail deposits, both at banks and building societies, in the hope that such a measure would be less distorted by the kind of structural changes which are now affecting the traditional institutionally based definitions of money. Banks and building societies have been moving closer in terms of personal retail financial services offered, and this trend seems likely to continue (see the Green Paper, "Building Societies: A New Framework", July 1984, HMSO, Cmnd. 9316). Their customers are also becoming financially more sophisticated. These factors should lead to increased competitiveness in the setting of interest rates on deposits, and this, plus an increased reliance by both banks and building societies upon wholesale funds at the margin, is likely to make the spread between deposit and lending rates of increasing importance in determining both the overall and the relative rates of growth of financial intermediaries.

The cost of bank intermediation, the interest spread, has been reduced by competitive innovation during the period of liability management, and may have contributed quite significantly to the overall growth in banks' books. Corporate borrowing has been persistently large, in part reflecting the drying-up of the fixed rate debenture market (though there have been a few signs of a prospective revival of this market in the last couple of years as longer-term interest rates have declined), and, in attempting to neutralise the expansionary effect on £M3, the authorities have needed to undertake persistently heavy funding operations outside the banking system, thereby reducing net public sector indebtedness to the banks.

Whilst the authorities have been notably successful to date in funding operations, the continuing growth of bank lending ahead of the monetary targets remains a matter for concern. One possibility may nevertheless be that the current inflated path of lending will prove to be a temporary phenomenon, in other words that the problem may go away. It is hard to envisage bank borrowing by the non-bank private sector remaining well in excess of the growth of nominal incomes for an indefinitely extended number of years. Yet it has now been so for quite a long period.

The growth of bank intermediation associated with corporate switching from fixed to floating rate loans was associated with the onset of high and volatile inflation. The progressive reduction of price in-flation during recent years could perhaps influence companies' financing decisions and encourage some return to fixed rate issues outside the banking sector. The authorities have been attempting to foster the corporate capital market in various ways, and may continue to strive to that end. Alternatively, banks might come to follow the example of their European counterparts by issuing less liquid forms of liability that would not be classified as money, though the experience of the "corset" period, mentioned earlier (see section 3.), is discouraging in this respect. We will continue to look at these and other possibilities, but they are all essentially structural changes, with an uncertain outcome. Shorter term policy will continue to rely on the traditional instruments, fiscal, funding and interest rates.

REFERENCES

Bank of England, *Quarterly Bulletin*, several issues.

Committee on the Working of the Monetary System, The Radcliffe Report, August 1959, Cmnd. 827.

Financial Statement and Budget Report, several issues.

Fisher, D. (1968), "The Demand for Money in Britain", *The Manchester School*, Vol. 36, no. 4, December.

Goodhart, C.A.E. (1984), *Monetary Theory and Practice*.

Green, C.J. (1984), "The Demand and Supply of Bank Credit in the United Kingdom: A Survey", Bank of England, mimeo, May.

The Green Paper, "Monetary Control", March 1980, MHSO, Cmnd. 7858.

Jao, Y.C. (1983), "A Libertaian Approach to Monetary Theory and Practice", *Discussion Paper*, no. 23, November, Department of Economics, University of Hong Kong.

Mills, T.C. (1982), "The Information Content of the UK Monetary Aggregates, *BEQB*, University of Leeds and Bank of England, April.

Sprenkle,C.M. and Miller,M.H. (1980), "The Precautionary Demand for Narrow and Broad Money", *Economica*, no. 47, November.

4. MONETARY CONTROL: THE GERMAN EXPERIENCE

H. Schlesinger

1. INTRODUCTION

Fifteen or twenty years ago, the topic "Monetary Conditions for Economic Recovery" would hardly have provoked a controversial debate among leading English speaking central bankers, economic policy makers and academics. Participants with a German language background – among whom some of our Dutch friends might discreetly be included – would probably have presented singularly conservative views on the stabilisation function of monetary policies, which many of you might have received with scepticism if we had met, let us say, in the mid-1960s. Confronted, however, with unusually high unemployment figures as we face today, most economists (including those from Germany), would have concluded in the end that European economies should be actively reflated – although speakers from various countries might have disagreed on the appropriate amount of discretionary demand stimulus. Looking specifically at the rôle of central banks, academic opinion leaders would probably have argued that some deliberate easing of monetary conditions was being called for, obliging the monetary authorities to actively promote low levels of market interest rates and keep the supply of reserves to the commercial banking system reasonably ample.

Statistically speaking, European unemployment figures are, indeed, historically high today, and, taken as such, appalling. This negative verdict includes Germany where the registered number of people out of work still exceeds 2 million. Nevertheless, many of us will be inclined to judge the policy problems at hand quite differently from what might have been a consensus view among professional economists, if similarly dismal employment conditions had existed during the 1960s or early 1970s.

Monetary Conditions for Economic Recovery, ed. by C. van Ewijk and J.J. Klant

2. A BROAD CONSENSUS VIEW

We place a high degree of emphasis on supply-side considerations, as we discuss the causes and possible cures of the existing under-utilisation of human and physical resources in many of our countries. We are prepared to accept the notion that "rational" expectations be-haviour of economic agents and the disappearance of fiscal and money illusion are likely to frustrate any attempt to use fiscal and monetary policy instruments in a traditional anticyclical manner. Moreover, the recognised need for removing structural budget and balance of pay-ments deficits and stubborn inflation seems to call for deliberate fiscal and monetary restraints in a number of "stagflation-ridden" economies in which internal and external financial disequilibria persist.

How could one define monetary conditions conducive to economic growth and recovery in the new policy environment? A fairly broad consensus view could, perhaps, be expected to develop, if the following policy principles were taken as a common starting point: major central banks responsible for relatively strong national currencies should keep a fairly firm grip on their domestic money supply, with inflation-prone or smaller countries possibly linking their exchange rate to "hard currencies", so that everywhere people can be convinced that inflation will be definitely brought under control.

Monetarist and non-monetarist economists are likely to share the view that conditions for a resumption of sustained economic expansion would improve, if both the speed and variability of inflation can be reduced perceptibly in a lasting manner, and it is accepted almost universally that inflation can, at least in the long-run, be regarded as a monetary phenomenon. The consistent control of monetary aggregates and the monetary targeting techniques developed by leading central banks since the mid-1970s have therefore become an important policy innovation which is widely appreciated both, in academic circles and by the public at large, and these new features of monetary control should retain their value in the 1980s.

There are modern Keynesians, who in John Hicks' words, at some stage, discovered on the theoretical plane that Keynes himself "must surely in some sense, perhaps a very weak sense, have been a monet-arist" (see Hicks (1974)). They no longer doubt the importance of money and of prudent monetary management. In a more practical sense, Alexandre Lamfalussy from the BIS once characterised the stylised position of what he labels a "conservative Keynesian demand-management" economist. This new type of conservative "feels guilty about his neglect of the rising inflationary pressures during the 1970s" and therefore came "to attach prime importance to the fight against inflation" during the early years of the current decade (see Lamfalussy (1981)). As a "pragmatic monetarist", which approximately designates my own position and the views held by key economists at the Deutsche Bundesbank, I could only notice such shifts towards a more conservative type of economic thinking on the part of earlier Keynesian economists with satisfaction, since they reassured the German central bank that its own cautious perception of the stabilisation function of monetary policy had found wide acceptance elsewhere in the course of the past decade.

I could not pretend, however, that the quantitative framework used by major central banks since the second half of the 1970s, which I think should be maintained, could be regarded as a German invention. The Federal Reserve System and the Bank of England had established internal guidelines for the growth of monetary aggregates before the Bundesbank first announced a monetary growth target for the year 1975 in public. The decision to adopt the new policy framework in Germany was, moreover, not easily taken, its technical design had to be adapted to changing economic conditions during the past ten years, and not all members of the Bundesbank's Central Bank Council could unequivocally be labelled "pragmatic monetarists". Let me therefore briefly review the history of monetary targeting in Germany and, in this factual manner, give you a more concrete idea why I think that our present policy concept still meets the requirements of our present economic situation.

3.   MONETARY TARGETING IN GERMANY

As you may know, prices have been brought firmly under control in Germany by now, while the real economy is likely to recover comparatively slowly. Some people may therefore be tempted to preach the old gospel of easy monetary policies once more in order to encourage a stronger expansion of domestic demand in Germany, while the longer-term requirements of credible target-oriented monetary policies may all too easily be neglected again. The circumstances under which targeting practices were introduced in Germany were, after all, quite different from present economic conditions. In the Federal Republic a monetary target for the coming year was publicly announced for the first time at the end of 1974. This meant that monetary policy was committing itself in a publicly accountable manner in several respects: stability of the purchasing power of money remained, as practised before and stipulated by the Bundesbank Law of 1957, the supreme ultimate policy objective. But an intermediate monetary target was specified, namely the annual growth of the central-bank money stock. And the Bundesbank since that time had to gear the use of its traditional interest rate and liquidity policy instruments to this intermediate target, or at least to pay visible attention to it. (For a more detailed description of the Bundesbank's targeting practices and the implementation of its annual monetary objectives see Schlesinger (1982) and Dudler (1982).)

The basic significance of the innovations introduced in the mid-1970s need hardly be explained. It must be pointed out, however, that the transition to monetary targeting constituted a bold step in the beginning, because it was not very clear at first how our promises were to be kept; we therefore spoke initially of an "experiment" only. The Bundesbank had always paid attention to the development of monetary aggregates. Representatives of the Bundesbank, however, with few exceptions, viewed "monetary rules" sceptically until well into the last decade, and in some cases still do so today. It is true that the monetary target is set annually by the Central Bank Council almost "unanimously" (which of course does not rule out the possibility of abstentions), as far as the intention of defining such a target is concerned (but not with respect to the actual figure). Naturally, however, it cannot be taken for granted in a political body that all the members of the Council are equally strongly convinced of the rationale of this practice. It is therefore worth asking: how did this process of rethinking, which affected the Deutsche Bundesbank around the middle of the last decade and other major central banks a little later, come about?

The transition to monetary targeting was prepared on the intellectual plane by the debate on monetarism of the 1960s and 1970s. In

the course of this the arguments of the monetarist school gained increasing acceptance. After a long period of neglect of monetary policy
in the years immediately following the Second World War, it generally
became recognised that monetary stabilisation policy has a key rôle to
play in fighting inflation. The "discovery" (and in the case of Germany: a greater emphasis) of the fact that over the longer term general
inflationary processes are dependent on excessive monetary expansion
led at the same time to monetary aggregates becoming more respectable
again as information and control variables for monetary policy.

The decisive factor in this change of view was, however, the
concrete experience of inflation since about the end of the 1960s.
"Creeping inflation", which had previously been taken over lightly in
many countries, developed in the words of Harry G. Johnson into
"briskly walking inflation". Economic policy was marked by full employment targets and sometimes even "guarantees". And the predominant
economic theory – this means mainly theory written in English – found
nothing negative, but really only positive features in the inflationary
climate, which whitewashed over all the social tensions. Faith in the
Phillips-curve prevailed and dominated policies; Samuelson and Solow
once described it as "a menu of choice(s) between different degrees of
unemployment and price stability" – they denied at the same time that
"every creeping inflation inexorably becomes a trotting one" (see
Haberler (1984)).

Monetary policy accommodated the inflation – known as anti-cyclical
monetary policy under the banner of full employment – more or less
voluntarily. Central-bank policy was often mistakenly geared to nominal
market interest rates or lagging economic indicators like consumer
prices or the unemployment figure – the two indicators which are the
only ones of interest to the politicians, but which are certainly insufficient for monetary policy and may even mislead it.
The Federal Republic and Switzerland, which were "islands of stability"
for quite a long while, did not remain unaffected by the spirit of the
times. Things were made particulary difficult for them by the fact that
any success they scored in domestic stabilisation policy was nullified by
inflows of funds from abroad. Under conditions of fixed dollar exchange
rates up to the collapse of the fixed rate system in 1973, the rising

global inflation rate spread to those countries, too, and monetary policy lost its credibility as well as effectiveness. The additional boost given to inflation by the global commodity boom of 1972-73, the first oil crisis and the quickening pace of wage rises in Germany called for thorough domestic stabilisation, and the collapse of the Bretton Woods System, i.e. the abandonment of the obligation to intervene against the US dollar, made this possible. The Bundesbank had to make it clear that it was able and willing to pursue a policy of a rigorous stabilisation. It therefore came to the conclusion, with the full support of the Federal Government and the German Council of Economic Experts, that it would be useful to provide all those involved in economic decision-making with an explicit monetary framework for the planning of expenditures and prices by setting a monetary target. This was coupled with the expectation that it would be possible to commit all areas of economic policy to joint efforts at stabilisation and to lower the cost of the anti-inflation policy.

This background makes it plain that turbulent circumstances were instrumental in helping the new monetary strategy to achieve a breakthrough in practice. The fact that today a fairly large number of central banks in industrial countries have opted for a concept of monetary targeting owes less to the tenets of monetarism, few of which are accepted without reservations, than to the failure of earlier criteria.

Outstanding examples of favourable experience with monetary targeting since 1975 are two periods of successful price stabilisation policy in Germany. First, in the second half of the 1970s we managed to bring down the rates of price and wage rises in Germany to a reasonably tolerable level and in particular to break the inflation psychology that had been spreading; in other words, to restore confidence in the domestic value of our currency. Second, at the beginning of the 1980s the Bundesbank successfully resisted the threat of a "vicious spiral" of depreciation and inflation, which in the form of a general "flight from the Deutsche Mark" was threatening to undermine confidence in the external value of our currency (which would have consequences to the domestic value of money).

In both cases the monetary targets proved their worth by enhancing the willingness of the central bank's decision-making bodies to take decisions. Moreover, the Federal Government and the Bundesbank were united in making serious efforts to achieve stabilisation, and finally, the credibility of the central bank's determination to pursue a stabilisation policy increased. To put it in the words of Karl Klasen, the President of the Bundesbank at that time: in the absence of the monetary target, we would not have responded so early or so often.

The pragmatic policy objectives of monetary targeting quite certainly do not conform in every respect to the ideas of the monetarists. Neither the Bundesbank nor other major central banks have announced medium-term monetary targets to date. As a matter of fact, however, a medium-term basic orientation is involved in our policy. This applies to the derivation of the target, the most important variable of which is the growth of production potential (not of anticipated actual production). But we have fairly often made adjustments over the shorter term, say, in the event of stubborn domestic inflationary pressures. Now and then there have been situations in which a recommended "gradualism" would have seriously weakened the credibility of monetary targeting (e.g. 1974-75 and 1979-80, after years of excessive monetary expansion). Besides, exchange rate disturbances have repeatedly prompted us to modify our monetary targets.

4.   MONETARY TARGETING AND THE EXCHANGE RATE

I would like to say a little more on the external aspect of the problem. On the one hand, on the transition to floating in 1973, monetary policy in Germany gained the room for manoeuvre necessary for effectively pursuing national monetary and price stabilisation objectives. On the other hand, in retrospect many central-bank experts are more than a little disappointed to see that exchange rate relationships between the major key currencies have developed in anything but "textbook fashion". Particularly in relation to the dominant US dollar, there have been marked fluctuations not only in nominal but also in "real" exchange rates, and their implications for the national economy are unsatisfactory: they exaggerate successes in fighting inflation (Germany in 1978, United States in 1983-84) as well as inflationary tendencies; they change the pattern of foreign trade in a manner that cannot be maintained in the long run. In other words, exchange rate movements may jeopardise the ultimate objectives of one's own monetary policy. We were faced with a conflict situations of considerable proportions in 1977-78 and 1980-81. In the first case an excessive "real" appreciation of the Deutsche Mark threatened German competitiveness, tended to dampen the propensity to invest and endangered the upswing that had finally got going. At that time the Bundesbank responded by bringing down domestic interest rates to a historically low level and stabilising them there. In the end it had to accept a marked overshooting of its monetary targets. The excessive monetary expansion accepted at that time could be offset only gradually thereafter, and the consequences of the second oil crisis could be combatted only slowly. In particular, the hope entertained by some that, in the event of a corrective deprecia-tion, an overshooting in the other direction could be prevented by measures of our own, proved illusory. In the light of this negative experience and some other technical reasons, we subsequently an-nounced "conditional target corridors" for the growth of the central-bank money stock, i.e. we emphasised the conditions on which we intended to keep monetary expansion more in the upper or more in the lower half of the chosen target range (of 3 percentage points).

In 1980-81, when a "depreciation inflation spiral" was looming, this formulation enabled us to implement, more or less "according to plan", monetary targets in the bottom half of the range without simply aban-doning the principles of monetary targeting. In this way, however, it proved possible to stabilise exchange rate movements, to work towards the adjustment of Germany's excessive current-account deficit and to avoid a dangerous secondary round of inflation at home.

In general we try to ride out exchange rate fluctuations as long as possible without abandoning the basic stance of our monetary policy at home. At the end of last year, for example, we abstained from explicit conditionality altogether when we announced our monetary target of 4-6 per cent for 1984, not at the least because we thought that external developments, presented no serious risks. The fact that the Bundes-bank, contrary to many expectations, has so far not responded more strongly in its monetary policy to the considerable swings in dollar interest rates and the dollar exchange rate also fits into this picture. Whether we shall be able to adhere to this stance does not depend on ourselves alone. This is without doubt one of the most important fields for research and experimentation, in which theorists and central banks alike must gain further experience.

5. CONCLUDING REMARKS

This brings me to the end of my account of monetary targeting in Germany. I can sum up our experience as follows: we should continue with this practice. Views on the subject among my colleagues at the Bundesbank are I think similar, although, needless to say, this must be decided anew every year. This is not much of a problem if the preceding year has passed off quite well - both in terms of monetary targeting and also in terms of general economic conditions. Unemployment and comparatively low rates of economic growth are, unfortunately, likely to be with us for some time to come. It would, however, be a great mistake to try to cure our remaining illnesses by resorting to myopic "easy money" policies again and thus risk jeopardising the domestic and external stabilisation gains which we have been able to achieve in a rather painful way in recent years.

REFERENCES

Dudler, H.J. (1982), "The Implementation of Monetary Objectives in Germany - Open Market Operations and Credit Facilities" in Meek, P. (ed.), *Central Bank Views on Monetary Targeting*, Federal Reserve Bank of New York, New York, May.

Haberler, G. (1984), "The Slowdown of the World Economy and the Problem of Stagflation - Some Alternative Explanations and Policy Implications", prepared for the Worldbank.

Hicks, J. (1974), *The Crisis in Keynesian Economics*, Oxford.

Lamfalussy, A. (1981), "Rules versus Discretion: An Essay on Monetary Policy in an Inflationary Envirnment", *BIS Economic Papers*, no. 3, April.

Schlesinger, H. (1982), "The Setting of Monetary Objectives in Germany", in Meek, P. (ed.), *Central Bank Views on Monetary Targeting*, The Federal Reserve Bank of New York, New York, May.

5. MONETARY CONTROL: THE DUTCH EXPERIENCE

Some reflections on the liquidity ratio

M.M.G. Fase

1. INTRODUCTION

This paper is about the problems of interpreting monetary developments in the Netherlands. It is common to judge monetary policy by its results in terms of the intermediate policy targets chosen. This pragmatic approach is prompted by the fact that our knowledge of the ways policy instruments, monetary variables and real variables are inter-related, is far from complete.

In the Netherlands, monetary policy is traditionally a quantitative policy with the national liquidity ratio as the central indicator or inter-mediate target. Its main instrument comes in the form of the credit restrictions imposed on the money-creating banking system as a whole. The choice of a quantity policy entails that to a large extent interest rate movements are the policy result rather than its objective. Apart from the theoretical consideration that prices and quantities cannot be controlled simultaneously, this is also due to the fact that the Dutch economy is a very open economy where external capital transactions go unhindered. Nevertheless there is some scope for influencing interest rate levels, viz. via the so-called narrow monetary policy. This is the policy directed at the money and foreign exchange markets.

The present study centres on the broad rather than on the narrow monetary policy pursued. A few years ago Kessler (1980) presented an analysis of Dutch monetary policy in the light of the ultimate aims of macro economic policy over the past decade or so. His most important conclusion was that a policy stance different from the one actually taken would not have been preferable. This paper focuses on monetary control experience in the Netherlands over the past 15 years by looking in detail at a number of actual or possible intermediate targets of Dutch

Monetary Conditions for Economic Recovery, ed. by C. van Ewijk and J.J. Klant

monetary policy. Each assessment has more than one intellectual dimension. First there is the assessment made immediately after the period considered. It is this assessment which is done in practice and therefore carries the most weight for preparing the actual policy stance. However, such an assessment is often based on information which later turns out to have been provisional. Therefore an assessment made at a later date when much more complete information is available may be informative too. This approach, which is an assessment in retrospect, provides our second dimension. Of course, this second approach is, in a sense, academic in nature. However, it gives an overview in the longer term perspective and thus may help to determine a position vis-à-vis short-term signals. This paper deals with these two aspects in section 4. Prior to this, sections 2 and 3 give an outline of the way monetary policy makes itself felt in the economy. Next to the monetary transmission discussed in section 2, section 3 deals briefly with the choice of the most appropriate monetary indicator or intermediate target.

The paper thus provides a reflection on the main indicator of Dutch monetary policy. It will be built up around five topics, viz.:
- the way the money supply is supposed to influence the economy;
- the connection with the choice of the policy indicator;
- the efficacy of the liquidity ratio as a central monetary indicator;
- the question to what extent the assessment of the policy pursued is distorted by the monetary indicator used;
- the question whether there are appropriate alternatives to the traditional liquidity ratio.

2.   TRANSMISSION MECHANISM

The ultimate target of monetary policy is to influence quantities in the real economy, such as employment, inflation, economic growth and external relations. The latter are embodied in the balance of payments and the exchange rate. To achieve these policy goals monetary policy is only one of the possible means, particularly because monetary policy cannot bear the burden alone. Therefore, the monetary instrument requires the support of other instruments of macro-economic policy, viz. budgetary and wage policy.

Monetary policy makes itself felt through its instruments such as credit restrictions, discount policy, open market transactions and the quotas for borrowing. These instruments exert their influence on the economic target variables via the so-called transmission channels. Much has been said and written about these monetary transmission channels. Roughly speaking, two points of view can be distinguished.

The oldest view is very general and finds its source in the old quantity theory approach, which confronts flows of money with flows of goods and services. According to this view, an excess of money or liquid assets will lead to price increases and real exchange rate effects which remedy the macro-economic disequilibria. The basis for this line of thought is provided by the famous Fisher equation, $MV=PT$, which forms the pivot of the quantity theory. The other viewpoint is more specific and in line with the view that monetary variables exert a specific influence on the balance sheets of the different sectors of the economy as a whole and thus on categories of expenditure. In more concrete terms, this means that real and nominal interest rates, capital costs, financial wealth and proxies of monetary disequilibria figure as explanatory variables in expenditure equations.

In contrast to the first, general view, the second specific view is based on an elaborated theoretical reasoning about the working of the economy, which is very often supplemented with empirical knowledge. It is thus in line with the long tradition of formulating specific behaviour for economic aggregates going back to the Keynes of the General Theory, Tinbergen and Klein. It is therefore not surprising that users of empirical macro-models usually advocate the second standpoint. Proponents of some form of the quantity theory, who do not think it very appropriate to model the economy in detail, mostly hold the more general point of view. Modern monetarism is one of the various guises of this view. Monetary thinking at the central banks, too, has - partly as a result of their policy responsibility - been strongly influenced by the general quantity theory approach, although the more specific view-point can also be found there (see e.g. Zijlstra (1979)).

The above distinction is most notably a didactic schematization. At the theoretical level it corresponds with an aggregative versus an allocative approach of monetary policy. Practice comes in greater gradations. As already indicated, policy makers employ both viewpoints in arriving at a judgement. On the one hand, they will confine themselves to overall indices to assess the monetary situation, while on the other, they will, in the use and dosage of the available instruments, take into consideration how these will affect the economy. This means that monetary policy is in fact pursued along two lines. The use of certain instruments is meant to call forth particular reactions. At the same time, however, this policy aims at creating the economic climate that is considered a condition for the achievement of the policy targets aimed at.

The degree of success achieved by the monetary policy conducted cannot simply be determined in quantitative terms. This is partly due to the circumstance that the use of the monetary instrument is not the only factor influencing the ultimate policy objective. Apart from its current impact monetary policy also includes both a longer-term socio-psychological influence on the economic climate and the development of new instruments. Therefore it is, in a sense, also a conditioning policy. In reality monetary policy, in the terminology of Tinbergen, assumes both a quantitative and a qualitative form. Entirely apart from the views on the working of monetary policy actually chosen, there is the practical need to employ monetary indicators or intermediate targets for the formulation and assessment of monetary policy.

3. MONETARY INDICATORS

The acknowledgement that our knowledge of the working of the economic system is incomplete does not only form the basis for the existence of the two points of view set out above. It also forms a justification for the common use in discussions about monetary policy of the set of concepts: operational target/intermediate target or indicator/ ultimate target. This paper is mainly concerned with the intermediate targets or indicators of monetary policy. A monetary indicator aims at representing the effect of monetary influence on the ultimate targets of economic policy. The intermediary target provides the guideline for the performance of policy instruments. The operational target is the translation of the intermediate target into operational terms for the policy maker. As for the central bank it is assumed that a change in this intermediary target reflects the monetary influence on the ultimate objective of policy.

It must be noted here that a final assessment of the stance of monetary policy must be made against the background of the general aims of economic policy. As indicated before, the means employed to that end consist of more than monetary policy instruments alone.

The eligible variables for the stance of monetary policy ensue from the theoretical view on the monetary transmission. Advocates of the quantity theory or aggregative approach will attach great importance to the money supply or, in view of the controllability by the monetary authorities, the base money supply, M0. Proponents of the point of view which sees transmission as a chain of changes in wealth will, in principle, be prepared to accept a wide range of financial assets as indicators, next to the money supply. In addition, the role of indicator can also be fulfilled by long-term interest rates as a proxy for capital costs.

A problem with the different possible indicators is that they do not depend on the policy instruments alone. This means not only that changes in the relevant variables reflect the influence of monetary policy, but also that they are the result of economic developments which are taking place elsewhere, and thus elude the influence of monetary policy. The degree of this dependency, therefore, is a constraint on the choice of a monetary indicator. The question whether monetary policy should be formulated in terms of quantities of assets, such as the money supply, or in terms of interest rate levels – in short interest rate target vs. quantity target – can be reduced to testing for this constraint. The possible uncontrolled variability in the indicators furthermore makes it necessary to exercise great caution in the assessment of actual monetary developments. That is why such an assessment cannot be considered in isolation, but must be viewed against the background of the actual economic circumstances.

4.   MONETARY DEVELOPMENTS IN THE NETHERLANDS, 1970-84

In this section the authentic and retrospective approaches to the assessment of monetary policy will be attempted. The insights gained with these two approaches need not necessarily coincide.

For the first approach, the President's General Surveys contained in consecutive Annual Reports are the most authentic source of informa-

tion. The second approach attempted here provides an historical overview with the aid of the statistical knowledge now available. In both
approaches attention will be paid to the liquidity ratio, which has been
the main monetary indicator and the central monetary policy target
throughout.

4.1. The liquidity ratio in the Annual Reports: a close reading

Each year, the President's General Survey in the Banks's Annual
Report contains a discussion of movements in the liquidity ratio in the
year under review and their implications for the monetary policy to be
pursued in the near future. In addition, the General Survey presents,
from time to time, the philosophy underlying the Bank's monetary
policy. In this section, selections from the discussions on these topics
will be quoted. They form the basis for the most authentic policy
assessment possible.

As the *1967 Report* reports an increase of the liquidity ratio of 1
percentage point and the remark that for 1968 this trend will have to
be closely watched, we start with a quotation from President Zijlstra's
second Annual Report. This *1968 Report* contains both a discussion of
the Bank's monetary philosophy underlying the use of the liquidity
ratio. It reads:

"...to ensure uninterrupted circulation of the national income there
should be a certain minimum quantity of primary and secondary liquidity
in proportion to the national income, that proportion being the liquidity
ratio. This minimum liquidity ratio, which may be described as a kind
of minimum stock, is not constant. It falls as the efficiency of the
payments mechanism increases. ...If this ratio is above the minimum
required, the difference forms a potential source of inflation. ...The
use of monetary policy, in the form of applying quantitative credit
restrictions, brings down the actual liquidity ratio closer to the required minimum" (pp. 19-20).

At the end of 1968 this ratio was 38% according to the Annual
Report. This was considered too high. An interesting remark is:

"...In any case what is always involved is a deliberate influencing of
the liquidity ratio by controlling domestic liquidity creation... If domestic liquidity creation is not kept under control, use of the other
policy instruments may be tantamount to beating thin air" (p. 28).

The *1969 Report* not only states that the 1.5 percentage point
reduction of the ratio aimed at was not achieved, owing to inflationary

financing by the public authorities. However, it also formulates the target for 1970:

"...For liquidity as a whole the aim is to reduce the ratio by 1-1.5 points. A decisive factor in achieving this goal will again be the development of the public finances and the nation liquidity surplus (or deficit)" (p. 24).

The *1970 Report* also goes into the problems of monetary policy, saying explicitly:

"...That despite these development the liquidity ratio did fall, if only fractionally, is due to the fact that net national income rose faster than initially assumed when monetary policy was formulated. In so far as this sharper rise was only a nominal one, the associated decline in the liquidity ratio is not the reflection of an effective monetary policy but only the result of stronger inflation" (p. 13).

For *1971*, the *Report* reads:

"...In the year under review the effectiveness of monetary policy was again considerably undermined by the inflow of funds abroad. The sharp rise in national income, in money terms, completely absorbed the increase in liquidity stemming from abroad; in the course of 1971, the liquidity ratio even dropped by half a percentage point...". (p. 17).

The *Report for 1972* again contains fragmentary remarks about the philosophy underlying the policy. Despite the marginal decline in the ratio from 33.5% to 33%[1], the following remark about the public authorities' financing behaviour is noteworthy:

"...As a result ƒ 3.4 billion of liquidity was mopped up, thus preventing any current highly liquid conditions from fuelling forthcoming overspending in the private sector. The liquidity absorption was particularly necessary owing to a further huge inflow of liquid funds from abroad in 1972, totalling ƒ 3.2 billion..." (p. 12).

In the *1973 Report* the liquidity ratio does not figure in the President's General Survey.

The *Report for 1974* states that the ratio has undergone an increase of 3 percentage points, reading:

(1) In 1968 the ratio had still been 38%. The 5 percentage point decline cannot be explained by means of the consecutive passage quoted from the General Surveys. Closer analysis of the data shows that nearly 4 percentage points of the decline are the result of revisions of the series, of which those of 1969 (2.15 percentage points) and 1972 (2.0 percentage points) are the most important. See also table 1.

"...Economic conditions showed such clear signs of weakening that the government decided to introduce far-reaching measures to stimulate the economy. Consequently, the Bank withdrew its plans to apply severe credit restraint... Monetary policy should by its nature be conducted as a quantitative policy, with the level of interest rates following from it..." (p. 21).

The *1975 Report* again includes a discussion of the principles - in line with criticism on the part of some monetarists - underlying the monetary policy in a wider perspective. It reads:

"...If inflation is entirely or largely absent, and if there ar no external disturbances to contend with, the basic principle of monetary policy is relatively easy to formulate. In this case, the money supply should move in line with the growth in real national income; moreover, it is advisable to calculate the real increase on a long run trend basis rather than an annual basis. The money supply should include the whole range of money and near money, subject to adjustments which may have to be made in special circumstances. The success of such a policy will be evidenced by the stability over time (with some cyclical variation) of the ratio of the money supply to NNI, in other words the national liquidity ratio. Such a policy is an effective means of preventing inflation, since it leaves no margin for price increases..."

The remark that, compared with 1972, the ratio in 1975 is nearly 4 percentage points higher, is followed by the statement that:

"...At all events, the increased liquidity of the economy may be deemed normal in that it coincides with a phase of economic recession..." (pp. 18-19).

In *1976*, too, the ratio went up further, and the *Report* again presents a discussion on the principles of monetary policy in the Netherlands. We read:

"...It must also be borne in mind that the rapid increase in the liquid-ity ratio since 1971 includes a large cyclical and thus endogenous component which will probably disappear as economic conditions im-prove. But an autonomous component will undoubtedly remain to be dealt with by appropriate policy measures. A reduction in the liquidity ratio of (on average) 1 percentage point per year during the medium-term period until 1980 - a time-span adopted frequently for present policy purposes - would seem to be the minimum objective; otherwise monetary policy is condemned to play a passive role or, to use a phrase that is much in vogue, to assume a largely accommodating character...It would be wrong to assume that a monetary target, expressed in terms of a liquidity ratio, differs essentially from a policy expressed in terms of a desired rate of growth in the money supply...It is likewise er-roneous to assume that a monetary target expressed in terms of a desired liquidity ratio presupposes an accommodating policy..." (pp. 20-21).

The *1977 Report* takes again a look at the future of monetary policy. It reads:

"...The Bank therefore resolved to orientate monetary policy towards a gradual decline in the liquidity ratio over a number of years. The resulting monetary policy, aimed at a reduction in the ratio of one percentage point per year, could not be introduced until May 1977, so that a fall in the ratio could scarcely be expected for that year as a whole..."

It also says that:

"...In the present circumstances, it seems advisable for monetary policy to aim at stabilizing the liquidity ratio at its end-1977 level" (pp. 18-19).

In *1978* the reduction of the national liquidity ratio aimed at does indeed take place. The *Report* notes, however, that:

"...Such a decline does not, of course, provide adequate evidence of healthier monetary conditions unless it is accompanied by a fall in the rate of inflation, a condition which has, in fact, been fulfilled..." (p. 20).

According to the President's General Survey of *1979* such a reduction was not repeated in 1979. It reads:

"...The year under review was the third year in which the credit restrictions, introduced at the beginning of 1977, were operative... Until the present the ratio has not fallen by more than one percentage point in all. The increasing tendency towards monetary financing by the public authorities...was a disruptive factor" (pp. 19-20).

The General Survey of the *1980 Report* does not mention the ratio. It does say, however:

"...Domestic liquidity creation, i.e. from domestic sources, ...was again high relative to the growth in nominal net national income. Not surprisingly, this relatively large money creation found its way abroad... As in 1979 the public authorities caused the excessive creation of liquidity..." (p. 18).

The *1981 Report* is the first published under President Duisenberg. He writes that:

"...Monetary policy in the Netherlands was, is and will continue to be directed at achieving a level of liquidity creation such that the external value of the guilder remains as stable as possible, and its domestic value is at the same time stabilized to the maximum possible extent, or, in other words, inflation is restricted to the extent that monetary policy is capable of achieving this aim..."

On the liquidity ratio he notes that:

"...The fall in the liquidity ratio in 1981 is the result of a slowdown in money creation in aid of industry, which in a sense is to be regretted, a moderate amount of inflationary financing by the public authorities and an inflow of liquidity from abroad connected with the turnround of the balance of payments on current account..." (pp. 24-25).

The *1982 Report* deals briefly but clearly with the liquidity ratio, reading:

"...Despite the public authorities' abstinence from monetary financing, and with private sector bank borrowing more or less stable at a low level, the domestic money supply increased sharply (9.5%). The liquidity ratio (M2 as a percentage of net national income) consequently went up to 39%, some 3% higher than in early 1977, when liquidity conditions were regarded as being so easy...The easy liquidity conditions do not constitute an obstacle to economic recovery and, though not entirely devoid of risk, they are considered acceptable by the Bank for the time being, given the economic situation..." (p. 24).

In 1983 liquidity conditions remained easy. Much attention is paid to this development by the President in his General Survey in the *1983 Report*. He writes:

"...For a considerable period of time the creation of new money has substantially exceeded both the long-term and the actual growth of net national income in nominal terms, so that the liquidity ratio (M2 as a percentage of net national income) rose sharply, from just over 35% in 1979 to 41% at end-1983..."

The President's conclusion is that by placing their debt with the banking system, the public authorities are largely to blame for this development. He goes on to say that:

"...It is not without concern that the Bank views the development – which was described as exuberant above – of the money supply. A level of unemployment which is unprecedented since the depression in the 1930s is not an 'environment' in which monetary restrictions can be contemplated as a matter of course. Nothing can be allowed to impede the economic recovery which is really getting under way in the market sector, but at the same time the conditions which will permit the recovery to be durable must be sustained. One such condition is controlled growth of the money supply so as to prevent inflation from flaring-up again, the prospect of which would cause confidence to decline and interest rates to rise..." (pp. 26-27).

So much for the quotations relating to the liquidity ratio and the underlying philosophy taken from the General Surveys of President Zijlstra (1967-1981) and President Duisenberg (from 1982 onwards). They do not require further exegesis; nevertheless we shall take a closer look at the course of the liquidity ratio as the main intermediate target or monetary indicator in Dutch monetary policy.

4.2. A closer look at the liquidity ratio

What can we learn from the above selected reading? First of all that, despite the openness of the economy, the money supply is and should be regarded as an independent and controllable variable. The instrument by means of which the money supply can be controlled is almost invariably restriction of domestic money creation ensuing from banklending to the private sector. Insofar as the excess in the supply of money comes from the two other sources, viz. from the public sector and from abroad, it should be compensated for by monetary policy.

Second, as from 1975, the consecutive General Surveys report that efforts to bring about a reduction in the ratio have proved unsuccessful, for reasons which are, incidentally, entirely valid. The question arises here whether the almost constant failure to achieve the policy target is not caused by the choice of the ratio as an intermediate target. On the other hand, it is clear from developments between 1968 and 1972, when a 5 percentage point decline was achieved, that this indicator does not preclude the possibility of a substantial decrease[1].

Third, it should be noted that the Bank's monetary philosophy is discussed at increasingly shorter time intervals (1968, 1972, 1975, 1981, 1982, 1983), indicating that the rationale of the liquidity ratio as a monetary indicator has become less self-evident both inside and outside the Bank.

Finally, the quoted paragraphs recognize explicitly that the execution of monetary policy requires an interpretative approach, which is substantially different from straightforward monetarism, advocated sometimes in those days (cf. Zijlstra (1979)).

As far as the monetary philosophy is concerned, a characteristic aspect is the judgemental approach, which takes as a basic startingpoint that monetary conditions should not cause disturbances in the economy as a whole. This is in line with the old quantity theory *cum* neutral

(1) See also footnote on page 100.

money approach. It means that the monetary authorities did not opt for a specific approach to the transmission mechanism. The monetary assessment centres on the growth of the money supply, which must be such that it does not lead to price inflation or exchange rate effects. The national liquidity ratio serves as the yardstick. This liquidity ratio shows the money supply, M2, as a percentage of net national income. This M2 is traditionally defined as the sum total of notes and coin, demand deposits, time deposits, liquid savings, foreign exchange balances and short-term claims on the public authorities insofar as held by the general public.

A major role is played by the assumption that this ratio is a controllable variable whose numerator functions, to a large extent, as an independent variable (see especially the 1968 Report). Dutch monetary policy consequently centres on the money supply, M2, and is thus a quantity policy which accepts the ensuing interest rate levels. On one or two occasions the General Surveys suggests the target to be the growth rate of the money supply, which should correspond with the long-term growth of real output. The policy target during the period reviewed is, however, always formulated in terms of the liquidity ratio, with stabilization of the domestic and external value of the guilder as the ultimate target. The policy seeks to control the domestic liquidity creation due to net bank lending. This is, as it were, the operational target, for the sake of brevity not discussed in this paper (see Annex I for a tabular survey).

As far as the national liquidity ratio is concerned, the Annual Reports rarely mention the realization of the planned reduction. As a matter of fact, the Annual Reports show a more or less steady increase, at least for the recent period, of the ratio. There are several ways to look at this tendency. A first interpretation may be that Dutch monetary policy, measured by its results, was not very tight, not to say expansionary. A second interpretation may be that the liquidity ratio has become a less appropriate intermediate target, which has made the interpretation of Dutch monetary development unnecessary difficult. For several reasons, given below, I believe the latter is probably the case.

In this connection it is interesting to look at the relevant figures as shown in consecutive Annual Reports. Table 1 gives the figures for

1967-1983. It shows the liquidity ratio as given in the successive Annual Reports for the years concerned and for the preceding years. Analysis of these data brings several interesting facts to light.

In the first place, the actual change in the ratio from one year to the next turns out, in retrospect, to deviate fairly substantially from that observed in the year under review. This is especially true of the years 1975-78, be it that the final changes turn out to be alternately higher and lower than those observed in the first instance. Despite the sometimes considerable differences between the initial and the final changes in the liquidity ratio, the average difference over the years considered is not too large. At 0.05, the average absolute change is, retrospectively, barely higher than that initially measured. Only in 1979-81 successive adjustments result in a reversal of signs.

In the second place, the table shows considerable differences, for a number of years, between the liquidity ratios upon which policy analysis in the relevant year was based, and those used later. Retrospectively, the ratio usually turns out to be lower. In some years the difference is substantial, amounting to 2-3 percentage points, whereas there is seldom a negligible difference. The small difference recorded in the most recent years is misleading because these figures can, as experience shows, by no means be considered definitive.

For this there are several plausible explanations. The most important of these is the fact that the national income figures are regularly adjusted before a definitive figure is achieved. In addition, the volume of M2 is also subject to small statistical changes - or breaks in the series -, as a consequence of the way it is compiled. This variation over time raises the question whether this does not detract from the ratio's role as a monetary indicator. The question becomes all the more pressing when it is realized that in the course of time the liquidity ratio may have become increasingly endogenous in character. Because of this endogeneity the liquidity ratio may, but not necessarily, introduce a tendency towards an accomodating policy. The numerator of the liquidity ratio consequently needs to be adjusted for some of these endogenous variations to such an extent that doubts may arise about the efficacy of this policy indicator. These doubts are strengthened further by the facts that the ratio approach in practice - as table 1

Table 1 – Liquidity ratios, 1967–1983

According to Annual Report for	Liquidity ratio in																
	1967	1968	1969	1970	1971	1972	1973	1974	1975	1976	1977	1978	1979	1980	1981	1982	1983
1967	37.7																
1968	37.5	38.1															
1969	35.7	36.7	36.3														
1970	35.6	36.6	36.1	36.0													
1971	35.6	36.6	36.1	36.1	35.3												
1972	34.5	35.6	34.4	34.4	33.2	32.6											
1973		35.6	34.8	34.8	33.3	32.7	35.1										
1974			34.8	34.8	33.3	32.6	35.3	38.1									
1975				34.8	33.5	32.8	35.4	38.6	37.3								
1976					33.5	32.6	35.0	38.7	36.8	40.1							
1977						32.6	34.7	38.0	36.1	40.3	38.6						
1978							35.1	38.2	36.0	39.8	37.4	36.1					
1979								38.2	35.7	39.3	37.2	36.0	36.0				
1980									35.7	39.5	37.3	36.8	36.9	36.1			
1981										37.5	35.5	34.6	34.6	35.6	34.9		
1982											35.3	34.7	34.3	35.0	35.1	37.4	
1983												34.7	34.3	35.0	35.1	36.7	39.0
Change in reviewed year (percentage points)		0.6	-0.4	-0.1	-0.8	-0.6	2.4	2.8	-1.3	3.3	-1.7	-1.3	0	-0.8	-0.7	2.3	2.3
Last change		1.1	-0.8	0	-1.3	-0.9	2.5	3.1	-2.5	1.8	-2.2	-0.6	-0.4	0.7	0.1	1.6	2.3
Difference between first and definitive figures	3.2	2.5	1.5	1.2	1.8	0	0	-0.1	1.6	2.6	3.3	1.4	1.7	1.1	-0.2	0.7	2.3

Source: Annual Reports, Table 3 of Statistical Annex.

shows – has the disadvantage of being highly sensitive to data revisions[1]. As the liquidity ratio concerns also M2 (for almost three decades) one may wonder whether it does take into account sufficiently financial innovations and the implied altering liquidity services provided by the components of M2.

4.3. Closer analysis of some monetary indicators

On the basis of the analysis of a number of economic time series, an attempt has been made to classify the turning-points in the cyclical development. The outcome of this analysis for the years 1967-83 is summarized in table 2.

Against the background of this cyclical classification, a number of possible monetary indicators for the Netherlands are shown. The following indicators have been considered:
- M1 ratio (M1 as a percentage of net national income);
- liquidity ratio (M2 as a percentage of net national income);
- growth rate of base money, M0;
- growth rate of the money supply, M1; – growth rate of the money supply, M3, i.e. M2 + savings deposits at money-creating institutions;
- growth rate of the money supply, M3S, i.e. M3 + savings at institutional investors and savings banks;
- real capital market rates.

(1) This is especially true of the later years, when trend reversals played a major role. If this is taken into account as well as certain statistical adjustments, the figures from 1976 onwards in table 1 will read as follows.

According to Annual Report for	Liquidity ratio in							
	1976	1977	1978	1979	1980	1981	1982	1983
1981	36.0	35.7	35.7	35.4	36.5	36.2		
1982		35.7	35.6	35.0	35.7	36.3	38.9	
1983			35.6	35.1	35.9	36.5	38.6	41.0

TABLE 2

Turning-Points in the Dutch Cyclical Situation, 1967-1983

Turning-points		Duration in quarters			
trough	peak	expansion	contraction	peak-peak	trough-trough
1967:IV	1970:II	10	7	–	17
1972:I	1973:IV	7	7	14	14
1975:III	1977:I	6	5	13	11
1978:II	1979:IV	6	12	–	–
1982:IV					

The classification in table 2 corresponds to a major extent with that of Van Duijn (1978) but has been updated on the basis of a greater number of series and a somewhat different method of analysis than Van Duijn's (see Fase & Bikker (1985)).

The result is shown in figure 1 where the shaded areas indicate periods of cyclical slowdown. Where the ratios are concerned, inspection of the upper part of figure 1 suggests a rather unsystematical pattern over the corresponding cyclical periods. Thus the M1 ratio turns out to decline in periods of increasing economic activity while the M2 ratio shows a reverse development. In the period of declining economic activity there is also seldom parallelism between the developments of the two ratios.

If we look at the growth rates of the various monetary aggregates defined above – M0, M1, M2, M3 and M3S – also depicted in figure 1, the charts again do not show a clear and consistent pattern. In periods of declining economic activity the growth rates of the various aggregates are usually lower than in periods of increasing activity. This means that, irrespective of the measure used, there are no indications of counter-cyclical monetary policy. The only remarkable factor is that the growth rate of M2 declines in periods of growing economic activity, but shows very little variation – except in 1973-1975 – in periods of declining economic activity. As is the case for the M1 and M2 ratios, such a pattern is less clearly discernible for the other monetary aggregates.

TABLE 3

Annual Growth Rates of Monetary Aggregates

Period	Average annual growth rate (%) of:								
	M0	M1	M2	M3	M3S	GNP	$\hat{p}$	$\hat{e}_1$	$\hat{e}_2$
In upward phase of the trade cycle									
72:II–73:IV	2.3	6.8	17.8	14.6	13.6	13.9	8.9	4.4	5.3
75:III–77:I	8.4	11.3	16.6	15.3	14.6	15.0	7.8	5.6	3.3
78:II–79:IV	2.0	3.3	5.3	8.9	8.8	7.5	4.9	2.2	2.6
82:IV–84:I	0.3	8.3	9.1	4.3	4.3	2.8	4.0	-0.7	-2.3
In downward phase of the trade cycle									
70:II–72:I	8.5	17.2	9.6	13.3	12.6	12.9	8.4	1.7	2.9
73:IV–75:III	11.9	14.6	13.5	12.9	12.3	11.3	10.1	3.3	3.0
77:I–78:II	5.5	8.7	4.4	9.6	10.1	9.3	5.1	2.2	4.3
79:IV–82:IV	3.2	5.4	7.4	8.0	8.0	4.3	5.7	0.6	-2.0

Explanatory note: the growth rate has been calculated on the base of centered four quarters moving averages; $\hat{p}$ means percentage change in consumer price index; $\hat{e}_1$ means effective appreciation of the guilder against competitors; $\hat{e}_2$ means effective appreciation of the guilder against suppliers.

This conclusion, only based on graphical inspection, is supported by the analysis of the growth rate of the various monetary aggregates and the change in the two ratios, shown in table 3.

4.4. Provisional conclusions

In general, a monetary indicator must meet a number of require-ments. In the first place it should be closely connected with the ulti-mate goals of economic policy. Secondly it should be, to a major extent, free from endogenous variations. In this context the main question is to what extent the indicators mentioned earlier comply with these require-ments.

Insofar as monetary policy is a cyclical policy, inspection of the charts of figure 1 shows that for the various monetary indicators a

Fig. 1 A number of monetary indicators 1970-1983

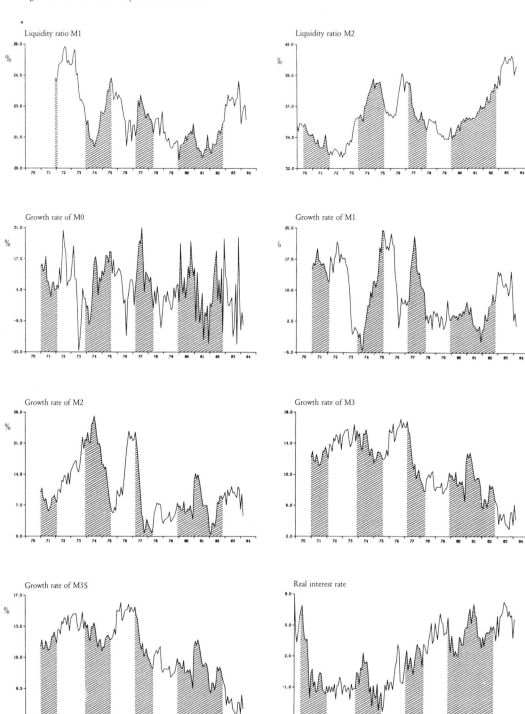

Note: The shaded area indicates periods of cyclical contraction

change in them is not followed by a predictable change in the cyclical situation. An exception is possibly formed by the growth rate of M2, but here too there is no question of a strong link. A strong link with cyclical conditions would mean that the relevant indicator contains a major endogenous component. As the indicator used is more composite in nature, this endogenous element increases. There are, for example, various substitution processes, involving shifts to and from the monetary aggregates considered, which have been brought about by interest rate considerations. Model simulations with the Bank's macromodel MORKMON (see Fase (1984)) also suggest that the significance of these processes must not be neglected. In addition, cyclical variations in nominal national income add an extra endogenous element to the numerator of the ratios considered. As to controllability, the Bank attempts to manage directly net credit expansion of banks by means of credit ceilings on lending to the private sector. However, net credit expansion is only one out of three sources of money creation, the others being the public sector and the balance of payments. The ability of monetary policy to neutralize these sources of money creation is limited in a context of continuing large surpluses on current account. This applies to both the liquidity ratio and the other monetary indicators presented before. In view of this it is interesting to examine the question whether there is an alternative to the monetary aggregate M2 or the derived liquidity ratio.

5. POSSIBILITIES FOR AN ALTERNATIVE INDICATOR

5.1. Introduction

The monetary aggregates used above have all been obtained by simple summation of the components. Apart from the fact that this is in low repute in index number theory, the question arises whether this method makes enough allowance for innovations and gradual changes in the financial system during the past 15 years. In a sense, the Bank's practice to include in the money supply that part of savings that is considered liquid reflects this idea. The same is true of the discussions within the Bank on the interest rate induced switching phenomena which have led to a sharper administrative definition of savings in the monthly reporting to the Bank for monetary supervision purposes. Incidentally, this is also the main source of monetary statistics in the Netherlands. The switching from low to high-interest-bearing financial assets was at the time a result of the supposed changing behaviour towards interest rate differentials. Such switching was to some extent accompanied by a rise in the interest earned and a reduction in the liquidity of the combined assets. This was apparently a desired substitution for the holders of financial portfolios. Foreign exchange speculation, if and insofar as financed from demand depositis or savings deposits, is not reflected in the usual monetary aggregates. Insofar as this was accompanied by money creation - for example by the taking up of short-term credit for the financing of foreign exchange transactions - it does show up in the usual monetary aggregates. In the use of the traditional M2 series, allowance must be made for these problems by means of the application of corrections which take the liquidity of M2 into account on an *ad hoc* basis as it were.

For a more systematic approach to possible endogenous changes or financial innovations, the money supply would have to be measured while taking into consideration the liquidity services provided by the components. This means that in the case of aggregation, weights must be assigned to the components, which correspond with the degree of liquidity. A useful method to achieve that goal is the construction of an index figure. In view of recent theoretical and statistical results by applying index number theory to monetary aggregates, special attention has been given here to the Törnquist-Theil Divisia index. (see e.g. Barnett (1981, 1984)). This index provides a method of monetary aggregation where, on the basis of micro-economic maximizing behaviour, an index series is constructed without *a priori* assumptions on the form of the aggregation function. By way of experiment, this has been attempted here in order to assess the monetary development in the Netherlands from a different perspective.

5.2. The method of the Törnquist-Theil Divisia Index

The starting-point of this method is that holders of assets pay a "user price" for the liquidity reserves provided by these assets. Together with the size of the asset - the amount - this price is included in the Divisia Index. The user price for asset i in period t, $\Pi_{i,t}$, is defined as follows:

$$\pi_{i,t} = \frac{R_t - r_{i,t}}{1 + R_t}$$

with $\pi_{i,t}$ the "user price" of component i, R_t the interest rate on assets without a liquid character and $r_{i,t}$ the interest rate on component i.

Although interest rates are used to set up the index series it can be proved that the Divisia Index is in fact only a function of the amounts of the components, rather than the interest rates. Thus the objection sometimes raised that the series may not be used to explain rate levels, can be brushed aside. The Divisia Index gives, as it were, the developments of the liquidity services performed. It does not represent pure substitution.

The Törnquist-Theil Divisia Index is calculated as follows:

$$Q_t = Q_{t-1} \times \prod_{i=1}^{n} (M_{i,t} / M_{i,t-1})^{0.5 \times (S_{i,t} + S_{i,t-1})}$$

with Q_t the index, $M_{i,t}$ the amount of asset i, $S_{i,t}$ the expenditure part of asset i so that

$$S_{i,t} = \pi_{i,t} \ M_{i,t} / \sum_{i=1}^{n} \pi_{i,t} \ M_{i,t}$$

In logarithmic form the Divisia Index can be easily formulated in growth rates as follows:

$$\ln (Q_t) - \ln (Q_{t-1}) = \sum_{i=1}^{n} Z_{i,t} \cdot (\ln M_{i,t} - \ln M_{i,t-1})$$

with $Z_{i,t} = 0.5 (S_{i,t} + S_{i,t-1})$.

The growth rate of the amount of liquidity Q, thus constructed, is therefore the weighted sum total of the growth of the asset M_i with a moving average of the "expenditure part" (calculated with the above user price) of the relevant asset as a weight.

TABLE 4

Definitions of Monetary Aggregates

Monetary aggregate	Component	Interest rate
M1	CH+DB+DG	., RBG, RGG
M2	M1+TV+SOE+KOSRO	ditto, RK, RSB, RSCH
M3	M2+SEB+SBB	ditto, RT
M3S	M3+STFI+SBFI+SGFI	ditto, RSFI, RT1

Explanatory note: The meaning of the symbols is explained in Annex II.

5.3. Data and results

In principle, the adoption of the Törnquist-Theil Divisia Index requires that all potential assets with liquid characteristics, together with the corresponding interest rates, are included in the index function. The available data, however, do not allow this. This leads to a less ambitious approach using a realistic level of disaggregation. Moreover, our experimental study was confined to the monetary aggregates M2, M3 and M3S. The data for the various assets are end-of-quarter figures and have been adjusted for breaks in series. The composition of the aggregates and interest rates used are summarized in table 4. Our approach implies that logically the number of assets included could be extended to a larger set. By restricting ourselves to the asset considered we impose zero weights to the remaining candidates, because we assume them to be illiquid.

For the interest rates, the monthly averages of the last month of the relevant quarter have been taken. In view of the major variance and the inevitable asynchronism of fluctuations in the various series, end-of-quarter figures would have been less suitable. A possible drawback of the use of quarterly averages here would be the fact that the variability in the interest rate levels would be smoothed out and interest rates would only appear as averages in the index function.

An inverted interest rate structure implies a negative user price. This is not consistent with the basic assumption that there exists a price for the liquidity services provided by the assets considered. To

Fig. 2 Comparison of the conventional liquidity ratio and the liquidity ratio derived from DIVISIA index (%)

A Liquidity ratio for M2 and M2DIV

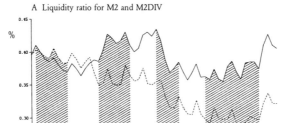

Note: M2__; M2DIV....

B Liquidity ratio for M3 and M3DIV

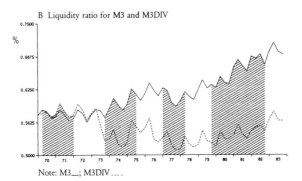

Note: M3__; M3DIV....

C Liquidity ratio for M3S and M3SDIV

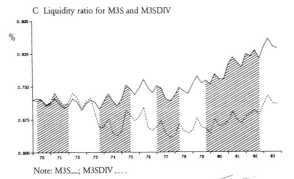

Note: M3S__; M3SDIV....

Note: The shaded area indicates periods of cyclical contraction

Fig. 3 Changes in the liquidity ratios on an annual basis (percentage-points)

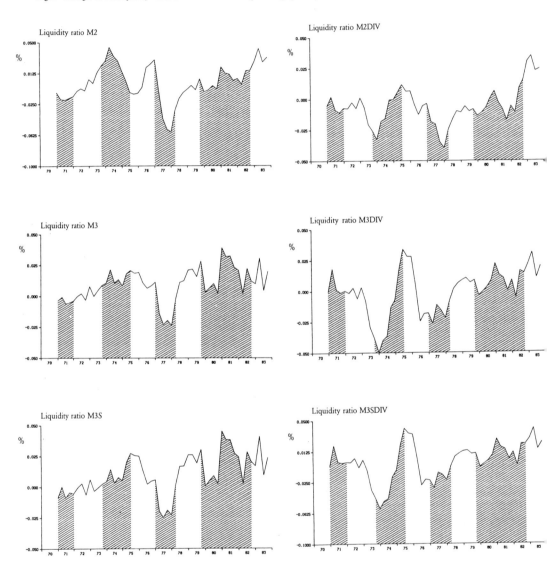

Note: The shaded area indicates periods of cyclical contraction

avoid this situation, the interest rate data have been adjusted for periods with an inverted interest rate structure by interpolating the normal pattern of the historically observed interest rate structure in the Netherlands. This seems to be justified by the fact that the inverted rate structure in particular periods – 1976:3, 1978:3,4 and 1979:4-1980:1 – was mainly due to exchange rate developments within the EMS. As a matter of fact, the resulting narrow monetary policy did not affect the money supply substantially (see Van Hellenberg Hubar (1981)). As a proxy for an interest rate for assets not having liquid characteristics we used the interest rate for private loans with a period to maturity of 20 years.

The empirical analysis yields an index series – the so-called Törnquist-Theil Divisia Index – for the monetary aggregates concerned. These series, together with the corresponding aggregates resulting from simple summation, converted into indices, are shown in annex III.

Figure 2 shows the three alternative liquidity ratios and the corresponding ratios derived from the Törnquist-Theil Divisia index. It is striking that, although the Divisia series shows the same fluctuations for all aggregates considered, the underlying trend lags behind that in the conventional simple sum series. Moreover, all Divisia ratios are increasingly lower than the conventional ratios. This means that the Divisia series suggests a lower degree of liquidity of the economy as a whole than the conventional sum indices of M2, M3 and M3S. Another interesting feauture is the absence in the Törnquist-Theil Divisia series of the accelerated growth of the money supply M2 during 1972-1974. This can be explained by the fact that it was this very period which saw a sharp growth of the time deposits component, which is given a lower weight in the Divisia Index. In the period 1979-1981, too, the growth rate of the Törnquist-Theil Divisia aggregates is less than that of the simple sum aggregate series. This is also due to the smaller weight assigned to the growth of time deposits. An economic interpretation for this must be that the conventional liquidity ratios include an increasing component of liquid assets only held for purposes other than transactions.

Finally, figure 3 shows the changes on an annual basis in the conventional and the Divisia series for the various ratios distinguished.

Inspection of the figures reveals that, with the exception of M3 in the beginning of 1973, the differences are to be found in the levels of the ratios rather than in the changes.

5.4. Interpretation and comparison

To conclude this exercise in monetary aggregation we have attempted to summarize our main results by the traditional sample moments statistics. Table 5 displays the results together with the corresponding statistics for simple sum aggregates.

From this table it may be concluded that the growth rate of the Divisia M2 aggregate is on average considerably lower than that of the simple sum M2 aggregate, being 7.9% and 10.5% respectively. The

TABLE 5

Sample Moments of Average Annual Rate of Growth of Monetary Aggregates, GNP and Prices (%)

	mean	standard deviation	coefficient of variation
M0	5.6	9.6	1.7
M1	9.2	7.0	0.8
M2	10.5	6.3	0.6
M2DIV	7.9	4.2	0.5
M3	11.0	3.6	0.3
M3DIV	9.5	3.2	0.3
M3S	10.7	3.1	0.3
M3SDIV	9.6	3.0	0.3
Nominal GNP	9.6	4.9	0.5
Consumption price	6.9	2.4	0.3
Appreciation of Guilder	2.4	3.8	1.6

standard deviation of Divisia M2 is almost half that of the traditional M2, indicating that the time path of M2 is much more volatile than that of Divisia M2. As to the aggregates M3 and M3S there is a smaller difference between the simple sum and Divisia aggregates whereas the spread is almost identical. However, the coefficient of variation shows a remarkable constancy for each pair of monetary aggregates, being almost identical for the M2 and M3 variants respectively. In terms of absolute volatility, however, we may conclude that the Divisia aggregate for M2 suggests a tighter monetary policy with less uncertainty than the traditional M2 indicator.

6.   SUMMARY AND CONCLUSION

The principal aim of this study was to investigate to what extent the assessment of the monetary policy pursued in the Netherlands is influenced by the indicators used. In this connection, attention was paid in particular to the liquidity ratio which has traditionally served as the central monetary policy variable in Dutch monetary analysis.

In this paper two approaches were used. First, the annual reports were reviewed as far as the liquidity ratio was concerned. It was noted that, despite policy intentions, the ratio did not decrease substantially. Moreover, we showed that this indicator has – at least in the Annual Reports – undergone frequent and important changes in the course of the years, sometimes causing the ultimate change to be materially smaller than it was supposed to be. Apart from uncertainties as to the figures, the liquidity ratio as indicator has a major drawback in that the ratio is in part of an endogenous nature. Additionally, it is highly determined by demand. The endogenous nature means that the ratio must never be viewed by itself. The demand-determined nature reduces its controllability for the monetary authorities.

Second, a few alternative approaches were suggested. A first alternative to the ratio approach is the examination of the growth rates of the various monetary aggregates. Grouped by cyclical phases, it does not yield a consistent basis for assessing the policy pursued. The second alternative was the construction of a monetary index – the Törnquist-Theil Divisia Index. Expressed as a ratio, the index shows a steady downward trend. This is in line with the view, formulated in the Annual Report for 1967, that the ratio should reflect the increasing efficiency of payments – and thus the higher velocity of circulation. If and to the extent that the picture presented by the Divisia monetary aggregate is correct, this means that the liquidity of the Dutch economy

- which the liquidity ratio seeks to approximate - has not increased continually since 1975 and that the current high ratio is less disquieting than is suggested by examination of the bare figures. A simular conclusion results if we look at the average annual growth rate of the Divisia M2 aggregate.

Consequently, in this view the starting position for economic recovery in the Netherlands is much less marked by excess liquidity than is assumed on the basis of the more traditional approach. Hence, the danger of inflation fuelled by monetary ease would appear to be less threatening. However, this conclusion is wholly based on the hypothesis that the Divisia monetary aggregate represents an appropriate monetary indicator.

REFERENCES

Barnett, W.A.(1981), *Consumer demand and labor supply: goods, monetary assets and time*, Amsterdam-New York-Oxford.

Barnett, W.A.(1984), "Recent monetary policy and the Divisia monetary aggregates", *The American Statistician*, 38, 165-172.

Duyn, J.J. van (1978), "Dating postwar business cycles in the Netherlands", *De Economist*, no. 126.

Fase, M.M.G.(1984), *MORKMON: een kwartaalmodel voor macro-economische beleidsanalyse*, Monetaire monografie no. 2, De Nederlandsche Bank, Deventer (also published as: MORKMON: a quarterly model of the Netherlands economy for macro-economic policy analysis).

Fase, M.M.G. and Bikker, J.A. (1985), "De datering van economische fluctuaties: proeve van een conjunctuurspiegel voor Nederland 1965-1984, maart, De Nederlandsche Bank N.V., Report 8502.

Hellenberg Hubar, B.A.J.M. van (1981), "De omgekeerde rentestructuur als nationaal en internationaal verschijnsel" in *Omgekeerde rentestructuur: oorzaken en gevolgen*, NIBE, Amsterdam, 7-29.

Kessler, G.A. (1980), "The impact of Dutch monetary and exchange rate policies on employment", mimeo (also published in G.A. Kessler; 1980, "De invloed van het Nederlandse monetaire beleid en wisselkoersbeleid op de ontwikkeling van de werkgelegenheid", *Maandschrift Economie*, 45, 53-80).

Zijlstra, J. (1979), "Central Banking: a moderate monetarist view", paper presented at the Bank of Israel, Mimeo.

ANNEX I Money supply (as % of net national income)

	1967	1968	1969	1970	1971	1972	1973	1974	1975	1976	1977	1978	1979	1980	1981	1982	1983
1. Increase in floating public debt	0.95	1.49	0.81	0.57	-0.32	-2.36	-0.87	-0.60	1.08	1.11	0.59	1.22	1.66	1.60	0.35	-0.73	-0.24
2. Short-term bank credit to private sector	2.67	2.44	1.15	1.23	12.7	1.61	3.91	3.69	1.03	2.46	3.27	3.80	3.09	2.15	1.13	0.75	0.23
3. Long-term operations of money-creating institutions																	
a) Capital market lending	2.44	3.40	3.49	3.33	3.64	5.22	4.21	3.46	3.76	5.18	5.09	6.35	5.45	3.68	3.14	3.41	4.13
b) Capital market borrowing (-)	-0.04	-0.05	-0.11	-0.28	-0.27	-0.16	-0.53	-0.31	-0.93	-0.29	-2.36	-2.75	-2.24	-1.89	0.04	-0.06	-0.62
c) Increase (-) in long-term liabilities	-2.67	-2.23	-2.68	-3.03	-3.59	-2.73	-1.61	-1.37	-4.73	-1.79	-4.59	-5.16	-4.42	-2.52	-3.65	-1.14	-0.05
Net total	-0.27	1.12	0.69	0.02	-0.21	2.34	2.07	1.78	-1.89	3.09	-1.86	-1.56	-1.21	-0.72	-0.48	2.21	3.46
4. Items in transit and statistical discrepancies	-0.28	-0.30	-0.25	0.09	-0.39	-0.41	-0.19	-0.40	-0.22	-0.07	-0.35	-0.44	0.09	-0.41	-0.43	-0.72	-0.61
5. Total domestic liquidity creation (1 to 4)	3.06	4.74	2.40	1.91	0.35	1.18	4.92	4.48	-0.00	6.59	1.65	3.02	3.63	2.61	0.57	1.51	2.83
6. National liquidity surplus	0.39	-0.08	0.88	1.52	2.14	2.24	1.39	1.89	1.93	0.23	-0.40	-1.61	-1.24	-1.32	1.19	1.34	0.83
7. Increase in money surplus (5 + 6)	3.46	4.66	3.28	3.43	2.49	3.42	6.31	6.37	1.93	6.82	1.25	1.40	2.39	1.29	1.76	2.85	3.66

Explanatory note: the quarters 1963:4–1967:2; 1969:1–1972:2 and 1977:2–1981:2 were periods of direct credit control. From March 1978 onwards, net liquidity creation by the banking sector rather than bank lending has been the means of monetary control.

ANNEX II - Symbols

Abbreviation	Description
CH	Notes and coin.
DB	Demand deposits with banks.
DG	Demand deposits with giro institutions.
TV	Time deposits + foreign-currency balances + short-term debt of local authorities.
SOE	Liquid savings.
KOSRO	Short-term debt of central government.
SEB	Genuine savings with banks.
SBB	Savings certificates to bearer with banks.
STFI	Fixed-term and other deposits with financial instutions.
SBFI	Savings certificates to bearer with financial institutions.
SGFI	Checking account deposits with financial institutions.
RBG	Interest rate on checking accounts at banks.
RGG	Interest rate on checking accounts at giro institutions.
RK	Interest rate on temporary loans to local authorities.
RSB	Intrest rate on savings deposits at banks.
RSCH =	$\frac{1}{2}$(RSCH3-RSCH1)
RSCH1	Interest rate on 1-year Treasury paper.
RSCH3	Interest rate on 3-month Treasury paper.
RT =	$\frac{1}{2}$(RT3B+RT1B)
RT3B	Interest rate on three-month fixed-term savings account at banks.
RT1B	Interest rate on one-year fixed-term savings accounts at banks.
RSFI	Interest rate on savings deposits at financial institutions.
RT1	Interest rate one one-year fixed-term savings accounts.

PART II

INTERNATIONAL MONETARY COORDINATION

6. INTERNATIONAL MONETARY POLICY TO PROMOTE ECONOMIC RECOVERY

W.H. Buiter

1. INTRODUCTION

The purpose of monetary policy is to ensure that money does not matter. There are three reasons why money may matter for real economic performance. First, to the extent that monetary growth is causally connected with inflation, insufficient or excessive money growth (even if fully predictable) will cause the actual inflation rate to differ from the optimal one. The optimal inflation rate is the one that produces satiation with costlessly produced non-interest-bearing money balances. It is associated with a zero nominal interest rate. If the real interest rate is positive, the optimal inflation rate will be negative. This result is both well-known and practically uninteresting. Equally obvious is the second reason why money may matter. Monetary policy should not introduce extraneous, unnecessary noise into the economic system. Even in an idealized flexible price economy, randomization of monetary policy will be costly if the realizations of the stochastic money supply process are not immediately and fully observable by private agents. Adopting non-stochastic policy rules as a *known*, contingent (conditional or flexible) function of current or past observables.

The third reason why money may matter hinges on the presence of nominal inertia or stickiness in the behaviour of wages and/or prices. Given such "Keynesian" features, tight monetary policy will not result in a transition to a lower price level or inflation rate at full employment. Even if in the long run, reductions in money growth are associated with equal reductions in the rate of inflation, the real-time transition or traverse may involve persistent and significant periods of excess capacity and involuntary unemployment. Well-designed monetary policy minimizes these output or unemployment costs of achieving a

Monetary Conditions for Economic Recovery, ed. by C. van Ewijk and J.J. Klant

sustained and sustainable reduction in the rate of inflation. To minimize the "sacrifice ratio"[1], it will often be beneficial to use the instruments of fiscal policy in conjunction with monetary policy. The two are of course linked through the government's budget identity, but there are infinitely many combinations of changes in taxes, spending, borrowing and external financing that are consistent with a given sustained change in the rate of monetary growth. Alternative complementary fiscal packages may have greatly different implications both for the adjustment process and for the nature of the ultimate equilibrium.

In an open economy, external policies and events will alter the current and anticipated future constraints faced by the domestic policy maker. Thus, under a credible fixed exchange rate regime, the domestic rate of inflation cannot be systematically higher or lower than the world rate of inflation. Foreign monetary and fiscal policy actions affect the domestic economy through goods markets (e.g., by altering world demand for home country traded output), through interest rate linkages and, in the case of an endogenous exchange rate regime, through spot and forward exchange markets. Freely floating exchange rates do not, except in very special and practically unimportant cases, insulate a country from external real and financial shocks, nor do they prevent the spillover of domestic disturbances into the rest of the world. Only the most naive zero-capital mobility, trade balance view of exchange rate determination could lead one to believe that "decoupling" through exchange rate flexibility is an option.

The existence of mutual spillovers is not by itself sufficient for policy coordination. It could be the case that policy actions are properly "priced" so that even decentralized, non-cooperative policy design leads to Pareto-efficient outcomes. Merely to state this possibility is almost sufficient to refute it. The two main reasons are that market prices are not sufficient indices of marginal social value and that national policy makers are not sub-atomistic, competitive agents. Even in highly abstract, idealized representations of competitive, market-clearing

---

(1) The sacrifice ratio is the cumulative undiscounted net output or unemployment cost of achieving a one per cent steady-state reduction in the inflation rate.

economies such as the overlapping generations model, the incompleteness of the set of markets (reflecting, e.g., the difficulties one is likely to encounter when attempting to make binding private contracts with the dead and the unborn) prevents prices in the markets that do exist from being accurate social shadow prices. Other reasons for the non-existence of a complete set of Arrow-Debreu markets are adverse selection and moral hazard. The insufficiency of market prices for harmonizing non-cooperative policy actions is especially serious when labor, goods or credit markets are in disequilibrium (or in non-Walrasian equilibrium) and non-price rationing occurs. In addition, the non-atomistic nature of national policy makers means that they do not necessarily treat market prices or other policy makers' actions as parametric when designing policies that are optimal from a national perspective. Government behaviour in countries other than Andorra, Lichtenstein, Luxembourg, etc., is more properly viewed as a non-cooperative dynamic game against other governments and against markets with anticipating (even if competitive) private agents. In these markets some governments will be large participants.

To assert that, given externalities and non-competitive behaviour by governments, there exists scope for global welfare improving policy coordination schemes that move the world economy closer to the contract curve, is not to argue that there may not also be many "cooperative" schemes that will result (or in the past have resulted) in reduced global welfare. Nor does the merely *qualitative* proposition that there exist welfare improving arrangements for international cooperation and coordination deny the possibility that the *quantitative* significance of the improvement could be slight and/or highly uncertain. The task of quantifying the fruits of international policy coordination is an important one but lies beyond the scope of this paper. In what follows I propose to study the design of efficient disinflationary policies in an interdependent economic system. The formal vehicle for this analysis is a small and simple analytical two-country macroeconomic rational expectations model[1]. I will start with the case of the flex-price New Classical

(1) The analysis relies heavily on the single-country analysis of efficient disinflationary policy in Buiter and Miller (1983b). The two-country model is a slight extension of the model used in Miller (1982).

wonderland in which credibility of monetary policy is necessary and sufficient for costless disinflation. The consequences of successive concessions to realism can then be traced in a relatively straightforward manner. The consequences of unilateral and coordinated policy design and implementation are emphasized throughout.

In what follows, "first-best" policies which eliminate inflation at a stroke without output or unemployment costs will almost always exist, and can be derived by inspection. It will therefore not be necessary formally to specify an objective functional penalizing deviations from zero inflation and from full employment or capacity output. The paper does not deal at all with the "incentive-compatibility" of the first-best policies, i.e., with whether these policies are time-consistent.

2. A MODEL IN WHICH CREDIBILITY OF MONETARY POLICY IS NECESSARY AND SUFFICIENT FOR A COSTLESS SUSTAINED REDUCTION IN INFLATION

The various models to be considered in this paper will differ from each other only as regards the specification of the inflation process. They will have a common set of portfolio balance equations and output market equilibrium equations. These are given in equations (1)-(7). Starred variables relate to the foreign country, unstarred variables to the home country. All variables except for interest rates, measures of fiscal stance and tax rates are in logarithms. The notation is as follows: m is the nominal stock of money, p the consumer price index, y real output, r the short nominal interest rate, e the nominal exchange rate, measured as the number of units of home currency per unit of foreign currency, f is an index of fiscal stance, v the value added deflator at factor cost, τ_i the indirect tax rate, ℓ a measure of real money balances, c international competitiveness or the real exchange rate and μ the instantaneous proportional rate of growth of the nominal money stock.

All parameters are non-negative. $\dot{x}$ denotes the right-hand side time derivative of x. Expectations are formed rationally. E_t denotes the conditional rational expectation operator at time t.

(1a) $\qquad m - p = ky - \lambda r$

(1b) $\qquad m^* - p^* = k^* y^* - \lambda^* r^*$

(2a) $\qquad y = -\gamma(r - E_t \dot{p}) + \delta c + \varepsilon(m-p) + \beta f + \eta y^*$

(2b) $\qquad y^* = -\gamma^*(r^* - E_t \dot{p}^*) - \delta^* c + \varepsilon^*(m^* - p^*) + \beta^* f^* + \eta^* y$

(3) $\qquad E_t \dot{e} = r - r^*$

(4a) $\qquad p = \alpha v + (1-\alpha)(e+v^*) + \tau_i , \quad 0 < \alpha < 1$

(4b) $\qquad p^* = \alpha^* v^* + (1-\alpha^*)(v-e) + \tau_i^* , \quad 0 < \alpha^* < 1$

(5a) $\qquad \ell \equiv m - v$

(5b) $\qquad \ell^* \equiv m^* - v^*$

(6) $\qquad c \equiv e + v^* - v$

(7a) $\qquad \mu \equiv \dot{m}$

(7b) $\qquad \mu^* \equiv \dot{m}^*.$

Equations (1a) and (1b) are standard domestic and foreign money demand functions. Demand for domestic output, in (2a) is a decreasing function of the real interest rate and an increasing function of competitiveness, of real money balances, of the degree to which fiscal policy is expansionary, as measured by f , and of the foreign level of economic activity. The demand for foreign output is specified analogously in (2b).

The money stock is to be interpreted as narrow money, say the monetary base. Domestic money is held only by domestic residents, for domestic transactions purposes. There is no direct currency substitution. This seems reasonable as domestic money is dominated as a store of value by short domestic bonds and foreign money by short foreign bonds. Between these two interest-bearing assets there is perfect substitutability. Equation (3) represents uncovered interest parity, the outcome of perfect markets and risk-neutral speculative behaviour. The consumer price index is a weighted average of the two national value added deflators as shown in (4a) and (4b). Indirect taxes can drive a wedge between factor costs and market prices[1].

In the New Classical wonderland of this section, output is always equal to its capacity or full employment level, i.e.

$$(8a) \qquad y = \bar{y}$$

$$(8b) \qquad y^* = \bar{y}^*.$$

What permits this is the perfect flexibility of the domestic and foreign price levels and (in the background) of domestic and foreign money wages. GDP deflators have the flexibility normally associated with the exchange rate and other financial asset prices. The domestic and foreign rates of inflation can be expressed as in (9a,b).

$$(9a) \qquad \dot{p} = -\dot{\ell} + (1-\alpha)\dot{c} + \mu + \dot{\tau}_i$$

$$(9b) \qquad \dot{p}^* = -\dot{\ell}^* - (1-\alpha^*)\dot{c} + \mu^* + \dot{\tau}_i^* .$$

Equivalently (except at those instants at which "news" arrives), we can look at the expected rates of inflation given in (9'a) and (9'b):

$$(9'a) \qquad E_t \dot{p} = -[\lambda^{-1}+\gamma^{-1}\varepsilon]\ell + [(\lambda^{-1}+\gamma^{-1}\varepsilon)(1-\alpha)-\gamma^{-1}\delta]c + [\lambda^{-1}+\gamma^{-1}\varepsilon]\tau_i$$

$$- \gamma^{-1}\beta f + (\lambda^{-1}k+\gamma^{-1})\bar{y} - \gamma^{-1}\eta\bar{y}^*$$

$$(9'b) \qquad E_t \dot{p}^* = -[\lambda^{*-1}+\gamma^{*-1}\varepsilon^*]\ell^* -[(\lambda^{*-1}+\gamma^{*-1}\varepsilon^*)(1-\alpha^*) - \gamma^{*-1}\delta^*]c$$

$$+(\lambda^{*-1}+\gamma^{*-1}\varepsilon^*)\tau_i^* - \gamma^{*-1}\beta^* f^* - \gamma^{*-1}\eta^*\bar{y}+(\lambda^{*-1}k^*+\gamma^{*-1})\bar{y}^*$$

[1] For a justification of the absence of explicit consideration of the government budget identity, see appendix II.

ℓ , ℓ^* and c form a minimal set of state variables for our model. The state equations can be written as:

$$
)\quad \begin{bmatrix} E_t \dot{\ell} \\ E_t \dot{\ell^*} \\ E_t \dot{c} \end{bmatrix} = \begin{bmatrix} a_{11} & a_{12} & a_{13} \\ a_{21} & a_{22} & a_{23} \\ a_{31} & a_{32} & a_{33} \end{bmatrix} \begin{bmatrix} \ell \\ \ell^* \\ c \end{bmatrix} + \begin{bmatrix} b_{11} & b_{12} & b_{13} & b_{14} & b_{15} & b_{16} & b_{17} & b_{18} & b_{19} & b_{1,10} \\ b_{21} & b_{22} & b_{23} & b_{24} & b_{25} & b_{26} & b_{27} & b_{28} & b_{29} & b_{2,10} \\ b_{31} & b_{32} & b_{33} & b_{34} & b_{35} & b_{36} & b_{37} & b_{38} & b_{39} & b_{3,10} \end{bmatrix} \begin{bmatrix} \mu \\ \mu^* \\ \tau_i^* \\ \tau_i \\ f \\ f^* \\ \bar{y} \\ \bar{y}^* \\ \dot{\tau}_i \\ \dot{\tau}_i^* \end{bmatrix}
$$

where the a_{ij} and b_{ij} coefficients are given in Appendix I .

The system given in (10) has three non-predetermined, forward-looking or jump state variables. The domestic and foreign value added deflators, v and v^* are flexible, market-clearing prices, as is the nominal exchange rate e . The boundary conditions for $\ell \equiv m-v$, $\ell^* \equiv m^* - v^*$ and $c \equiv e + v^* - v$ take therefore the form not of given initial conditions but of the terminal or transversality condition that the solution to (10) should lie on the stable manifold (if this exists). For this terminal condition to generate a unique, convergent solution trajectory for ℓ , ℓ^* and c , given the actual and anticipated future values of the ten forcing variables, the characteristic equation of (10) should have three unstable roots, i.e., roots with positive real parts. It is easily seen that if there are no real balance effects in the two countries' IS curves ($\varepsilon = \varepsilon^* = 0$) the three characteristic roots are $\rho_1 = \lambda^{-1}$, $\rho_2 = \lambda^{*-1}$ and $\rho_3 = [\gamma^{-1}\delta + \gamma^{*-1}\delta^*]/[\alpha + \alpha^* - 1]$. The first two are always positive, the third will be positive if $\alpha + \alpha^* > 1$, i.e., if on average the residents of each of the two countries have a preference, at the margin, for spending on own output. If both α and α^* exceed one half, this condition will be satisfied[1]. The characteristic

(1) If $\alpha + \alpha^* = 1$, the exchange rate is constant, $e \equiv 0$ and $p = p^* + \tau_i - \tau_i^*$.

roots are continuous functions of the a_{ij} in equation (10). A sufficient condition for (10) to have 3 unstable characteristic roots is therefore $\alpha + \alpha^* > 1$ and small real balance effects.

The steady state conditions of the model have the familiar long-run classical or monetarist properties. The same set of steady-state conditions, given in (11) below, will also characterize the other variants of the model analyzed in this paper, although the latter exhibit "Keynesian" behaviour outside the steady state.

(11a) $\dot{p} = \dot{v} = \mu$

(11b) $\dot{p}^* = \dot{v}^* = \mu^*$

(11c) $\dot{e} = \mu - \mu^*$

(11d) $r = r^* + \mu - \mu^*$

(11e) $y = \bar{y}$

(11f) $y^* = \bar{y}^*$

(11g) $r = \dfrac{(\delta^*\gamma + \delta\gamma^*)\mu + \delta\varepsilon^*\lambda^*(\mu-\mu^*) + \delta^*\beta f + \delta\beta^* f^* - [\delta^*(1-\varepsilon k) - \delta\eta^*]\bar{y} - [\delta(1-\varepsilon^* k^*) - \delta^*\eta]\bar{y}}{(\gamma+\varepsilon\lambda)\delta^* + (\gamma^*+\varepsilon^*\lambda^*)\delta}$

(11h) $c = \dfrac{(\gamma^*+\varepsilon^*\lambda^*)\varepsilon\lambda\mu - (\gamma+\varepsilon\lambda)\varepsilon^*\lambda^*\mu^* - (\gamma^*+\varepsilon^*\lambda^*)\beta f + (\gamma+\varepsilon\lambda)\beta^* f^*}{(\gamma+\varepsilon\lambda)\delta^* + (\gamma^*+\varepsilon^*\lambda^*)\delta}$

$\quad + \dfrac{[(\gamma^*+\varepsilon^*\lambda^*)(1-\varepsilon k) + (\gamma+\varepsilon\lambda)\eta^*]\bar{y} - [(\gamma+\varepsilon\lambda)(1-\varepsilon^* k^*) + (\gamma^*+\varepsilon^*\lambda^*)\eta]\bar{y}^*}{(\gamma+\varepsilon\lambda)\delta^* + (\gamma^*+\varepsilon^*\lambda^*)\delta}$

(11i) $\ell = k\bar{y} - \lambda r + (1-\alpha)c + \tau_i$

(11j) $\ell^* = k^*\bar{y}^* - \gamma^*(r-\mu+\mu^*) - (1-\alpha^*)c + \tau_i^*.$

In the long-run, real interest rates are equalized and the real exchange rate is constant. Differences in monetary growth are reflected

in the rate of depreciation of the exchange rate. The world real interest rate rises with fiscal expansion at home and abroad. An increase in
capacity output at home or abroad lowers the long-run real interest rate
if $\delta^*(1-\varepsilon k)-\delta\eta^* > 0$ and $\delta(1-\varepsilon^*k^*) - \delta^*\eta > 0$ respectively. If there is
no real balance effect at home or abroad, a change in the rate of
growth of the nominal money stock at home (abroad) raises the domestic
(foreign) nominal interest rate one-for-one and leaves the long-run real
interest rate unaffected. If there is a real balance effect at home
an increase in monetary growth at home raises the nominal interest rate
at home less than one-for-one. The real interest rate (at home and
abroad) is reduced.

Absent real balance effects, changes in money growth rates leave
the long-run real exchange rate unaffected. With a real balance effect
at home, higher money growth at home means a long-run depreciation of
the real exchange rate. The mechanism is that, if $\lambda > 0$, higher money
growth and domestic inflation lowers the real stock of money balances
and thus the demand for output. An improvement in competitiveness is
required to rebalance the output market. Fiscal expansion at home
causes long-run real appreciation while fiscal expansion abroad has the
opposite effect. It should be clear that a proportional shift in the *levels*
of the domestic or foreign money stock paths will not affect the nominal
or real interest rate or the real exchange rate but will be associated
with equal proportional shifts in the levels of the path of p, p^* or e.

Linear dynamic rational expectations models in continuous time can
in general be represented as in equation (12)

$$(12) \quad \begin{bmatrix} \dot{x}(t) \\ E_t\dot{y}(t) \end{bmatrix} = A \begin{bmatrix} x(t) \\ y(t) \end{bmatrix} + bz(t)$$

where x is an n_1 vector of predetermined state variables, y is an $n-n_1$
vector of non-predetermined state variables, and $z(t)$ is a vector of
exogenous or forcing variables. We assume that A is diagonalizable and
has n_1 stable and $n-n_1$ unstable characteristic roots. The boundary
conditions for (12) are given by:

(13a) $x(t_0) = \bar{x}(t_0)$ (n_1 initial conditions)

(13b)   The solution should lie on the stable manifold ($n-n_1$ terminal conditions).

Let Λ be a diagonal matrix whose diagonal elements are the characteristic roots of A. We partition Λ as follows:

$$\Lambda = \begin{bmatrix} \Lambda_1 & 0 \\ 0 & \Lambda_2 \end{bmatrix}.$$

Λ_1 is the $n_1 \times n_1$ matrix whose diagonal elements are the stable roots of A while Λ_2 contains the unstable roots. Let V be an $n \times n$ matrix whose rows are linearly independent left-eigenvectors of A. We partition A, B, V and $V^{-1} \equiv W$ conformably with x and y as follows:

$$A = \begin{bmatrix} A_{11} & A_{12} \\ A_{21} & A_{22} \end{bmatrix}; \quad B = \begin{bmatrix} B_1 \\ B_2 \end{bmatrix}; \quad V = \begin{bmatrix} V_{11} & V_{12} \\ V_{21} & V_{22} \end{bmatrix}; \quad V^{-1} \begin{bmatrix} W_{11} & W_{12} \\ W_{21} & W_{22} \end{bmatrix}.$$

We also define $D \equiv V_{21}B_1 + V_{22}B_2$.

The solution to the two-point boundary value problems (12), (13a) and (13b) is given by:

(14a) $\displaystyle y(t) = -V_{22}^{-1}V_{21}x(t) - V_{22}^{-1}\int_t^\infty e^{\Lambda_2(t-\tau)} DE_t z(\tau)\, d\tau$

(14b) $\displaystyle x(t) = W_{11}e^{\Lambda_1(t-t_0)}W_{11}^{-1}\bar{x}(t_0) + \int_{t_0}^t W_{11}e^{\Lambda_1(t-s)}W_{11}^{-1}B_1 z(s)\, ds$

$\displaystyle \qquad - \int_{t_0}^t W_{11}e^{\Lambda_1(t-s)}W_{11}^{-1}A_{12}V_{22}^{-1}\int_s^\infty e^{\Lambda_2(s-\tau)} DE_s z(\tau)\, d\tau\, ds$ (1).

(1) See Buiter (1984a).

In the classical model of equation (10) the x-vector of predetermined variables vanishes, $y^T(t) \equiv [\ell(t), \; \ell^*(t), \; c(t)]$ [(1)], and $z^T(t) \equiv [\mu, \; \mu^*, \; \tau_i, \; \tau_i^*, \; f, \; f^*, \; \bar{y}, \; \bar{y}^*, \; \tau_i, \; \tau_i^*]$. Thus:

$$
(15) \quad
\begin{bmatrix} \ell(t) \\ \ell^*(t) \\ c(t) \end{bmatrix}
= -V_{22}^{-1} \int_t^\infty
\begin{bmatrix}
e^{\rho_1(t-\tau)} & & 0 \\
0 & e^{\rho_2(t-\tau)} & 0 \\
0 & & e^{\rho_3(t-\tau)}
\end{bmatrix}
DE_t
\begin{bmatrix}
\mu(s) \\ \mu^*(s) \\ \tau_i(s) \\ \tau_i^*(s) \\ f(s) \\ f^*(s) \\ \bar{y}(s) \\ \bar{y}^*(s) \\ \dot{\tau}_i(s) \\ \dot{\tau}_i^*(s)
\end{bmatrix}
ds
$$

The crucial aspect of equation (15) is that the state variables depend only on current anticipations of future values of the forcing variables. Current and past behaviour of the exogenous variables and the policy instruments matters only to the extent that it influences expectations of the future.

From the general dynamic specification of the model in equations (1)-(8) and from the steady state conditions in equation (11), or from equations (9a), (9b) or (9'a), (9'b) and (10) the following result can be obtained by inspection. The initial situation is one of constant values of all forcing variables (i.e., $\dot{\tau}_i = \dot{\tau}_i^* = 0$).

Proposition 1: In the flexible price model, the credible announcement of an immediate, permanent reduction in current and future monetary growth by $\Delta\mu$ in the home country is necessary and sufficient for an immediate, sustained reduction in domestic inflation by $\Delta\mu$. It will be

(1) y^T denotes the transpose of y.

obvious that in this model with its instantaneous market-clearing features there will never by any output costs of bringing down inflation.
Lack of credibility about future monetary growth may, however, prevent a desired reduction in inflation, no matter how faithfully the
authorities restrict the current monetary growth rate. E.g., the possibility of the election at some future date of an inflation-prone government may prevent even a very conservative government from translating
monetary deceleration during its term of office into corresponding
reductions in inflation. It is not sufficient to commit oneself, one must
also be able to commit one's successors. The recognition of this dilemma
is behind some of the calls for embedding monetary policy in a constitutional framework (or tying it into a constitutional straight jacket,
depending on one's point of view) in order to safeguard it against
political manipulation.

The response of the system to the immediate credible permanent
reduction in domestic monetary growth is especially transparent when
there are no real balance effects ($\varepsilon = \varepsilon^* = 0$). The transition to the
new steady state with the lower rate of inflation is instantaneous. All
real variables other than the domestic rate of inflation and the domestic
stock of real money balances remain unchanged. The domestic nominal
interest rate declines by the same amount as the reduction in domestic
monetary growth and domestic inflation. Foreign inflation remains unchanged. The rate of depreciation of the domestic currency ($\dot{e}$) also
declines by the amount of the reduction in μ and $\dot{p}$. Real competitiveness remains constant. Note however, that both the domestic value
added deflator v and the nominal exchange rate undergo an immediate
discontinuous or discrete drop at the time of the policy announcement
with $\Delta v = \Delta e = \lambda \Delta \mu$. The reason for this is apparent in the domestic
money demand function (1a). Lower money growth and lower inflation
imply a correspondingly lower nominal rate of interest. This raises the
demand for real money balances. With the level of the nominal money
stock given (only its instantaneous rate of change has declined by a
finite amount) and output exogenous, the required jump increase in $m-p$
must be effected through a discrete decline in p. With real competitiveness constant, the decline in p is made up of equal discrete reductions
in v and e. The picture is drawn in Figure 1. Note that there are no

Figure 1 An unexpected permanent reduction in money growth at $t=t_0$

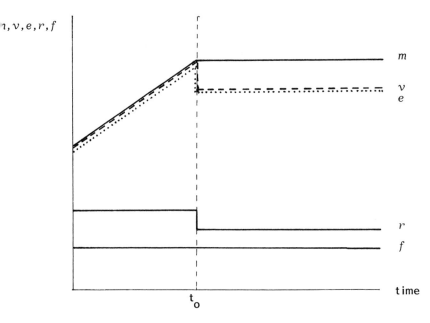

m, v, e, r, f

externalities or indeed any real external effects of the domestic anti-inflation program. Coordination is redundant.

When there are non-zero real balance effects, immediate credible permanent reductions in domestic money growth again result in an immediate transition to the new steady state equilibrium with domestic inflation reduced by the amount of the reduction in money growth and with foreign inflation unchanged. This time, however, the real interest rate at home and abroad and the real exchange rate will be affected.

Since $\dfrac{\partial r}{\partial \mu} = \dfrac{\delta^* \gamma + \delta(\gamma^* + \varepsilon^* \lambda^*)}{\delta^* (\gamma + \varepsilon \lambda) + \delta(\gamma^* + \varepsilon^* \lambda^*)}$ (across steady states), the domestic (and foreign) real interest rate rises when the domestic money growth rate is cut if $\varepsilon > 0$. The domestic nominal interest rate declines less than one-for-one when μ is lowered, while the foreign nominal interest rate $r + \mu^* - \mu$ rises. Since $\dfrac{\partial c}{\partial \mu} = \dfrac{(\gamma^* + \varepsilon^* \lambda^*) \varepsilon \lambda}{(\gamma + \varepsilon \lambda) \delta^* + (\gamma^* + \varepsilon^* \lambda^*) \delta}$ (across steady states), a reduction in domestic money growth worsens domestic competitiveness if $\varepsilon > 0$. The reason is that a lower value of μ raises the real interest rate equally at home and abroad. The domestic nominal interest falls, however, while the foreign nominal interest rate rises. The domestic stock of real balances thus goes up while the foreign nominal interest rate rises. The domestic stock of real balances thus goes up while the foreign real money stock declines. To equilibrate the domestic and foreign output markets domestic competitiveness must decline (foreign competitiveness must improve). In this case the credible announcement of the immediate, permanent reduction in μ is accompanied by a discrete drop in v and a discrete increase in v^*. While c falls, the impact effect on e is ambiguous.

There are several ways of avoiding these spillovers from domestic monetary growth reductions on real variables that concern foreigners. The home country could stop its real interest rate (and thus the world real interest rate) from rising by contractionary fiscal policy with $\Delta f = \frac{\varepsilon\lambda}{\beta}\Delta\mu$. This would also stabilize the real exchange rate and stop the foreign nominal interest rate from rising. The foreign country cannot use fiscal policy alone to stabilize both its real interest rate and its real exchange rate. To prevent the real interest rate from rising, contractionary fiscal policy is called for (with $\Delta f^* = \frac{\varepsilon\lambda\,\delta^*}{\beta^*\delta}\Delta\mu$) while to stop foreign competitiveness from improving, expansionary fiscal policy abroad is called for with $\Delta f^* = \frac{-(\gamma^*+\varepsilon^*\lambda^*)\varepsilon\lambda}{(\gamma+\varepsilon\lambda)\beta}\Delta\mu$. It is clear from equations (11g) and (11h) that the foreign money growth rate μ^* and the foreign fiscal stance, f^* can be used jointly to stabilize the real interest rate and the real exchange rate. This does mean, of course, that the foreign country cannot choose to stabilize its real exchange rate and its real interest rate while maintaining its previous rate of inflation.

It is possible for the two countries jointly to choose any pair of inflation rates $\dot{p}$ and $\dot{p}^*$ while maintaining the old real interest rate and competitiveness by using both money growth rates and fiscal instruments appropriately.

3. MODELS IN WHICH SMART DEMAND MANAGEMENT IS NECESSARY AND SUFFICIENT FOR A COSTLESS, SUSTAINED REDUCTION IN INFLATION

The main reason for spending time with the classical model in which, given credibility, nothing can go wrong, is that it provides good insight into what can go wrong in more realistic and useful models.

It is generally accepted that the level of money wages and the GDP deflator are not like the foreign exchange rate or the stock market index. A common alternative view is that the value added deflator (or the wage) changes only gradually over time in response to excess demand or supply pressure, e.g., through an augmented Phillips curve:

(16) $\dfrac{d}{dt}(v - \theta\tau_d) = \psi(y - \bar{y}) + \pi, \; \psi > 0 \; ; \; 0 \le \theta \le 1$

(16') $\dfrac{d}{dt}(v^* - \theta^*\tau_d^*) = \psi^*(y^* - \bar{y}^*) + \pi^* \; , \; \psi^* > 0 \; ; \; 0 \le \theta^* < 1.$

In (16) it is recognized that the direct tax rate may influence the behaviour of before-tax wages and other factor payments. The two extreme possibilities are that it is the rate of change of after-tax factor rentals ($v - \tau_d$ and $v^* - \tau_d^*$ with $\theta = \theta^* = 1$) or the rate of change of before-tax factor rentals (v and v^* with $\theta = \theta^* = 0$) that is determined through the Phillips-curve mechanism. $v - \theta\tau_d$ and $v^* - \theta^*\tau^*_d$ are treated as sluggish or predetermined (i.e., incapable of making a discontinuous jump at a point in time). The sacrifice ratio depends crucially on the specification of the process governing π, the augmentation term in the Phillips-curve or "core inflation". Note that the old-fashioned non-augmented Phillipscurve, $\dot{v} = \psi(y - \bar{y}) + \bar{\pi}$ where $\bar{\pi}$ is exogenous (e.g. zero) implies an infinite sacrifice ratio. To keep inflation at a lower level forever, the output or unemployment gap $y - \bar{y}$ has to be in-creased and kept at this higher level forever.

There are at least three well-known models of the inflation process which combine the view that $v - \theta\tau_d$ (the prive level) moves sluggishly with the view that π (core inflation) moves flexibly. Two are re-presented in (16) plus (17) or (18) below, the third in (19a), (19b), (19c),

(17) $\pi = \mu \; ; \quad \pi^* = \mu^*$

(18) $\mu = \dot{p} \; ; \quad \mu^* = \dot{p}^*$

(19a) $\dot{\tilde{v}} = \Omega(w-\tilde{v})$; $\dot{\tilde{v}}* = \Omega*(w*-\tilde{v}*)$

(19b) $E_t\dot{w} = \Omega(w-\tilde{v}-\psi(y-\bar{y}))$; $E_t\dot{w}*$; $\Omega*(w*-\tilde{v}*-\psi*(y*-\bar{y}*)($

(19c) $v = \tilde{v} + \theta\tau_d$; $v* = \tilde{v}* + \theta*\tau_d^*$.

The first model (17) has core inflation equal to current money growth (Dornbusch (1980)), Buiter and Miller (1981)). The second (18) has core inflation given by $\dot{p}$ or $\dot{p}*$, the right-side derivative of the price level path of the classical, flex-price model of the previous section. This means that core inflation equals the rate of change of the price level in the classical equilibrium model except at those points where that rate of change becomes infinite and the classical equilibrium price level make a discrete jump. Price equations such as (16) and (18) have been used by Mussa (1981) and Barro and Grossman (1976).

Equations (19a), (19b), and (19c) represent a contract model in which the level of the current contract wage, w , depends on current expectations of future values of $\tilde{v}$ and excess demands and the current value added deflator depends on past contract wages. This model is due to Calvo (1982a, b, c) and can be viewed as a continuous time version of Taylor's model of overlapping, staggered 2-period nominal wage contracts (Taylor (1980)). The interpretation of (19a), (19b) and (19c) is clear when we solve for v and w explicitly as follows:

(20a) $\tilde{v}(t) = e^{-\Omega(t-t_0)}\tilde{v}(t_0) + \Omega\int_{t_0}^{t} w(s)e^{-\Omega(t-s)}ds$

and

(20b) $w(t) = \Omega\int_t^\infty E_t[\tilde{v}(s) + \psi(y(s) - \bar{y})]e^{-\Omega(s-t)}ds + e^{\Omega t}E_t \lim_{\tau\to\infty} e^{-\Omega\tau}w(\tau)$

or

(21a) $v(t) = v(t_0) + \theta[\tau_d(t) - \tau_d(t_0)] + K(t-t_0) + \Omega^2\psi\int_{t_0}^{t}\int_s^\infty E_s(y(z)-\bar{y})dzds$

and

(21b) $w(t) = v(t) - \theta \tau_d(t) + K + \Omega \psi \int_t^\infty E_t(y(s) - \bar{y}) ds$

in (20a) and (20b) is an arbitrary constant of integration, to be determined by a terminal boundary condition. It is easily seen that in models with a well-defined steady state rate of inflation and monetary growth $\overset{\infty}{\mu}$, the arbitrary constant K is equal to $\overset{\infty}{\mu}/\Omega$. Note that while $\tilde{v}$ is predetermined in (20a), the current contract wage w is, among other things, an increasing function of current expectations of future excess demand and of the transversality condition determining steady-state inflation through K. Since w is flexible, the rate of change of the value added deflator, $\dot{\tilde{v}}$, is flexible (see equation (19a)). The effect of direct taxes on v if $\theta > 0$ also introduces an element of domestic cost flexibility. All three models in equations (16)-(19) thus have flexible core inflation. It may therefore appear that a credible announcement of an immediate, permanent reduction in money growth would again be sufficient (and necessary) for reducing domestic inflation without output costs. This is not correct, because an immediate transition to a lower rate of inflation would require, if the interest-elasticity of demand for money balances is negative, that the stock of real money balances is increased. In the classical flex-price model, the price *level* drop shown in figure 1 brought about the necessary increase in real money balances. Absent price *level* flexibility, the authorities must either increase the *level* of the nominal stock of money balances, or cut direct or indirect taxes so as to reduce the market price level for any given level of after-tax factor income or prevent the fall in nominal interest rates associated with lower steady state inflation by having expansionary fiscal policy. Therefore:

Proposition 2: In the model with a predetermined price level but flexible core inflation, credible, immediate, permanent reduction in money growth in the home country is necessary for an immediate, costless, sustained reduction in domestic inflation by the same amount. In addition, the authorities must either generate an immediate increase in the level of the real money stock (by a 'jump' in the nominal money stock or by direct or indirect tax cuts, with all fiscal variables adjusted in such a way as to keep aggregate demand equal to full employment supply) or engage in a set of fiscal measures (e.g., an increase in) that prevent a decline in the domestic nominal interest rate. Only the first of these two options avoids international spillover effects (assuming no real balance effects).

In all three of these models therefore, one country's inflation can be eliminated costlessly and at a stroke, given credibility of announcements of future money growth and given a policy for mimicking or avoiding the need for, the price level drop shown in figure 1.

We can write the domestic monetary equilibrium condition as

$$(22) \quad m - \tilde{v} - \theta\tau_d = k\bar{y} - \lambda r + (1-\alpha)c + \tau_i$$

Note that $\tilde{v} \equiv v - \theta\tau_d$ is predetermined.

To achieve an instantaneous transition to a new low-inflation steady state, if the foreign country does not change any of its policy instruments, the home country's policy instruments should satisfy:

$$(23) \quad \Delta m - \theta\Delta\tau_d - \Delta\tau_i + \frac{\beta(\lambda\delta^* + (1-\alpha)(\gamma^* + \varepsilon^*\lambda^*))}{\Lambda}\Delta f$$

$$= -\frac{\lambda[\delta^*\gamma + \delta\gamma^* + \delta\varepsilon^*\lambda^* + (\alpha-1)(\gamma^* + \varepsilon^*\lambda^*)\varepsilon]}{\Lambda}\Delta\mu$$

where $\Lambda = (\gamma+\varepsilon\lambda)\delta^* + (\gamma^* + \varepsilon^*\lambda^*)\delta$

If there is no real balance effect at home or abroad, the "money jump" policy with $\Delta m = -\lambda\Delta\mu$ would be the simplest way to proceed. The *level* of the nominal money stock is raised once-and-for-all at the same time that its rate of growth is lowered. While such a policy combination may appear to be prone to credibility problems, it should be noted that it would be implemented automatically if the government announced a credible nominal income target rather than a monetary growth target. A nominal income target is of course a "velocity-corrected" monetary target which would automatically allow for the decline in velocity associated with the transition to a lower rate of inflation. The jump in real money balances can, from (23) also be achieved with an unchanged nominal money stock, through a cut in indirect taxes balanced in terms of revenue by an increase in direct taxes, provided $\theta < 1$, i.e. provided indirect taxes have a larger immediate effect on the price level than direct taxes[1].

Absent real balance effect, changes in m or τ_i would permit costless and instantaneous domestic disinflation without any real spill-overs to the foreign country. The real interest rate, the real exchange rate and the foreign country's nominal interest rate would be unaffected.

Expansionary domestic fiscal policy (an increase in f at the same time that μ is reduced) will not in general be consistent with an immediate costless transition to a lower inflation steady state, except for a closed economy or a small open economy. Even without real balance effects, an increase in f will be associated with a higher long-run real interest rate and a long-run appreciation of the domestic real exchange rate. The short-run result of such a policy combination would be to start a boom abroad, stimulated by the improvement in foreign competitiveness. The combination of domestic money growth reductions and fiscal stimulus that would satisfy the desired new low inflation domestic steady state conditions, would in all likelihood create a transitional slump at home. With a real balance effect even the money jump and indirect tax cut policies will have repercussions abroad. The domestically correct steady state policy combination is again likely to cause a slump at home and a boom abroad.

If the domestic authorities adopt a money jump or indirect tax cut policy[2] in conjunction with the money growth deceleration when real balance effects are present, the foreign authorities will in general need to change two policy instruments to stay at full employment. They could, e.g., accept a higher real (and nominal) interest rate and an improved level of foreign competitiveness by implementing a discontinuous, once-and-for-all reduction in the level of the foreign nomi-

---

(1) Remember that, with public spending constant, we must have $\Delta\tau_d + \Delta\tau_i = 0$
(2) "Indirect tax cut policy" refers to a constant revenue change from indirect to direct taxes. There are therefore no direct aggregate demand effects of such a policy.

nal money stock (or an increase in foreign indirect taxes if $\theta* < 1$) and a change in $f*$. The same result holds qualitatively whether or not real balance effects are present, if the home country lowers money growth and raises f at the same time.

A combined common reduction in money growth rates at home and abroad will cause a global slump unless both countries undertake simultaneously money jump policies, indirect tax cuts or fiscal stimuli. If there are no real balance effects, money jumps or indirect tax cuts in the two countries permit and immediate, costless global disinflation at a constant real interest rate and real exchange rate. Even if there are real balance effects, an immediate costless global disinflation will be possible, with money jumps or indirect tax cuts in both countries, at a constant real exchange rate but a higher real interest rate, if the two countries have identical structures. Without this restriction, however, the two fiscal instruments f and $f*$ will have to be used jointly with the reductions in money growth and the money jumps or indirect tax cuts to achieve efficient global disinflation.

How important are the costs of badly-designed disinflation policy? Consider as a simple illustrative example the wage-price block of equations (4a), (16) and (17) where core inflation equals the rate of growth of the money stock. A little manipulation yields

$$(24) \quad -\int_t^\infty (y(s) - \bar{y})ds = \frac{1}{\psi} \{[m(\infty) - p(\infty) - (m(t) - p(t))] + \theta[\tau_d(\infty) - \tau_d(t)]$$

$$+ [\tau_i(\infty) - \tau_i(0)] + (1-\alpha)[c(\infty) - c(0)]\}$$

The cumulative net undiscounted output cost given in (24) increases with the amount by which real money balances must be increased in the long run. Without a nominal money stock jump, the long-run change in $m-p$ equals $-\lambda\overset{\infty}{\Delta}r$ where $\overset{\infty}{\Delta}$ means long-run or steady state change. In the simplest case, without real balance effects, $\overset{\infty}{\Delta}r = \overset{\infty}{\Delta}\mu$. The sacrifice ratio is therefore

$$(25) \quad SR \equiv \frac{\int_t^\infty (y(s) - \bar{y})ds}{\overset{\infty}{\Delta}\mu} = \frac{\lambda}{\psi} - \frac{\theta}{\psi\overset{\infty}{\Delta}\mu}\overset{\infty}{\Delta}\tau_d - \frac{1}{\psi\overset{\infty}{\Delta}\mu}\overset{\infty}{\Delta}\tau_i + \frac{(\alpha-1)}{\overset{\infty}{\Delta}\mu}\overset{\infty}{\Delta}c \ .$$

A unilateral reduction in μ has a sacrifice ratio of λ/ψ, increasing

in the interest sensitivity of money demand and decreasing in the slope
of the Phillips curve. As is clear from (24) or (25) money jumps or tax
cuts could reduce the sacrifice ratio to zero. Note, however, that a real
appreciation of the currency ($\overset{\infty}{\overset{\sim}{\Delta}} c < 0$) also lowers the sacrifice ratio.
The problem is that while $\frac{(1-\alpha)}{\psi} \overset{\infty}{\overset{\sim}{\Delta}} c$ enters the domestic cost calculation
$\frac{\alpha^*-1}{\psi} \overset{\infty}{\overset{\sim}{\Delta}} c$ enters the foreign cost calculation. The anti-inflationary gains
of real exchange rate appreciation are strictly beggar-thy-neighbor. In
addition, the short run gains from exchange rate appreciation accruing
to a single country may well overstate the long-run gains. Note that
without real balance effects $\overset{\infty}{\overset{\sim}{\Delta}} c = 0$ after a unilateral reduction in μ. As
is shown, e.g., in Buiter and Miller (1983a), any initial antiinflationary
gains due to exchange rate appreciation must be "handed back" as the
loss of competitiveness unwinds in the long run, since in their
model $\overset{\infty}{\overset{\sim}{\Delta}} c = 0$. Of course the *timing* of the anti-inflationary successes will
be different when the exchange rate is permitted to appreciate sharply
in the short run and early reductions in inflation may be worthwhile in
themselves, even if the net output cost of fighting inflation is not
affected. It should also be pointed out that the model (like all models in
this paper) is assumed to be structurally invariant with respect to the
class of policy changes under consideration. It may be that the "short
sharp shock" of a sudden exchange rate appreciation permits one to
"overwrite" the existing inflation equations. The sluggishness or inertia
of the price-wage mechanism could vanish when the government invests
in credibility by engineering a brutal appreciation of the exchange rate.
I do not consider that possibility in this paper. In any case, the
foreign government would be disinvesting in credibility by suffering a
brutal depreciation of the exchange rate.

The moral of this section is that if there is only price *level* inertia
but no *inflation* inertia, well-designed aggregate demand management
policy (changes in μ, m, f, μ^*, m^* and f^*) are sufficient to ensure
efficient, i.e. costless and instantaneous unilateral or joint reductions
in inflation [1]. When a greater degree of inertia is attributed to the
wage-price process, this fairly optimistic conclusion vanishes.

---

(1) Of course, indirect tax cuts may be helpful, if $0 \leqq \theta < 1$, even if f
is kept constant.

4. MODELS IN WHICH GENIUS OR GOOD LUCK ARE NECESSARY FOR A COSTLESS, SUSTAINED REDUCTION IN INFLATION

Many economists have a view of the wage-price process that implies considerably more sluggishness and inertia than has been permitted in any of our models considered thus far. Multi-period contract models such as Taylor's (1980) are one well-known example.

Some of the essential features of this entire class of models are represented by the simplest possible "adaptive" core inflation process. It is characterized by a sluggish price level and, subject to some qualifications (4a) and (16) are combined with (25). For the foreign country equations (4b) and (16') are joined with (25'):

(25) $\quad \pi = \xi(\dot{p}-\pi)$, $\xi > 0$

(25') $\quad \dot{\pi}^* = \xi^*(\dot{p}^* - \pi^*)$.

It is easily checked that for the home country the sacrifice ratio is now given by:

$$SR(t) \equiv \frac{\int_t^\infty (y(s)-\bar{y})\,ds}{\overset{\infty}{\Delta}\pi} = \frac{\int_t^\infty (y(s)-\bar{y})\,ds}{\overset{\infty}{\Delta}\mu} = \frac{1}{\xi\psi} - \frac{1}{\psi\overset{\infty}{\Delta}\mu}[\theta\overset{\infty}{\Delta}\tau_d + \overset{\infty}{\Delta}\tau_i] + \frac{(\alpha-1)}{\psi\overset{\infty}{\Delta}\mu}\overset{\infty}{\Delta}c.$$

Note that a money *level* jump no longer helps to avoid or even reduce the output costs of bringing down inflation[1]. Barring changes in tax rates or in the real exchange rate, both v and π are predetermined and the sacrifice ratio depends only on the slope of the short-run Phillips-curve, ψ, and the speed of adjustment of core inflation, ξ.

---

(1) It may still be a useful (or even essential) component of a complete policy package capable of achieving an instantaneous transition to a lower rate of inflation steady state.

The foreign sacrifice ratio is given by:

$$SR^*(t) = \frac{1}{\xi^* \psi^*} - \frac{1}{\psi^* \overset{\infty}{\Delta} \mu^*} \left[\theta^* \overset{\infty}{\Delta} \tau_d^* + \overset{\infty}{\Delta} \tau_i^* \right] + \frac{(1 - \alpha^*)}{\psi^* \overset{\infty}{\Delta} \mu^*} \overset{\infty}{\Delta} c .$$

Following Okun (1978) we can, as was discussed in the previous section, use direct or indirect tax cuts to break core inflation. Unless $\theta = 1$ and direct tax increases fully offset the price level effect of equal revenue indirect tax cuts, and indirect tax cut financed by a direct tax increase can melt core inflation. Even if $\theta = 1$ a net cut in overall taxes can have the desired effect on core inflation. This exercise is then of course complicated by the fact that tax cuts implemented for their cost-reducing effects will also have aggregate demand effects (i.e., f would increase). Public spending will then have to be adjusted in such a way as to maintain aggregate demand at full employment. Note the opposite effect of changes in c on the domestic and foreign sacrifice ratios. If the home country through its policy actions were to achieve a long-run appreciation of its real exchange rate (a decline in c) then the foreign country would, if its inflation objectives are constant, be forced to suffer a cumulative net loss of output. But for this output loss the depreciation of the foreign country's real exchange rate would result in a rise in foreign core inflation.

Note that if some form of incomes policy could shock core inflation, i.e., jump π, the output cost of bringing down inflation could be reduced or even eliminated altogether without recourse to changes in the tax structure (while keeping the aggregate demand effect of fiscal policy constant) or to beggar-thy-neighbor, zero-sum attempts at "competitive loss of competitiveness".

The rewards from a successful incomes policy would be enormous. The mechanism for achieving it, theoretically and in the light of historical experience, is problematic. With centralized wage bargaining and strong unions capable of delivering on the shop floor wage agreements negotiated centrally, it might be possible to achieve an anti-inflationary breakthrough this way. With decentralized, non-synchronized and non-cooperative wage bargaining someone has to go first while everyone wishes to go last. Proposals for "real wage insurance" through the public purse, floated briefly in the U.S.A. under Carter, may be helpful here. Tax-based income policies are, if anything, primarily a means for lowering the natural rate of unemployment (for raising $\bar{y}$). They may, however, when they are introduced, also serve to break the momentum of on-going core inflation.

Proposition 3: If there is both a predetermined price level and quasi-predetermined, adaptive, core inflation, the policies required if both countries are to achieve an instantaneous and costless disinflation are the following. Both countries have to announce and implement credible reductions in the rate of growth of their nominal money stocks. Tax cuts (or indirect to direct tax changes) have to be implemented to break core inflation. The lower velocities associated with a successful transition to lower inflation rates will have to be accommodated by a once-and-for-all increase in the level of each country's nominated money stock. Public spending in each country is to be adjusted so as to maintain aggregate demand at its full employment level. Credible nominal income targeting could be a substitute for the money *growth* deceleration and money *level* increase. Incomes policy, if effective, could be a substitute for tax cuts.

It might be argued that the view of core inflation embodied in equations (25) and (25') is both too "backward-looking" and too optimistic. Modern eclectic views of the wage-price process not only incorporate sluggishness in the level and rate of change wages but also forwardlooking behaviour. They also view   as strictly predetermined, i.e., unlike (25) and (25') changes in the price *level* brought about through changes in the exchange rate or tax rates, cannot move the level of π discontinuously. This view is represented in equations (26), (27) and (26'), (27'):

(26) $\quad \dot{\pi} = \xi_1(q-\pi)$, $\quad \xi_1 > 0$

(26') $\quad \dot{\pi}^* = \xi_1^*(q^* - \pi^*)$, $\quad \xi_1^* > 0$

(27) $\quad E_t\dot{q} = \xi_2(q-\dot{p})$, $\quad \xi_2 > 0$

(27') $\quad E_t\dot{q}^* = \xi_2^*(q^*-\dot{p}^*)$, $\quad \xi_2^* > 0$.

q is the current rate of wage contract inflation. π, core inflation, has the interpretation of "the going rate". It is a function of past contract inflation. Current contract inflation is a function of current expectations of the future state of excess demand and of what the "going rate" will be in the future.

Solving for q and π we find:

$$(27) \quad q(t) = \pi(t) + \xi_2 \int_t^\infty e^{(\xi_2 - \xi_1)(t-s)} E_t[\psi(y(s)-\bar{y})+\theta\dot{\tau}_d(s)+\dot{\tau}_i(s)+(1-\alpha)\dot{c}(s)]ds$$

$$(28) \quad \pi(t) = \pi(t_0)+\xi_1\xi_2\int_{t_0}^t\int_s^\infty e^{(\xi_2-\xi_1)(s-z)} E_s[\psi(y(z)-\bar{y})+\theta\dot{\tau}_d(z)+\dot{\tau}_i(z)+(1-\alpha)\dot{c}(z)]dzds.$$

This solution makes sense only if $\xi_2 \geq \xi_1$. When $\xi_2 = \xi_1$ (and provided the relevant integrals exist), (27) and (28) simplify to:

$$(27') \quad q(t) = (t)+ _2 E_t (y(s)-\bar{y})ds+ _2E_t[\quad_d^+ \quad_d^+ \quad_i^+(1-)c]$$

$$(28') \quad \pi(t) = \pi(t_0)+\xi_1\xi_2\int_{t_0}^t\int_s^\infty E_s\psi(y(z)-\bar{y})dzds+\xi_1\xi_2\int_{t_0}^t E_s[\theta\ddot{\Delta}\tau_d(s)+\ddot{\Delta}\tau_i(s)+(1-\alpha)\ddot{\Delta}c(s)]ds$$

In this model the current contract rate of inflation, q, is non-predetermined but core inflation or "the going rate" is strictly pre-determined. Barring changes in tax rates and in the real exchange rate, current contract inflation exceeds the going rate if the "present value" of currently expected future excess demand is positive. Current core inflation equals core inflation at some initial date plus an increasing function of the sum between that initial date and the current date of the present value of future excess demand expected at each instant between these two dates. Domestic current contract inflation can be reduced instantaneously by long-run tax cuts or long-run real exchange rate appreciation. Barring these two channels, only credible announcements of (policies causing) future recessions can bring down current contract inflation. Credibility remains central, but is no longer sufficient to avoid costs. Core inflation cannot be brought down instantaneously even when indirect or direct tax cuts or exchange rate appreciation are announced credibly. It is a function of the entire history of past expectations of future excess demands, tax cuts and real exchange rate appreciation. Barring the last two influences, it is (past expectations of) credible future recessions that bring down core inflation. Anticipated current and future reductions in nominal income growth or monetary growth can no longer be translated painlessly into lower inflation. They work if and to the extent that they create expectations of future recessions. Note that this can create some awkward credibility and time-consistency problems. Assume the authorities policies that will cause a deep recession at some future date. It is possible that inflation and core inflation are brought down to their desired level *before* the recession has actually started. What government, having licked inflation with the help of the *announcement efffects* of future recessions, would then create a recession merely to validate these past expectations? These expectations would be bygones and a government reoptimizing after inflation had been brought down would be tempted to cheat on its earlier policy commitments. Such a policy announcement would therefore not be credible.

Both global and single-country attempts to reduce inflation will, in the most realistic of our models, always take time. A single country may achieve its anti-inflationary objectives without unemployment and output costs by using cost-reducing tax cuts and real exchange rate appreciation. The world as a whole can rely only on tax cuts and, where feasible, incomes policy. The transition to the low inflation equilibrium will involve the internal and external coordination of time-varying trajectories for monetary growth (including money stock jumps), tax rates and public spending. If a serious research effort gets underway now, we may be ready with sensible policy packages when there is once again the perceived need to accord high priority to reducing inflation, after the next inflationary outburst.

6. CONCLUSION

This paper has considered anti-inflationary policy design in an open interdependent economic system. Policy instrument values or rules were treated as though imposed "exogenously". Both for positive analysis (how is policy actually determined?) and for normative analysis (how should policy be designed?) it is essential that policy behaviour should be endogenized through the explicit derivation of decision rules that reflect the objectives and the actual and perceived constraints (economic, technical, administrative, political, and informational) of the policy makers.

Finally, it is important not to be misled by the deterministic nature of the models considered in this paper, into believing that credibility and precommitment require inflexible policy design. Credibility means that pre-announced rules are followed faithfully. These rules can, indeed *should*, be contingent or conditional in nature. Provided the nature of the rules is understood by private agents – and this requires simplicity and transparence but not rigidity – and provided the government's record in sticking to its commitments can be monitored promptly and at little cost, optimal or even merely sensible policy design will always incorporate scope for flexible response to new information about the external environment and about actions of other players.

The widely known result, that in models with rationally anticipating, forward-looking private agents, optimal policy design will not in general be time-consistent, has led to a quite unwarranted resignation to the pursuit of time-consistent but suboptimal policies or even of time-inconsistent *and* suboptimal policies, such as the adoption of constant money growth rules. The moral is surely quite different. Time-inconsistency of optimal plans calls for institutional innovation and reform aimed at making the optimal policy time-consistent. New rewards, sanctions, threats or promises should be designed to render optimal policy incentive-compatible given the new purpose-built constraints. Institutional, and indeed constitutional innovation is bound to dominate resignation to the nth-best.

Appendix I

$$a_{11} = \lambda^{-1} - \frac{\alpha^* \gamma^{-1} \varepsilon}{1 - \alpha - \alpha^*}$$

$$a_{12} = \frac{(1-\alpha)\gamma^{*-1}\varepsilon^*}{1 - \alpha - \alpha^*}$$

$$a_{13} = (\alpha - 1)\left[\lambda^{-1} + \frac{\alpha^*\gamma^{-1}\varepsilon + \gamma^{*-1}(\varepsilon^*(1-\alpha^*) - \delta^*)}{\alpha + \alpha^* - 1}\right] + \frac{\alpha^*\gamma^{-1}\delta}{\alpha + \alpha^* - 1}$$

$$a_{21} = \frac{(1 - \alpha^*)\gamma^{-1}\varepsilon}{1 - \alpha - \alpha^*}$$

$$a_{22} = \lambda^{*-1} - \frac{\alpha\gamma^{*-1}\varepsilon^*}{1 - \alpha - \alpha^*}$$

$$a_{23} = (1 - \alpha^*)\left[\lambda^{*-1} + \frac{\tilde{\alpha}\gamma^{*-1}\varepsilon^* + \gamma^{-1}\varepsilon(1-\alpha) - \gamma^{-1}\delta}{\alpha + \alpha^* - 1}\right] - \frac{\alpha\gamma^{*-1}\delta^*}{\alpha + \alpha^* - 1}$$

$$a_{31} = \frac{\gamma^{-1}\varepsilon}{\alpha + \alpha^* - 1}$$

$$a_{32} = \frac{-\gamma^{*-1}\varepsilon^*}{\alpha + \alpha^* - 1}$$

$$a_{33} = \frac{\gamma^{-1}\delta + \gamma^{*-1}\delta^* - \gamma^{-1}\varepsilon(1-\alpha) - \gamma^{*-1}\varepsilon^*(1-\alpha^*)}{\alpha + \alpha^* - 1}$$

$$b_{11} = 1 \qquad\qquad ; \quad b_{21} = 0$$

$$b_{12} = 0 \qquad\qquad ; \quad b_{22} = 1$$

$$b_{13} = -\lambda^{-1} + \frac{\alpha^*\gamma^{-1}\varepsilon}{1 - \alpha - \alpha^*} \qquad ; \quad b_{23} = \frac{(\alpha^* - 1)\gamma^{-1}\varepsilon}{1 - \alpha - \alpha^*}$$

$$b_{14} = \frac{(\alpha-1)\gamma^{*-1}\varepsilon^*}{1 - \alpha - \alpha^*} \qquad ; \quad b_{24} = -\lambda^{*-1} + \frac{\alpha\gamma^{*-1}\varepsilon^*}{1 - \alpha - \alpha^*}$$

$$b_{15} = \frac{-\alpha^*\gamma^{-1}\beta}{1 - \alpha - \alpha^*} \qquad ; \quad b_{25} = \frac{(1-\alpha^*)\gamma^{-1}\beta}{1 - \alpha - \alpha^*}$$

$$b_{16} = \frac{(1-\alpha)\gamma^{*-1}\beta^*}{1 - \alpha - \alpha^*} \qquad ; \quad b_{26} = -\frac{\alpha\gamma^{*-1}\beta^*}{1 - \alpha - \alpha^*}$$

$$b_{17} = -\lambda^{-1}k + \frac{\alpha^*\gamma^{-1}+(1-\alpha)\gamma^{*-1}\eta^*}{1 - \alpha - \alpha^*} \quad ; \quad b_{27} = -\frac{[\alpha\gamma^{*-1}\eta^*+(1-\alpha^*)\gamma^{-1}]}{1 - \alpha - \alpha^*}$$

$$b_{18} = -\frac{[\alpha^*\gamma^{-1}\eta +(1-\alpha)\gamma^{*-1}]}{1 - \alpha - \alpha^*} \qquad ; \quad b_{28} = -\lambda^{*-1}k + \frac{\alpha\gamma^{*-1} + (1-\alpha^*)\gamma^{-1}\eta}{1 - \alpha - \alpha^*}$$

$$b_{19} = \frac{-\alpha^*}{1 - \alpha - \alpha^*} \qquad ; \quad b_{29} = \frac{1 - \alpha^*}{1 - \alpha - \alpha^*}$$

$$b_{1,10} = \frac{1 - \alpha}{1 - \alpha - \alpha^*} \qquad ; \quad b_{2,10} = \frac{-\alpha}{1 - \alpha - \alpha^*}$$

$$b_{31} = 0$$

$$b_{32} = 0$$

$$b_{33} = \frac{-\gamma^{-1}\varepsilon}{\alpha + \alpha^* - 1}$$

$$b_{34} = \frac{\gamma^{*-1}\varepsilon^*}{\alpha + \alpha^* - 1}$$

$$b_{35} = \frac{-\gamma^{-1}\beta}{\alpha + \alpha^* - 1}$$

$$b_{36} = \frac{-\gamma^{*-1}\beta^*}{\alpha + \alpha^* - 1}$$

$$b_{37} = -\frac{[\gamma^{-1} + \gamma^{*-1}\eta^*]}{\alpha + \alpha^* - 1}$$

$$b_{38} = \frac{[\gamma^{*-1} + \gamma^{-1}\eta]}{\alpha + \alpha^* - 1}$$

$$b_{39} = \frac{1}{\alpha + \alpha^* - 1}$$

$$b_{3,10} = \frac{-1}{\alpha + \alpha^* - 1}$$

Appendix II

The absence of explicit consideration of the government budget identity is justified as follows. In natural units (using upper-case letters) the domestic output market equilibrium condition and public sector budget identity (under a freely floating exchange rate regime) can be written as follows:

$$Y = F(r - E_t \frac{\dot{P}}{P} , \frac{EP*}{P} , \frac{M}{P}, G, T, Y*)$$

$$F_r < 0 \; ; \; F_C > 0 \; ; \; F_{M/P} \geqq 0; \; F_G > F_T < 0 \; , \; F_{Y*} > 0$$

$$\frac{\dot{M} + \dot{B}}{P} \equiv G + \frac{rB}{P} - T \; .$$

G denotes exhaustive public spending on goods and services, T total taxes net of transfers. B is the nominal stock of government bonds. βf , the effect of fiscal policy on demand in equation (2a) is given by $\frac{\partial \ln Y}{\delta G} dG + \frac{\partial \ln Y}{\partial T} dT$. Note that, if the balanced-budget multiplier is positive, then $F_G > |F_T|$.

I assume that as regards bond financing the domestic authorities throughout follow a "constant financial crowding out pressure" policy which consists in keeping constant the real stock of government debt B/P. The foreign authorities similarly keep $B*/P*$ constant. Thus $\dot{B} = B(\dot{P}/P)$ and $\dot{B*} = B*(\dot{P*}/P*)$. Whether or not B/P and $B*/P*$ are arguments in the money demand functions and/or the output demand functions, their constancy makes it unnecessary to consider them further. I am ignoring as of second-order importance the fact that domestic bonds may be held abroad and foreign bonds domestically. Let B^d denote domestic holdings of domestic government debt and B^f foreign holdings of domestic government debt. Then $B \equiv B^d + B^f$ and, by analogy, $B* \equiv B*^d + B*^f$. The proper argument in domestic behavioral relationships is $b^d \equiv \frac{B^d}{P} + \frac{EB*^d}{P}$; for foreign behavioral the proper argument is $b*^f \equiv \frac{B^f}{EP*} + \frac{B*^f}{P*}$. Even if $\frac{B}{P}$ and $\frac{B*}{P*}$ are constant over time, b^d and $b*^f$ could vary. If purchasing power parity (p.p.p.) held, then $\dot{b}^d + \dot{b}*^f = 0$. Without p.p.p., $\dot{b}^d + \frac{EP*}{P} \dot{b}*^f = (\frac{\dot{E}}{E} - \frac{\dot{P}}{P} + \frac{\dot{P*}}{P*})(\frac{EB*^d - B^f}{P})$.
Even if total (global) real bond wealth doesn't change, a redistribution

of a given total through current account deficits and surpluses (or through capital gains and losses) may change total demand for a country' output if the marginal propensity to spend out of bond wealth on that country's output differs between the two countries. I rule out any such "transfer effects" either on total spending on the individual countries' outputs. Given our bond financing assumption, we can write

$$\mu \equiv \frac{\dot{M}}{M} = \frac{P}{M} \, [G + (r - \frac{\dot{P}}{P}). \frac{B}{P} - T] \, .$$

Given M/P, G and $(r - \frac{\dot{P}}{P}) \frac{B}{P}$, the authorities can use total taxes net of transfers to choose the rate of monetary growth, μ. This still leaves them real spending, G, to set the current fiscal stimulus f at its desired value. Note, however, that since total tax receipts T (and G) are "assigned" to μ and βf, the indirect tax rate τ_i cannot be varied independently. Higher values of τ_i must be matched by a lower direct tax rate τ_d. For simplicity I will represent this requirement as $\tau_i + \tau_d = \bar{\tau}$.

REFERENCES

Barro, R.J. and Grossman, H.I.(1976), *Money, Employment and Infla-tion* Cambridge.

Buiter, W.H.(1984a),"Saddlepoint Problems in Continuous Time Rational Expectations Models: A General Method and Some Macroeconomic Examples", *Econometrica*, 52, May.

Buiter, W.H.(1984b), "Efficient Disinflation Policies", Note written for the Directorate General for Economic and Financial Affairs, Commission of the European Communities, May.

Buiter, W.H. and Miller, M.H. (1981), "Monetary Policy and Inter-national Competitiveness", *Oxford Economic Papers*, 33, July, Supplement.

Buiter, W.H. and Miller, M.H. (1983a), "Real Exchange Rate Over-shooting and the Output Cost of Bringing Down Inflation: Some Further Results", in J. Frenkel (ed.), *Exchange Rates and International Macroeconomics*, Chicago.

Buiter, W.H. and Miller, M.H. (1983b), "Cost and Benefits of an Anti-Inflationary Policy: Questions and Issues", NBER Working Paper No. 1252, December.

Calvo, G.A. (1982a), "Staggered Contracts and Exchange Rate Policy", Discussion Paper Series No. 129, Columbia University.

Calvo, G.A. (1982b), "Staggered Contracts in a Utility-Maximizing Framework", Discussion Paper Series No. 130, Columbia University.

Calvo, G.A. (1982c), "Real Exchange Rate Dynamics with Fixed Nominal Parities: On the Economics of Overshooting and Interest Rate Management with Rational Price Setting", Discussion Paper Series No. 162, Columbia University.

Dornbusch, R. (1980), *Open Economy Macroeconomics*, New York.

Miller, M.H. (1982), "Differences in the policy mix and consequences for the real exchange", University of Warwick, mimeo.

Mussa, M. (1981), "Sticky Prices and Disequilibrium Adjustment in a Rational Model of the Inflationary Process", *American Economic Review*, 71, December.

Okun, A. (1978), "Efficient Disinflationary Policies", *American Economic Review*, 68, Papers and Proceedings, May.

Taylor, J.B. (1980), "Aggregate Dynamics and Staggered Contracts", *Journal of Political Economy*, 88.

7. EUROPEAN MONETARY COOPERATION AND FINANCIAL STABILITY

P. de Grauwe[*]

1. INTRODUCTION

The large fluctuations of the dollar prior to 1979 gave the initial impetus for the establishment of the European Monetary System (EMS). This system aimed at creating an island of monetary stability in Europe, and in achieving this it would contribute to increasing investment and growth in Europe. In this paper we analyze to what extent these objectives have been achieved.

Since 1979 major changes occurred in the monetary regimes of a number of countries, in particular the US. These changes have certainly affected the ability of EMS countries to stabilize their exchange rates and their interest rates, and to achieve a greater degree of financial stability. The issue which arises here is to what extent the EMS was a better institutional arrangement than other more individual arrangements, to insulate the European financial markets from the shocks originating in the US. In order to answer this question we will contrast the experience of the EMS countries with those of some major non-EMS countries.

The switch in the economic policies in the US since 1979 has posed a serious challenge for European policy-makers. There is a general feeling that these policy-makers have failed in there response. The question, therefore, is still with us: How should Europe respond? One answer which, after having been discredited in the past, obtained academic respectability recently, is for Europe to engineer a coordinated

* I am grateful to Michael Emerson, Theo Peeters, and to the conference participants for criticism and suggestions, and to Guy Verfaille for research assistance.

fiscal stimulus. We will analyze this issue and argue that such an approach can only marginally reduce unemployment in Europe. For such a program to be successful one would need budget deficits in Europe that would dwarf the US-deficits. We conclude with some thoughts about the other options of economic policy in Europe.

2. THE EMS AND MACROECONOMIC PERFORMANCE

One of the main objectives of the EMS was to create a zone of monetary stability in Europe which would foster investment and growth. In a sense it can be said that the founders of the EMS considered monetary stability as an intermediate target, and growth and investment as the ultimate targets of the system. To what extent have these targets been achieved?

TABLE 1

Growth rates of GDP and of Investment
(Average during 73-78 and 79-83)

	GDP		Investment	
	(73-78)	(79-83)	(73-78)	(79-83)
Belgium	2.9	0.9	3.2	-4.2
Denmark	2.1	1.6	0.0	-4.1
Ireland	4.8	2.3	8.6	-1.8
Netherlands	3.7	0.4	2.1	-2.5
Germany	2.5	1.1	-0.9	1.1
France	3.4	1.5	1.8	-0.2
Italy	2.9	1.4	2.0	0.7
EMS	3.0	1.2	1.0	-0.5
US	3.2	1.3	3.9	-1.7
UK	2.3	0.9	2.1	-2.4
Japan	4.2	4.0	2.4	2.4
Austria	2.9	2.1	0.1	-0.8
Norway	4.7	2.8	6.9	-1.9
Sweden	1.8	1.5	-0.4	-0.1
Switzerland	-0.3	1.4	-5.7	2.7

Source: IMF, International Financial Statistics
Note : GDP and Investment are in constant prices.

As far as the ultimate targets are concerned, the record is dismal. As table 1 illustrates, the growth of output and investment was lower since the creation of the EMS, than during the period immediately preceding it. Obviously, it would be unfair to use this as evidence that the EMS was a failure. During the same period the world economy went through the worst recession since the second world war, which under any monetary regime would have affected the European countries. The relevant question then is whether the EMS has allowed its members to soften the blow produced by the world recession. In order to answer this question the economic record of the EMS countries is compared with the record of a number of other countries. The evidence, which is only suggestive, is also shown in table 1, and leads to the following observations. First, with the exception of Switzerland, all countries have experienced a decline of the growth rate of output during the post-EMS period. On average, however, this decline seems to have been more pronounced in the EMS countries than in the group of non-EMS countries included in the sample.

Second, investment activity declined on the average in the EMS as in most other countries[1]. There is no evidence, however, that this decline of economic growth and investment activity has been less pronounced in the EMS countries than elsewhere.

Third, it appears that the small EMS countries have suffered a stronger decline in their investment activity than the large EMS countries. During 1979-83 investment activity declined on average by 3% per year in the small EMS countries, whereas in the large EMS countries it increased by 0.5% per year. In the pre-EMS period, however, the small countries experienced a faster growth rate of investment than the large countries.

More ominously, the small EMS countries seem to have experienced a larger decline of their growth rates of output and of investment than the small non-EMS countries. We will come back to this phenomenon in a

---

(1) It should be emphasized that the recent strong upturn in the economic activity in the US is averaged out during 1979-83 because of the intensity of the US recession of 1980-81.

separate section where the experience of the small EMS and non-EMS countries is systematically compared.

This evidence, of course, is far from definitive. One could certainly argue that without the EMS things would have been even worse for its members. In order to evaluate this interpretation it is important to analyze how well the EMS has achieved its intermediate target, monetary stability. For it was through the achievement of greater monetary stability that the founders of the EMS hoped to contribute to better growth and investment prospects in Europe. The mechanism through which this was expected to happen was the following: a higher exchange rate stability in Europe would lead to less exchange rate uncertainty. European firms would therefore confront a lower level of risk concerning their rates of return. At given interest rates, this would lead to better investment prospects, and ultimately to better growth performance. This argument was generally thought to be even more important for the small countries, so that the expectation was that the small members of the EMS would profit from monetary stability in Europe in a disproportionate way.

3.   THE EMS AND EXCHANGE RATE STABILITY

We first look at the evidence concerning exchange rate stability. As far as short-term variability is concerned, the EMS can be called a success. The monthly changes of the EMS currencies against each other averaged close to 1 per cent since 1979, whereas the monthly variations of the dollar exchange rates were three times higher. Thus, the EMS has succeeded in reducing the risk concerning short-term changes in EMS bilateral exchange rates (for more evidence see Thygesen (1984) and EC-Commission (1984)).

It might be argued that the only objective of the EMS was the stabilization of the exchange rates in the short run. The EMS can then be called an unqualified success. This view, however, is unsatisfactory. What matters in most decisions about investment, output, export and import is the exchange rate outlook beyond the very short-term. In addition, for these decisions it is the change of the exchange rates relative to price levels (the real exchange rates) that matters. Changes in the real exchange rates measure whether currencies become cheaper or dearer in terms of goods and services, and thus are informative about the competitiveness of countries and their ability to export. For this reason one may also wish to know to what extent the EMS has contributed to real exchange rate stability over periods longer than a few months. In this paper we concentrate on the yearly changes of the

TABLE 2

Mean absolute change of real exchange rates

	1974-78	1979-83
Belgium	2.4	4.8
Netherlands	2.5	2.9
Denmark	2.6	3.8
Germany	1.6	2.5
France	4.6	1.6
Italy	3.8	2.6
Mean	2.9	3.0
US	3.2	5.1
UK	4.6	8.2
Japan	6.8	6.3
Austria	2.8	1.2
Norway	3.3	3.1
Sweden	3.6	3.0
Switzerland	6.7	4.5
Mean	4.4	4.5

Source: Morgan Guaranty, World Financial Markets.
Note : The exchange rate is defined as the effective exchange rate.

real exchange rates. Finally, we concentrate here on the *effective* exchange rates. This is a debatable approach. For, the objective of the EMS was to stabilize intra-EMS exchange rates. Nevertheless we choose to concentrate on the effective exchange rates as it is the overall level of exchange rate stability that matters for an individual country, and because it cannot be excluded that higher internal exchange rate stability in an exchange rate union is offset by more external exchange rate movements (see Marston (1982)).

Evidence on changes in the real (effective) exchange rates of the EMS currencies is provided in table 2, which compares the yearly changes of the real exchange rates five years before and five years after 1979, for both EMS and non-EMS countries. The following observations can be made. First, there does not seem to be evidence that real exchange rates within the EMS have changed less (on a yearly basis) since 1979. On average, real exchange rates were as variable (on a yearly basis) in the post-EMS as in the pre-EMS period. Note that both the pre- and post-EMS periods include years of substantial oil shocks, which must have increased real exchange rate variability in both periods.

It is also interesting to find that the two countries which, prior to the EMS, did not belong to an exchange rate agreement (France and Italy) reduced the degree of variability of their real exchange rate since they joined the EMS. This phenomenon, however, was completely compensated by an increased real exchange rate variability of the other EMS countries which, prior to 1979, had an exchange rate agreement (the "Snake"-arrangement)[1]. This suggests that the "Snake"-arrangement contributed to a tighter exchange rate relation among its member than the present EMS system does for the same countries. One explanation for this phenomenon could be that the "Snake"-arrangement was much more dominated by one country, Germany, than the EMS. A second observation one can make from table 2 concerns the non-EMS countries. Some countries (the US and the United Kingdom) have experienced a substantial increase in their real exchange rate variability. Others have stabilized the degree of real exchange rate variability (Japan, Norway and Sweden) or have reduced it (Switzerland and Austria). An interesting phenomenon is that, on the whole, the real exchange rates of major non-EMS countries have been more variable not only since 1979 but during the longer period 1973-83.

---

(1) In a recent paper Rogoff (1984) also finds that real exchange rate variability of the FF and the Lira has declined since the start of the EMS. His conclusion, however, that exchange rates within the EMS now have become more predictable does not take account of the observed increase in the variability of the other exchange rates in the system.

These observations suggest the following interpretation. The EMS countries are very open economies and highly integrated with one another. As a result, transactions costs (transport costs and impediments to trade) are low, compared with countries that are less integrated. Indeed, long-run real exchange rate changes were less pronounced in EMS countries than in major non-EMS countries before and after 1979. This interpretation, however, also suggests that the EMS has been powerless in reducing the long-run real exchange rate variability among participating countries. The fact that real exchange rates vary less within the EMS than outside reflects differences in openness and economic integration. It was observed throughout 1973-83 and cannot be used as evidence that the EMS succeeded in stabilizing the (yearly) real exchange rate movements.

We conclude that the EMS although successful in stabilizing nominal exchange rates in the very short run (daily, weekly or monthly), has had a mixed success in reducing the movements of its real exchange rates over a longer time horizon.

Why have EMS countries experienced difficulties to reduce real

TABLE 3

Inflation Rates (1974-78) and (1979-83)

	1974-78	1979-83
Belgium	9.2	7.1
Netherlands	7.9	5.3
Denmark	10.4	9.6
Ireland	14.3	14.7
Germany	4.7	4.8
France	10.7	11.8
Italy	16.4	17.0
Mean	10.1	10.0
Standard Deviation	3.9	4.7

Source: Ungerer, et alii (1983), and IMF, Internatinal Financial Statistics.

exchange rate movements? One element in the answer is that inflation rates among EMS countries have continued to be widely different. As is shown in table 3 inflation rates have diverged slightly more across countries after 1979 than during the period 1974-78. As a result, national price levels have diverged continuously. These divergences have led to periodic adjustments of nominal exchange rates, which due to their discontinuous character have led to substantial movements of the real exchange rates within the system. It should be pointed out

TABLE 4

Growth Rates of Money Stock (1974-78) and (1979-83)

	1974-78	1979-83
Belgium	8.6	2.6
Netherlands	11.5	4.4
Denmark	11.9	12.8
Ireland	17.4	8.2
Germany	10.9	3.7
France	11.5	12.0
Italy	18.0	16.1
Mean	12.8	8.5
Standard Deviation	3.5	5.2

Source: Ungerer, et alii (1983), and IMF, International Financial Statistics
Note: For Ireland the 1983 data are not available.

here that since the second half of 1983 the national inflation rates within the EMS have tended to converge. It is still too early to know, however, whether this phenomenon constitutes a permanent change towards a regime of greater convergence of inflation rates, or whether it is the result of temporary factors, in particular the European recession.

It is now well recognized that an important cause of high inflation differentials is the failure to co-ordinate national monetary polices. This failure is evident from table 4, showing the yearly growth rates of the money stocks (M1) in the EMS countries, before and after 1979. It can

be seen that although the growth rates of the money stocks have declined on average since 1979, differences in these growth rates have
increased. In fact, from 1979 to 1983 there appears to be less coordination of national monetary policies among EMS countries than during
the preceding period. It should, therefore, come as no surprise that
exchange rate uncertainty was not lower in the period 1979-83 than in
the period preceding 1979.

As in the case of inflation rates one observes some recent tendencies towards convergence of the growth rates of the national money
stocks. In 1983 for example the standard deviation of the growth rates
of the national money stocks had declined to 3%. A similar phenomenon
is observed in 1984 (see EC-Commission (1984)). Is this a sign that the
EMS is embarked on a path guaranteeing a more stable structure of
exchange rates?

The main problem in answering this question has to do with one's
belief of whether this recent change towards more monetary convergence
is a permanent or a transitory phenomenon. The history of the attempts
towards monetary integration in Europe during the last 15 years has
been characterized by frequent changes and reversals of policies.
Therefore, economic agents will remain sceptical about the permanent
nature of the recent movement towards monetary convergence. Only a
convergence of policies sustained over a long period will convince them
that a change in policy regime has occurred.

4.   THE EMS AND INTEREST RATES

A discussion about the contribution of the EMS towards monetary
stability in Europe would be incomplete without an analysis of the
trends and the variability of interest rates. To what extent did the EMS
contribute to more interest rate stability, and to what extent did the
system allow its members to insulate their financial markets from the
shocks originating elsewhere?

Since the start of the EMS in 1979, a major change occurred in the
operating procedures of the Federal Reserve. It is now generally accepted that this change affected the level and the variability of the
interest rates both in the US and in the rest of the world (see Bomhoff
(1983)). It is also clear that it made the objective of monetary stability

TABLE 5

Nominal and Real Interest Rates (Government Bond Yields); Average during 1974-78 and 1979-83.

	Nominal Interest Rates		Real Interest Rates	
	(74-78)	(79-83)	(74-79)	(79-83)
Belgium	8.7	12.1	-0.4	5.1
Netherlands	8.7	9.9	0.7	4.5
Denmark	13.8	17.5	3.4	7.8
Ireland	14.2	15.7	0.0	1.0
Germany	7.7	8.6	2.9	3.8
Italy	12.6	17.9	-3.8	0.9
Mean	10.7	13.7	0.3	3.5
US	8.1	11.7	0.2	2.8
UK	13.8	13.0	-1.8	1.7
Japan	8.1	8.2	-3.5	4.0
Austria	9.0	9.2	2.4	4.2
Norway	7.5	11.5	-1.5	2.2
Sweden	9.1	12.2	-0.8	2.1
Switzerland	5.2	4.6	0.4	0.1
Mean	8.7	10.1	-0.7	2.4

Source: IMF, International Financial Statistics
Note : The real interest rate is defined as the difference between the government bond yield and the observed rate of inflation. Thus, the real interest rate concept is an ex-post (realized) concept.

in Europe more difficult to achieve. The issue then becomes whether the EMS has been an institutional arrangement allowing for a better insulation of the domestic interest rates from the disturbances originating in the US than other arrangements.

Some evidence concerning this issue is provided in the following tables and graphs. We show both nominal and real interest rate developments.

Table 5 presents the average level of the nominal and the real interest rates (government bond yields) of the major EMS countries

TABLE 6

Measures of variability of nominal and real interest rates, (Government Bond Yields)

NOMINAL INTEREST RATES

	Standard Deviation		Mean Absolute Change	
	(74-78)	(79-83)	(74-78)	(79-83)
Belgium	0.2	1.5	0.5	1.4
Netherlands	0.7	1.1	0.9	1.3
Denmark	0.7	2.4	1.3	2.4
Ireland	2.2	1.4	2.7	1.8
Germany	1.7	1.0	1.2	1.4
France	0.5	2.3	0.9	1.8
Italy	1.7	2.6	1.4	2.0
US	0.3	1.5	0.6	1.5
UK	1.0	1.3	1.4	1.2
Japan	1.2	0.7	1.0	1.0
Austria	0.6	1.1	0.6	1.1
Norway	0.5	1.9	0.5	1.0
Sweden	0.8	1.1	0.5	0.9
Switzerland	1.4	0.7	1.0	0.7

REAL INTEREST RATES

	Standard Deviation		Mean Absolute Change	
	(74-78)	(79-83)	(74-78)	(79-83)
Belgium	2.9	0.7	2.6	0.8
Netherlands	1.7	0.8	1.5	1.2
Denmark	1.8	1.8	3.7	2.0
Ireland	3.7	2.4	5.5	2.4
Germany	0.5	0.7	1.0	0.9
France	1.5	2.2	1.6	1.3
Italy	3.3	3.4	3.3	3.4
US	1.7	4.3	2.0	2.7
UK	4.4	3.7	5.5	3.8
Japan	5.6	1.6	5.7	1.8
Austria	1.6	0.7	0.9	0.7
Norway	1.6	2.3	1.7	2.5
Sweden	1.0	2.3	1.3	3.1
Switzerland	2.6	1.0	1.5	1.6

Source: IMF, International Financial Statistics

during the five years preceding the EMS and during the period since its institution. These are compared with the interest rates of a number of other non-EMS countries. It can be seen that the level of the interest rates has in general increased substantially in the post-1979 period. This is especially the case for the real interest rates. There does not seem to be evidence that the EMS countries have been able to better withstand this upward movement of the real interest rates than non-EMS countries. In fact a striking exception to this trend is provided by Switzerland, a non-EMS country, whose real (and nominal) interest rate was lower in the post-EMS period.

Evidence about the variability of nominal and real interest rates is provided in table 6. We show the mean absolute yearly change and the standard deviation of both the nominal and the real interest rates. These are again compared for the EMS and some non-EMS countries. One observes, first, the substantial increase in the variability of the nominal and the real interest rate in the US since 1979. In most other countries nominal interest rate variability seems to have increased also. The major exception again is Switzerland, where the two measures of variability show a decline. In Germany and Japan the evidence suggests that nominal interest rate variability has changed little.

The evidence about real interest rate variability is mixed. Some countries experience an increase, others a decline in the variability of their real interest rates. There is, however, no tendency for the EMS countries to do better than the non-EMS countries in the sample.

A final piece of evidence is provided by the graphs of the nominal interest rates. These are presented in figures 1 to 4. In each figure the nominal interest rate developments in the different countries are compared with the US-interest rate development. The most striking aspect of this comparison is that the nominal interest rates in the EMS countries seem to have followed the cycles in the US interest rate more closely than the non-EMS countries in our sample. This is rather surprising if one remembers that a major objective of the EMS was to increase Europe's independence from the "vagaries" of financial developments in the US.

From this evidence about the level and the variability of the interest rates one can conclude that the EMS-countries have not been able to insulate their financial markets from the disturbances originating in the US in a more effective way than other major industrialized countries. There is even some evidence suggesting that EMS countries have been more affected in the short-run by US interest rate movements than the other countries in the sample. In addition, the case of Switzerland stands out. As a small country, using an individual approach in its exchange management it has achieved a surprising degree of financial stability, in a world of major financial disturbances.

One possible explanation why interest rate stability has been elusive in the EMS is the following. Large financial disturbances originating outside the system trigger new uncertainty about the EMS official exchange rates. In order to defend these exchange rates the monetary authorities adjust the interest rates within the system. Thus, external shocks tend to automatically produce interest rate movements within the system. It should be stressed that the source of the problem is not only the occurrence of outside shocks but also the absence of credibility of the official exchange rates.

The previous discussion also suggests that the nature of the co-operative arrangement embodied in the EMS provides little benefits to its members in terms of monetary and financial stability. In any case it does not seem to be superior to other non-co-operative arrangements. This may lead to the conclusion that in order to reap the benefits of monetary integration one has to go much farther than the degree of co-operation achieved in the EMS today. In a sense it can be said that the co-operation within the EMS is too little to have significant benefits for its members. The latter could achieve results in terms of monetary stability as well without the EMS.

5. THE EMS AND NOMINAL DISCIPLINE

It is sometimes argued that the EMS has worked as an external instrument of discipline for countries that otherwise would be tempted to follow inflationary policies. The cases of France and Belgium are often mentioned in this connection. To the extent that the EMS has offered such external nominal discipline it has provided a public good to its members, the benefits of which should be added to the cost-benefit analysis of the system.

174

FIGURE 1

Government Bond Yields

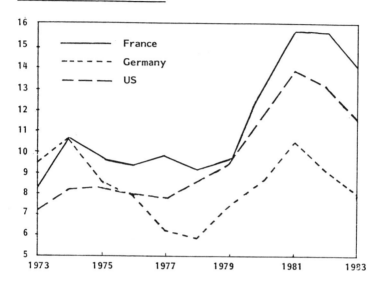

FIGURE 2

Government Bond Yields

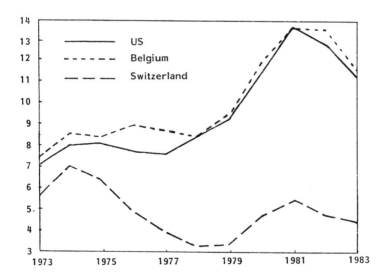

FIGURE 3

Government Bond Yields

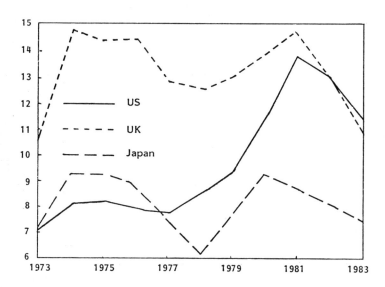

It is difficult to quantify this benefit. However, it is clear from the existing evidence that other exchange rate arrangements have also allowed countries to exert nominal discipline in their economies. To illustrate this, figures 4 and 5 show the average inflation rate in the EMS and compares this for the same group of non-EMS countries as the one analyzed in the previous tables. Both the weighted and the un-weighted average of the national inflation rates is shown.

The evidence clearly indicates that on the average the EMS coun-tries have not been able to disinflate their economies any better than the other major industrialized countries. On the contrary, the evidence seems to support the view that the EMS countries have been less suc-cessful in doing so. It should also be stressed that this slower dis-inflation in the EMS has not bee made possible by a higher growth rate of output and employment. As was illustrated in the previous sections the growth record of the EMS countries has not been more favorable than the growth record of the major non-EMS countries. Thus, it

176

FIGURE 4

Inflation in EMS and non-EMS Countries
(weighted average)

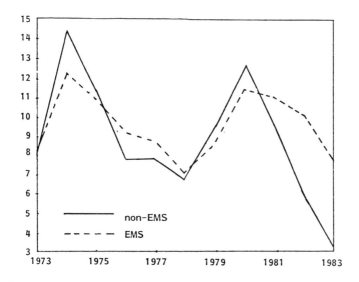

FIGURE 5

Inflation in the EMS and in the non-EMS Countries
(unweighted average)

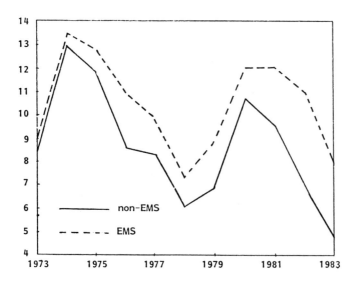

FIGURE 6

Average Growth Rates of GDP (1973-78 and 1979-84)

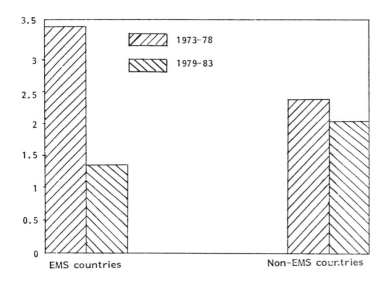

FIGURE 7

Average Growth Rates of Investment

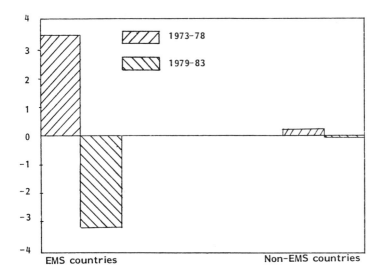

178

FIGURE 8

Yearly Absolute Change of Real Exchange Rates

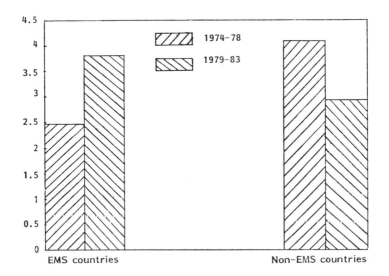

FIGURE 9

Real Interest Rates

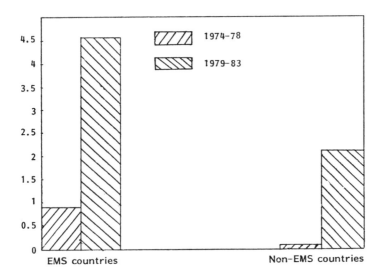

cannot be said that the EMS countries traded off more inflation for a better output and employment performance.

As far as exchange rate and interest rate stability are concerned, the EMS countries compare unfavorably with the small non-EMS countries. This is illustrated in figures 8 and 9. Figure 8 shows the mean absolute change of the real exchange rates of the four small EMS countries and of the four small non-EMS countries. A striking result is that this measure of real exchange rate variability increased for the small EMS countries, whereas it declined in the group of small non-EMS countries. Thus despite the increased international monetary disturbances since 1979, the small non-EMS countries succeeded in reducing their real exchange rate variability. And these countries achieved this without committing themselves into an explicit exchange rate union.

Finally, figure 9 shows that the small non-EMS countries have succeeded better than their EMS counterparts in limiting the upward movement of their real interest rates, so that during 1979-83 the level of the real interest rates in the former group was only half the level of the real interest rates in the group of small EMS countries.

The general picture that arises from this evidence is the following. The small EMS countries have fared worse than the small non-EMS countries in terms of growth and investment. This, of course could be due to factors quite independent from the EMS, (for example, domestic economic policies). Nevertheless the issue arises whether the EMS was in any way responsible for this.

The EMS was seen as a system that would lead to more exchange rate stability. In doing so it would lead to a lower degree of risk for investors, so that it could contribute to better investment and growth prospects. In this context it was often thought that the small countries would benefit most from the system. The facts are that small countries which chose to stay out of the system and which followed their own exchange rate policies achieved better results for the stabilization of their real exchange rates. In addition, these countries were also able to better insulate their economies from the interest rate shocks originating from the US. These are certainly striking results. They force us to re-think the costs and benefits of exchange rate agreements like the EMS for small open economies.

What could be the reason why the EMS seems to have been of so little help for the small members, in fact may even have harmed them, in their attempts to achieve more monetary and financial stability? One possible explanation, which is formulated here as a hypothesis in need of further testing is the following. The international monetary disturbances which occurred since 1979 have taken the form of large portfolio shifts out of a number of major currencies, in particular the DM, into the dollar. By tying their fate to the DM the small countries were exposing their financial markets to disturbances that were larger than if they had followed a more independent exchange rate policy. Their problems were compounded by the fact the German monetary authorities tried (unsuccessfully) to stem the tide by allowing the German interest rates to increase substantially. Thus the other EMS countries faced the worst of two worlds: a high real exchange rate variability coupled with high real interest rates. The countries which stayed out of this arrangement reduced the impact of these large disturbances on their domestic economies.

The previous discussion suggests that the EMS arrangement may have been unfavorable for some of its members given the nature of the shocks that occurred during 1979-83. This is in accordance with recent theoretical findings indicating that the optimality of exchange rate arrangements depends on the nature of the shocks that hit the economy (see e.g. Marston (1983)).

It is important to stress again that the superior macroeconomic performance of the four non-EMS countries analyzed here could be due to a better domestic economic policy in these countries. More research should be done here to find out how domestic policies and the exchange rate system have contributed to better macroeconomic results in these countries.

7. THE CHALLENGE OF US ECONOMIC POLICIES

The reversal in US policy making since 1979-80 has been dramatic. It has also challenged other countries to respond in a way that preserves their national interests. It is now generally felt that the major industrialized countries have failed to take up this challenge. As was documented in the previous sections, the EMS did not provide for an institutional framework facilitating such a common response.

This failure of European economic policies has spurred new pro-posals for joint action. The most recent one was formulated in a report to the EC-Commission by Layard, et alii, (see Layard, et alii (1984)). The central idea in this proposal is that the major European countries (and in particular Germany and the United Kingdom) should engineer a coordinated policy of (temporary) fiscal expansion, coupled to a policy of monetary accommodation. In the view of the authors, such a policy would allow European countries to absorb that part of the unemployment rate in Europe exceeding the "natural" unemployment rate (NAIRU). The latter is estimated at 7.5% in 1984. The observed unemployment rate in the EC being 10.5%, such a fiscal expansion could eliminate 3% points of the unemployment rate in the EC countries without giving rise to an acceleration of inflation.

The main weakness of the Layard (et alii) – proposal is the ab-sence of any estimate of the size of the fiscal stimulus in the EC needed to reduce aggregate unemployment from its current level of 10.5% to its "natural" level of 7.5%. In order to estimate the required fiscal stimulus we use the public investment multiplier on real GDP of 1.2 obtained in the Eurolink model (see European Economy (1983)). This multiplier is obtained assuming a concerted expansion of public investment in the four major EC-countries (Germany, France, Italy, and the United King-dom), and an accommodating monetary policy[1] (these are also the assumptions underlying the Layard proposal).

A second piece of information which is employed here is the em-pirical relation between the growth rate of GDP and the growth of employment. This relation was estimated for the EC-countries during the period 1960-83. In addition, this relationship is compared with the US. This allows us to compare the effectiveness of fiscal policies in the EC and in the US as a means to increase employment. The series of GDP growth and employment growth are represented in figures 10 and 11. The contrast between the US and the EC is obvious. The growth of

---

(1) In addition, this multiplier is obtained assuming fixed exchange rates among the four major countries in the EC. It is a weighted aver-age of the public investment multipliers of these four countries.

TABLE 7

Regression of Growth of Employment on Growth of Real GDP

	constant	GDP	R^2	DW	RHO
EC (1970-83)	-0.80	0.28	0.64	1.88	0.29
	(0.24)	(0.07)			
US (1970-83)	0.04	0.55	0.60	1.51	0.36
	(0.66)	(0.15)			

Source: EC-Commission, The European Economy, no. 18, Nov. 1983, and IMF, International Financial Statistics
Note: The numbers between brackets are standard errors.

employment in the US seems to be more closely related to the movements in the growth rate of GDP than in the EC.

This impression is confirmed by the results of regressing the growth rate of employment of GDP in the US and in the EC. Such a regression equation expresses the short-term relationship between output and employment growth. It has a similar interpretation as Okun's law. The results are shown in table 7.

The results indicate that the elasticity of employment growth with respect to the growth of GDP is about twice as high in the US than in Europe. The results of table 7 also imply that one needs a growth rate of GDP in the EC which is twice as high as the US growth rate in order to achieve the same growth in employment. Thus, in the EC a growth rate of GDP of 3.6% is needed to increase employment by 1%. In the US this growth rate of GDP is 1.8%. The reasons for this important "structural" difference between the EC and the US probably stem from the lack of flexibility of European labor markets compared to the US market. Factors that are responsible for this lack of flexibility of Europe's labor markets are the high tax rates on wage income, labor market regulations such as restrictions on hiring and firing, a social security system which discourages labor mobility.

The implications for the effectiveness of a fiscal expansion in the EC in creating jobs are far-reaching. Using the public investment multiplier of 1.2 and the employment elasticity of table 7, one can easily compute the size of the joint expansion of public investment in the four

FIGURE 10

Growth Rates of GDP and Employment in EC

FIGURE 11

Growth Rates of GDP and Employment in the US

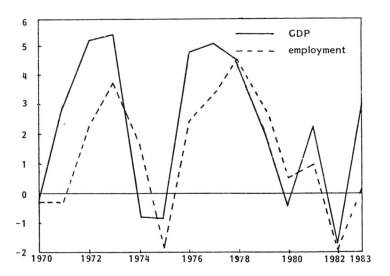

major EC-countries which would be needed to reduce unemployment by 3% points. Such an expansion would have to amount to 8.9% of GDP. It would in fact imply a tripling of public investment in the EC (which in 1984 amounted to 4% of the EC's GDP).

The implications for the budget deficits would also be substantial. Eurolink has computed the public investment multipliers on the budget deficits in the four major EC-countries. The weighted average for these four countries is 0.85; i.e. an increase of public investment of 1% of GDP leads to an increase of net lending of the public authorities of 0.85% (during the first year of the program). Thus, the joint public investment program would lead to an additional government budget deficit in these countries of 7.6% of GDP. Given the existing (uncorrected) budget deficit of approximately 5% of GDP, the fiscal expansion needed to reduce unemployment in the EC by 3% would lead to a budget deficit amounting to 12.6% of GDP. The magnitude of these numbers illustrate how ineffective even a joint fiscal expansion would be to fight Europe's unemployment problem. (For a similar point made concerning Japan see Hamada (1984)). It is also clear that the financing constraint would be formidable, making a coordinated fiscal stimulus unfeasible.

8.   CONCLUDING COMMENTS

Two conclusions can be drawn from the analysis of this paper. First, the EMS is an institutional arrangement which up to now appears to have been powerless in promoting monetary and financial stability in Europe. Evidence was shown indicating that the EMS has had only limited success in stabilizing real exchange rates over periods extending the short run, nor has it allowed its members to protect themselves from outside financial disturbances (in particular interest rate shocks) any better than other non-EMS countries. In fact, it was found that the small EMS countries were more subjected to real exchange rate and real interest rate shocks than comparable small European countries outside the EMS. Thus, it can be concluded that the EMS has been of little help for its members in confronting the worldwide economic disturbances since 1979.

The main reason for this failure of the EMS to achieve its objective undoubtedly is the fact that it is too loose as an institutional arrangement. If the EMS is to contribute to more monetary stability in Europe it must make a qualitative step forward towards monetary unification. The failure to do so reduces the EMS to an institution which is not more helpful for its members than an arrangement where countries follow their own preferred exchange rate policy.

The previous conclusion should not be interpreted as a plea to abolish the EMS. The EMS is an important experiment towards monetary unification. The danger of the present situation is that, as the benefits of the system are far from clear, the commitment towards monetary unification is weakened. Thus, the conclusion of this paper could be the following. Further steps towards the strengthening of the system are essential for its long-run survival. Only if these steps are taken one can hope that the objective of more monetary stability in Europe can be achieved.

The second conclusion of this paper is that policies of co-ordinated demand management in the EC can contribute very little towards the reduction of unemployment. Our calculations indicate that the major EC-countries would need to increase their budget deficits from the current level of 5% to 12.6% of their GNP in order to reduce the unemployment rate by 3% points. The financing constraints of such a program would be formidable.

The simple reason for this result is that the growth rate of GDP contributes very little to employment growth in the EC. The contrast with the US is striking where we found that the growth of GDP contributes twice as much to the creation of jobs than in the EC. The causes of this striking difference have to do with rigidities of the labor market and wage costs. These problems cannot be solved by programs to co-ordinate demand management. The latter can only lead to beneficial results if the supply-side problems of the European economies are tackled at the same time.

186

REFERENCES

Bomhoff, E.(1983), *Monetary Uncertainty*, Amsterdam, North Holland,

EC-Commission (1984),"Cinq Ans de Co-opération Monétaire en Europe", mimeo, March.

Hamada, K., and Kurosaka, Y (1984),"The relationship between production and unemployment in Japan: Okun's law in comparative
perspective", *European Economic Review*, June.

Layard, R.,Basevi, G.,Blanchard, O.,Buiter, W. and Dornbusch, R.,
(1984), "Europe: The Case for Unsustainable Growth", CEPS,
Brussels.

Marston, R.(1981),"Real and Monetary Disturbances in an Exchange
Rate Union", NBER Working Paper, no. 705, June.

Rogoff, K.(1984),"Can exchange rate predictability be achieved without
monetary convergence? Evidence from the EMS", Board of
Governors of the Federal Reserve System, *International
Finance Discussion Papers*, Washington DC.

Thygesen, N.(1984),"Exchange rate policies and monetary targets in the
EMS countries", mimeo.

Ungerer, H., et alii (1983),"The European Monetary System: The
Experience 1979-82", *IMF Occasional Papers*, no. 19, May.

8. THE OPTIMAL EXCHANGE-RATE SYSTEM AND ITS SIGNIFICANCE FOR ECONOMIC RECOVERY

H. Jager[*]

1. INTRODUCTION

Ever since the major currencies in the world abandoned the ex-change-rate system of fixed but adjustable parities in March 1973, the international monetary system gained ample experience with floating rates. After a period of euphoria, negative – but not altogether un-expected – effects of the transition to floating became perceptible. This led to a reorientation regarding which exchange-rate system to prefer. The results of that reappraisal, however, have until now been only moderately satisfactory, especially because, in general, they came about from analyses of a partial nature. By "partial" is meant the pursuance of only one of the many economic objectives while neglecting appro-priate adjustments in the accompanying economic policy.

In the present analysis an attempt is made to determine a hierarchy of exchange-rate regimes, without lapsing into such a partial approach. This is done by means of the determination of optimal eco-nomic policy. Subsequently, attention is given to the consequences of the choice of the exchange-rate system for economic recovery. In particular, its sensitivity for optimal economic policy under varying exchange-rate systems will be examined. Finally, some remarks will be made about the practicability of the exchange-rate regime which appeared to be optimal.

2. A RETURN TO FIXED EXCHANGE RATES?

Opinions differ about the functioning of floating exchange rates in the seventies. It is sometimes argued that the experience has been

* The author is grateful to the conference participants, and especially to Mr. J.L. Schneider for comments on an earlier draft, and Hans Amman for skilful research assistance.

relatively good (cf. Emminger (1982, p. 19)), in that floating rates allowed the world economy to absorb enormous shocks, in particular the two oil-price explosions, while it had no demonstrable effect on the growth in world trade – this despite the fact that theoretically a negative influence on the growth of world trade might have been expected as a result of increased uncertainty. Moreover, in the seventies the long-standing overvaluation of the U.S. dollar disappeared, capital controls were eliminated – especially in the United States and West Germany – and protectionism was continually reduced.

In contrast, majority opinion is that since the early seventies the exchange-rate movements have been excessive, erratic and, therefore, detrimental to the international trade and financial system (cf. De Grauwe (1983, p. 375)). According to this view the overvaluation of the U.S. dollar did indeed vanish after 1973, but as early as 1975-76 it appeared again. Furthermore, in the middle of the seventies the process of progressive trade liberalization which marked most of the post-war period reached a turning point. Since then, creeping protectionism in new forms, the "new protectionism", has been observed (cf. Bergsten and Cline (1982, pp. 10 and 11)), and the misalignment of exchange rates is considered an important additional source of this aggravation of protectionist pressure. There is, for example, evidence that this process was substantially supported by the overvaluation of the U.S. dollar, expecially against the Japanese yen, in 1976-77 and again in 1981-82 (cf. Bergsten and Williamson (1982, p 111).

With respect to the relationship between floating exchange rates and world trade hardly any empirical study until now shows a significant negative contribution of exchange-rate volatility to growth in international trade[1]. Notwithstanding this lack of empirical evidence, the dominant view is that the arguments for this relationship are theoretically sound and that it can be expected that the effect will only become noticeable in the longer term. Before floating exchange rates were introduced it was believed that the transition to floating would

---

(1) A recent exception to this rule is the study by Akhtar and Hilton (1984) which shows that exchange-rate uncertainty has a negative influence on trade between West Germany and the United States.

bring about a clear downward shift in the degree of international economic interdependence, while the autonomy of domestic economic policy
would increase considerably. Again, until now, empirical studies have
not supported these expectations (cf. Swoboda (1983), De Grauwe and
Fratianni (1984), and Thygesen (1984))[1]. These studies, however,
often – very properly – observed that the lack of a significant change
may be ascribed to the many disturbing influences which appear
because the methods employed compare two different periods.

Though these objections against floating exchange rates are stated
in very general terms, they already make it obvious that floating has
been experienced as unsatisfactory. This impression has in fact been
common since the dollar started to rise strongly in 1980. Fluctuating
exchange rates are not, therefore, an ideal system but, as Meltzer
observed recently, it is easier to criticise than to improve them
(Meltzer (1984)). It is, nevertheless, not surprising that in the last
few years the idea of a possible return to fixed exchange rates has
often re-emerged, although it almost never leads to any concrete proposal in that direction. The reason is that the pre-conditions for the
satisfactory functioning of fixed rates are very stringent.

A return to fixed but adjustable parities requires at least that
differences between countries in long-run inflation rates are close to
zero and that cyclical developments are practically completely synchronized. These conditions alone, however, are not sufficient. Greater
emphasis is being placed today on the importance of financial assets in
exchange rate determination (cf. Morgan Guaranty (1983)). Expected
return, its variability, and security are determinants of asset preference and, therefore, of foreign-currency preference. Exchange rate
changes will occur when national differences in these determinants are
changing. Factors influencing these determinants are, amongst others,
interest rates, confidence in economic policy management, and the
associated prospects of government budget deficits and of monetary
expansion. The reduced significance of the current account for ex-

(1) It has, however, to be noted that from a theoretical point of view
certain expectations can also be countered (see Jager (1984)).

change-rate determination has far-reaching consequences for the pursuance of fixed exchange rates. The necessity to develop a concerted macroeconomic policy for the main industrial countries in the world now goes far beyond the coordination needed to realise both small inflation differences and the synchronized cyclical development mentioned before. In fact, Shafer and Loopesko (1983, p. 69) are right when they state that maintaining fixed exchange rates necessitates a level of macroeconomic policy coordination which was never achieved on a sustained basis, even under the Bretton-Woods system.

In sum, the drawbacks of - nearly - pure floating exchange rates give rise to the question whether we can treat such an important price - as the exchange rate apparently is, considering its possibly substantial effects on the economies - under all conceivable circumstances with "benign neglect", i.e. as a residual outcome of other policies (see Emminger (1982, p. 25)). While it is important to analyse the preconditions necessary for a return to fixed exchange rates, it is also at least of equal importance to detect whether a fixed exchange-rate regime is to be preferred compared with its alternatives. Some degree of exchange-rate management seems to be inevitable, but the same may be true with regard to some degree of exchange-rate flexibility. Between these loose bounds there is still a variety of possible exchange-rate systems. It is, therefore, not surprising that there is recently a growing literature about optimal flexibility of exchange rates.

3.   METHODS TO APPROACH OPTIMAL FLEXIBILITY

Perhaps the most obvious way to determine the most favourable degree of exchange-rate management is to compare the outcome of the economic process in periods with different exchange-rate arrangements in force. Such an approach, however, has the disadvantage that some of the forms under discussion were never put into practice. It would, therefore, be virtually impossible to find a single country which applied all the exchange-rate systems in the past. This, however, is the least which is needed in order to avoid the situation where distortions which are caused by inter-country differences in economic structure, thwart the effects of the exchange-rate systems.

Even if the analysis is confined to just one country, however, the danger of distorting influences remains considerable, The mere design of economic institutions habitually presents changes in time in many more aspects than only the exchange-rate regime. Furthermore, it is wrong to decide in favour of one of the regimes on the basis of events that occurred *during* the period in which the regime was employed. One must, for example, keep in mind that the problems, which were created under the Bretton-Woods system and led to its abandonment, burdened the period *after* 1973. For this reason a comparison in time will lead too easily to completely ascribing economic developments to the functioning of the exchange-rate system of the time. This danger is continuously present, for example, in several of the studies cited in the preceding section, and in the studies contained in Williamson (1981). They likewise examine which exchange-rate system is to be preferred. It must be emphasized, however, that in general the authors of the latter studies were conscious of this flaw.

The remaining ways to gain insight into the desired exchange-rate system employ an economic model. Their drawback is that the economic structure may change when an alternative exchange rate system is put into practice. Information is absent, however, about the direction and extent to which the structure will be influenced by this alteration. In terms of the economic model this means that the influence on the parameter values and the specification of the economic relationships is lacking. This influence can, however, be of significance, especially that regarding the structure of exchange-rate expectations.

In a second, often employed, approach to the desired exchange-rate system an economic objective is pursued within the confines of an analytical economic model while simultaneously introducing a disturbance to the economy. The consequences of various exchange-rate regimes for the objective are then studied. Frequently used objectives in this approach are the maximizing of national income and of national consumption. The necessity to arrive at an analytical solution, however, imposes rather drastic restrictions on the size of the economic model. Consequently, the results of such exercises are conditional upon the rigorous assumptions used regarding the economic structure and economic objectives.

From the many studies of this approach it appears that the source and nature of the disturbance to the economy to a large extent determine whether a flexible rate or some variant of exchange-rate management is prefered. For example, the higher the variance of real shocks, the larger the desirability of fixed exchange rates, while a high variance of monetary shocks tends to raise the desirability of greater flexibility. In practice, however, the exact nature of a shock can usually neither be known to, nor be predicted by, policy makers. In addition, shocks of different natures will often occur concurrently. In the event of such considerable uncertainty about the shocks impinging on the economic system, policies that avoid the disastrous consequences of a broad range of – simultaneously occurring – shocks are preferable. In view of all these facts, the analytical approach just described does not appear very appropriate.

The objections against the analytical approach can be overcome by choosing one of the two approaches to the desired exchange-rate system which will be described below. One of them is the use of simulation studies. It is then possible to employ an econometric model which, in principle, is unrestricted in size and, therefore, much more differentiated compared with an analytical model. This offers scope for a substantially more realistic outcome. Since the relevance of an econometric model is limited to both the time period and country for which it has been estimated, this improvement is at the cost of the general validity of the results. An additional drawback, which a simulation study usually has in common with the analytical approach, is that the functioning of the exchange-rate systems is studied in isolation from other macroeconomic policy. This latter is, in other words, exogenously determined, whereas it is likely that, in practice, a change in the nature of the exchange-rate regime is coupled with changes in the actual time paths of instruments of economic policy. This lack of concomitant adjustment of the rest of macroeconomic policy is sometimes, only partly, eliminated by introducing a policy rule for one of the policy instruments. This restriction connected with the method in question is perceptible in, for example, the extensive simulation study in Kenen (1975).

The required policy interdependence finds expression in the approach which uses optimal control techniques. It allows one to determine the optimal time paths of the different economic instruments simultaneously. This important advantage in comparison with other methods is the main reason why it has been chosen for the present study. Nevertheless, the application of optimal control techniques has its restrictions too. When the approach uses an econometric model – as is done here – it has the drawback in common with simulation studies that the relevance of the outcome is restricted to both the period and country for which the model has been estimated. Moreover, it is doubtful that the introduction of an exchange-rate system which was not actually put into practice in the country and period considered, will not have an impact on the structure and, certainly, the coefficients of the econometric model used[1]. The point is that during the model's estimation period the behaviour of the economic agents was attuned to the existing exchange-rate arrangements. This drawback arises in optimal control studies as well as in simulation studies[2].

An obvious handicap that is specific for the application of optimal control techniques is the necessity to use a quantified macroeconomic objective function. In implementing the method this function is maximized – or minimized in the case of a loss function, as in the present study – under the constraints of the econometric model. Quantification of a macroeconomic objective function requires information about policymakers' preferences and target values. It appears to be difficult to gain insight into these desirabilities, because they are often of an implicit nature. Once constructed, however, such an objective function has the advantage that now the simultaneous realization of a number of economic objectives can be pursued and controlled. This is an important step towards greater realism of the results of theoretical studies.

(1) In discussions on the application of optimal control techniques this objection has frequently been raised. See, amongst others, Prescott (1977).
(2) This drawback is counteracted to a certain extent by the fact that the model's estimation period partly concerns years characterized by an adjustable peg, while in the rest of the period examined the guilder did not float against all the currencies. In addition, currencies are also susceptible to speculative attacks once par-value changes become an accepted way of relieving exchange-market pressures built up under fixed exchange rates. Both the final years of Bretton Woods and the so-called Snake arrangement show evidence in defense of this argument.

4. THE DECISION MODEL

In this study optimal control techniques are applied to an econometric model of the Netherlands' economy, combined with an objective function of the Netherlands' policy makers. The model is linear and has been estimated using quarterly data for the period 1967(I)-1976(IV) by means of two-stage least squares. The model, in principle Keynesian in nature, stresses the international economic relations of the Netherlands' economy. Since in the international trade component of an economic model, in particular, the adjustment lags are apt to be long, the model is very dynamic. The model includes a Phillips-curve, price indexation of wages and its feedback to prices, exogenously determined production, and budget constraints for the government and the money market.

The part of the model consisting of the international economic relations contains behavioural equations for the value as well as the price of both imports and exports of goods and services. The balance-of-payments identity determines the exchange rate. Apart from this feature of the so-called balance-of-payments approach to the exchange rate, the model possesses elements of portfolio-balance theory through the specification of a behavioural equation for the international capital flows. Because of its relevance for the explanation of the exchange rate, the model's international economic relations will be outlined here, and particularly in Appendix 1, in greater detail. The complete economic model, including its stability characteristics, has been presented in Jager (1981 and 1982).

Three explanatory variables appear to determine the speculative part of private capital flows. First, the difference between the actual exchange rate and the par value of the guilder makes a statistically significant contribution to the explanation of the Netherlands' speculative capital inflows. Since the effective exchange rate is used in the model, a positive difference between actual and par value of this rate expresses a strong guilder. Theoretically, this would have to stimulate the Netherlands' capital imports, which is in agreement with the facts, according to equation (1.7) in Appendix 1. This equation also shows that speculative capital inflows depend on, second, the trend in the exchange rate and, third, the tendency in official foreign-exchange market interventions. Since a rise in the exchange rate in the preceding two quarters contributes positively to capital inflows, speculators, apparently, have extrapolative exchange-rate expectations of the elastic type. These inflows are also promoted when the monetary authorities purchase foreign exchange.

The expectations scheme for the exchange rate that is found here supports the so-called bandwagon behaviour in the foreign-exchange market. The practical relevance of this behaviour has also been defended by, among others, Mayer (1982, pp. 24 and 41) and the Group of Thirty (1982, p. 14). This viewpoint is prompted by the consideration that exchange-rate expectations tend to be loosely held, especially over a period of months or more because of the relatively large white noise. For that reason, the expectations are to a great extent influenced by current events and speculators tend to take a short-term view, concentrating on making short-term gains (see Group of Thirty (1982, p. 14)). Another plea in favour of bandwagon behaviour is that, once the exchange rate starts to move, there are influences like the J-curve effect and the repercussions on domestic inflation that give rise to a self-reinforcing tendency in the exchangerate movement.

The decision model includes seven objective variables, *viz.* the growth of real gross national product (GNP), the stability of this growth, the rate of inflation, the balance on current account, the exchange-rate level (in relation to the currency's par value), and the stability of two terms of trade (or real exchange rates). One of these terms of trade is defined as the Netherlands' export price level related to that of competitors on foreign markets (or competitiveness on the export side), and the other as the price deflator of the Netherlands' GNP related to the Netherlands' import price level (or competitiveness on the import side). The econometric model lacks a sub-model of the labour market, so that full employment could not be included as an objective variable. This gap is partly filled by the presence of the growth of GNP and the close ties which are normally supposed to exist between the two variables. For the design of the loss function, the desired time paths of the objective variables are needed. These paths were derived from official publications. The same holds for the desired time paths of the instrumental variables, or control variables, in the model[1].

(1) For details concerning the desired time paths used for the economic objectives and instruments, see Jager (1981 and 1982).

The decision model contains six of these instruments of economic policy. They are: the short-run interest rate of the Netherlands Bank (the rate on advances), the government's nominal tax receipts, the government's net borrowing, the government's liquidity shortage, and official interventions in the foreign-exchange market. Moreover, the model allows the foreign assets obtained through these interventions to be converted to such long-term foreign assets that they lose the high liquidity which is necessary for reserve assets. The advantage of the existence of such a possibility is that the opportunity costs of monetary reserves can be partly circumvented through the higher rates of return of longer-term investments. In the analysis presented in the next section the exchange-rate arrangements differ in the design of both the time path of the parity and the size of the fluctuation margin around the parity. For this reason they also obtain the character of instruments.

The macroeconomic objective function which is employed is, as already mentioned, a loss function for the Netherlands' policy makers. The weights of this, quadratic, function have been derived by means of a method based on revealed preference. This method was, in essence, borrowed from Friedlaender (1973). With the aid of the econometric model, the weights of the objective variables have been obtained from the Netherlands' economic policy as it was actually conducted in the period 1967-70. As the Netherlands' economy showed a stable and, therefore, relatively predictable development in this period, it has been assumed that this policy is a good reflection of the policy preferred by the policy makers[1].

(1) Likewise, the weights of the instrumental variables are needed in the loss function. Apart from the information obtained from the method of revealed preference, the weights of various instruments and of the exchange rate have also been influenced by the necessity to keep their optimal time paths within politically acceptable limits and within the fluctuation margin around the parity, respectively, in the application of optimal control to the decision model. The following weights have been obtained. Growth of GNP: 19; stability of GNP growth: 15; balance on current account: 7; exchange rate and the two terms of trade: 5; government's borrowing in the capital market: 50; government's liquidity shortage: 50; conversion of monetary reserves to long term foreign assets: 50; and the rest of the policy instruments: 30.

The optimal policy for the decision model can be computed by means of the algorithm developed by Pindyck (1973). This algorithm, however, does not allow desired or target values for the objective and instrumental variables with an *endogenous* character. Some of the exchange-rate regimes between pure fixed and flexible rates, however, have an endogenous parity. This means that the parity in a certain period is determined by the optimal time paths of the model's state variables until then. The extension of the algorithm required for including endogenous target values is presented in Amman and Jager (1984). It is this extended Pindyck algorithm that will be used here.

5. THE OPTIMAL EXCHANGE-RATE SYSTEM

5.1. The exchange-rate systems

By means of optimal control techniques one can determine the optimal policy for each exchange-rate system distinguished. This is done for the time period 1970-76 using the decision model described above. Subsequently, these optimal policies can be compared. The system which is related to the optimum optimorum of these optimal policies, is called the optimal exchange-rate system. Since each exchange-rate system leads to only one optimal policy, this search for the optimal system results in an unique, unambiguous solution.

In the present analysis four exchange-rate systems are distinguished. The *first* system corresponds in its main features with the exchange-rate arrangement that actually existed for the guilder during the period under examination. The parity's desired time path in our first system is made identical to the actual parity of the guilder. The only difference is the numeraire, because here use is made of the effective exchange rate and not the nominal one. In fact, this desired time path is the same as the time series of Π^* (see Appendix II) and is, therefore, exogenous in the optimizing process. Since the Netherlands' policy makers have attempted from the beginning of the seventies to peg the guilder to a strong foreign currency facing relatively little inflationary prospects, *viz.* the Deutsche mark, the exchange-rate arrangement conducted, and thus our first exchange-rate system, can be described as the *strong-currency option* (see Thygesen (1979, p. 1)).

The *second* exchange-rate system in our set is the *floating exchange rate*. In our decision model it has been implemented by assigning the value zero to the marginal costs in the loss function connected with a deviation of the exchange rate from its target value. The explanation for this value is that under floating rates the divergence between the actual and par value of the currency's exchange rate is of no importance at all, but is undesirable only in so far as it influences the other objectives of economic policy in undesired ways. The costs of these undesired effects, however, already emerge as an increased disparity between the optimal and desired time paths for each of these other objectives. A second feature of floating rates is the complete lack of official interventions in the foreign-exchange market. This means that the sum of monetary reserves and longer-term investments of monetary reserves is determined beforehand for the whole period, except for the yields of the assets with which the sum is enlarged periodically[1].

The *third* exchange-rate system, which is distinguished, the *managed floating exchange rate*, has also been characterized by the exchange rate's weight in the loss function being equal to zero. The argumentation in favour of the introduction of this feature is similar to that for the floating rate. In the event of managed floating, official exchange-market interventions remain possible, so this arrangement lacks the second characteristic of freely floating exchange rates. It implies that under managed floating the monetary authorities can handle the exchange-rate developments by direct interventions, and counteract, if necessary, the undesired effects which the exchange rate might have under floating rates. By abstaining from official interventions, a floating rate regime has a substantial handicap. In fact, the transition to floating exchange rates is coupled with the loss of one of the instruments of economic policy.

---

(1) In the decision model this feature has been materialized by introducing the condition $\Delta RES^* = - \Delta B^*$ and assigning infinite costs to the use of these two instruments. In this way, both $(\Delta RES - \Delta RES^*)$ and $(\Delta B - \Delta B^*)$ will become zero, and thus likewise $(\Delta RES + \Delta B)$.

The *fourth* exchange-rate system which will be introduced in this study is a variant of a *crawling peg*. According to Williamson (1981, p. 4), a crawling-peg system has two essential characteristics. First, countries using this system accept the obligation to defend a par value (or peg) by maintaining the actual exchange rate within a fluctuation margin around the par value. Second, the crawling peg involves only gradual changes in the par value, and in smaller steps as opposed to the occasional large jumps which characterize the adjustable peg.

Under a crawling-peg system, the parity can be adjusted according to either a formula or an administrative decision. In general, adjustments of the peg according to an administrative decision will lead to a policy with the least loss when compared with any conceivable formula variant. The reason is that in a formula variant the parity adjustment is always tied to the change in the value of the formula chosen, whereas the decision variant lacks such a constraint. For that reason, here the latter variant will be employed[1].

In the following application the bounds of the fluctuation margin in the crawling-peg system as well as in the strong-currency option are set at -2.5 and +2.5 per cent of the par value. This bears a resemblance to the fluctuation margin which existed during the last years of the Bretton-Woods exchange-rate system and still exists in the European Monetary System. Under the floating and managed floating exchange rates, the par value entirely looses its significance. It is, therefore, realistic to remove the par value from private behavioural relations, that is from the equation for international capital flows. It fits in well with the aforementioned bandwagon behaviour in the foreign-exchange market, when the actual value of the exchange rate in the preceding period is substituted for the par value in the capital-flow equation. It is this substitution which has been carried into effect to determine the optimal floating and managed floating exchange-rate systems.

(1) The proposals which were advanced for an exchange-rate system that may reasonably be described as a crawling peg based on a formula, can be roughly divided into three categories, *viz.* formulas based on (1) changes in the level of national monetary reserves; (2) changes in the actual exchange rate; and (3) differences between national rates of inflation. For each of these categories optimal formulas have been determined and compared with each other in Amman and Jager (1985).

5.2. The results

Optimal policies are determined for all the exchange-rate systems introduced in the preceding section. For each of these policies, table 1 presents the total costs – or loss – and, moreover, the contributions of the time paths of the individual objective variables to the total costs.

In the total costs reported, the *de facto* costs of the exchange rate have been left out of consideration. This helps to achieve a fair-minded appraisal of the systems, since it is not relevant what exactly the time path of the exchange rate is even if a system has a fluctuation margin. The only purpose of the exchange rate's weight in the loss function is to ensure that the optimal time path of the rate stays within the fluctuation margin, if any, around the parity. As long as this goal is pursued successfully, a real loss in terms of economic costs is completely absent. Moreover, the attainment of this goal can easily be judged by looking to see whether the optimal exchange rate lies outside this margin. When this is so, the exchange rate's weight is increased to such a level that the optimal rate no longer crosses the margin. The costs in economic terms of this higher weight will appear in the form of a poorer realization of the desired time paths of the other means and ends because of the greater emphasis on a small difference between the optimal and the desired time path of the exchange rate.

In order to increase the comparability of the optimal policies, they are subjected to some conditions pertaining to the outcome in the last quarter of the period. First, it was required that the level of monetary reserves at the end of the period be roughly equal to that at the beginning. It is, thus, made impossible for an exchange-rate system to reduce total loss or costs by a net consumption of monetary reserves, and in so doing burden the policy that will be conducted in the next period. Despite this condition, the stock of the country's international liquidity appears to grow under all exchange-rate systems because a specified increase of the, officially held, *longer-term* foreign financial assets has been allowed. A second requirement was that substantial divergences in the use of sources for government expenditure over the entire period are prevented by assigning proper weights in the loss function to the three instruments of financing government expenditure.

From a comparison of the total costs presented in table 1, the

TABLE 1

Optimal Policy with Varying Exchange-Rate System [a]

Exchange rate system	Total Costs	Costs per objective variable					
		Real GNP level	change	Infla- tion	Current account	Change in terms of trade Export	Import
Crawling peg	8169*	5311*	78	181*	48*	200	486
Managed floating	8724	5378	65*	223	87	175	493
Strong- currency- option	9498	5463	67	404	55	132*	404*
Pure floating	9522	5507	77	406	51	279	449

a) An asterisk indicates the best record in the column.
b) Includes the costs of the instruments, besides those of the objective variables.

crawling-peg system appears to have the lowest costs and is, as a consequence, the optimal exchange-rate system. Managed floating comes next, while of the two remaining systems the strong-currency option must be preferred to pure floating. This sequence shows that, appar- ently, it is meaningful for monetary authorities to intervene in the foreign-exchange market. This result must, of course, not be confused with a plea in favour of sterilized interventions. In fact, the systems' optimal policies not only differ in intervention activities, but also in the time paths of all other instruments of economic policy.

From the costs - shown in table 1 - connected with the pursuance of a high level of real GNP it can be concluded that the optimal policy within the confines of the crawling-peg regime is also most successful in this respect, but the differences between the systems seem to be only small. This is demonstrated in table 2 by the fact that the highest real GNP's mean value for the entire period is ƒ 130.22 bln. in the case of the crawling peg, while the worst showing is for pure floating rates with a mean value of ƒ 130.06 per annum - which is only slightly lower. As a matter of fact, the exchange rate system with the best perfor-

TABLE 2

Means (μ) and Variances (σ^2) of the Optimal Time Paths of Relevant Variables[a)]

Optimal policy under:	Real GNP[b)]		Inflation[c)]		Current account[b)]	
	μ	σ^2 [d)]	μ	σ^2	μ	σ^2
Crawling peg	130.22*	0.93	6.80*	0.87*	2.24	0.46
Managed floating	130.16	0.36*	7.32	1.01	-0.25	0.74
Strong-currency option	130.09	1.05	9.52	1.27	3.16	0.43*
Pure floating	130.06	1.10	9.56	1.22	1.49	0.57

Optimal policy under:	Capital account[b)]		Exchange rate[c)]		Change in terms of trade				Reserves
					Export		Import		
	μ	σ^2	μ	σ^2 [d)]	μ	σ^2	μ	σ^2	σ^2
Crawling peg	-2.81	0.61	125.7	10.07	-1.84	2.78	7.20	4.19*	0.18
Managed floating	0.47	1.19	123.7	10.76	-2.24	1.68*	6.40	5.04	0.48
Strong-currency option	-4.13	0.88*	106.4	5.04*	0.68*	1.69	-0.32*	6.14	0.50
Pure floating	-1.47	0.57	107.2	4.67	0.56	4.15	-0.16	6.80	0.00

a) An asterisk indicates the best record in the column. The means are expressed as a value per annum, whereas the variances are calculated on a quarterly basis.
b) In bln. of guilders.
c) In per cent points.
d) This variance is determined for the deviations from the trend.

mance in tables 1 and 2 appears to lead to the highest level of real GNP in the final quarter. This property, in fact, also belongs to the crawling peg, with a level of ƒ 166.36 bln. on an annual basis; in this respect the worst result is for the strong-currency option with ƒ 162.16 bln. The values of managed floating and pure floating are ƒ 164.08 and ƒ 162.36, respectively.

The optimal crawling peg does not, however, show the most stable development of real GNP, as is illustrated by the third column of table 1. From this point of view, managed floating must be preferred, followed by the strong-currency option. In this respect, the crawling peg actually shows the worst outcome, although its performance is somewhat better in the second column of table 2, where the objective in question is materialized. In addition, the optimal crawling peg is characterized by the lowest inflation. This is shown in table 1 and also in the third column of table 2. The latter table indicates, furthermore, that the crawling peg also produces the least variability in inflation and that the effect of the exchange-rate system on inflation is substantially larger compared with its effect on the level of real GNP.

Regarding the pursuance of the desired time path of the balance on current account, again the optimal crawling-peg system has to be preferred, as shown in table 1, although, according to table 2, the most stable balance occurs in the case of the strong-currency option. The largest mean surplus also results from the strong-currency option, viz. ƒ 3.16 bln. on an annual basis, while managed floating has the smallest one.

Considering the data in the columns of the current account and the exchange rate in table 2, surprisingly it emerges that a higher mean value of the exchange rate is not always associated with a lower current-account surplus. Under the crawling-peg system, for example, the exchange rate clearly shows the strongest tendency to appreciate, while the current-account balance is almost the highest. Under managed floating, where the appreciation is also considerable, this connection is, however, completely different. The reason is, of course, that in optimal-control experiments all variables are changing simultaneously. As a consequence, the relationship between two variables will be influenced by the impact of alterations in the other variables. The two other exchange-rate systems exhibit only a modest appreciation and hardly differ with respect to the mean value of the exchange rate. These developments of the exchange rate, by way of its effect on import prices, probably explain to a considerable extent the diverging impact of the systems upon inflation. Figure 1 presents the complete optimal time paths of the exchange rate under the exchange-rate systems

FIGURE 1
Optimal Exchange Rate

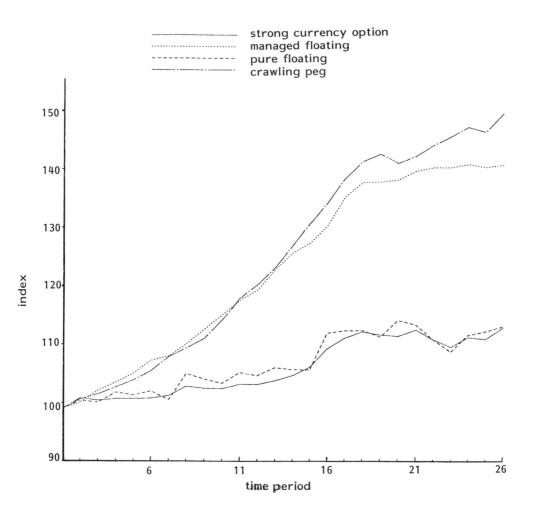

distinguished. It underlines the appreciation tendency, indicated before, regarding the crawling-peg system.

In table 2 a clear interdependence of the international capital flows and the exchange-rate characteristics does not emerge. During the period examined the guilder is strongest in the case of the crawling peg. Nevertheless, not that system but the managed floating rate leads to the smallest net capital outflow, while even pure floating - which is characterized by only a small currency appreciation - shows a small capital outflow compared to the system with a crawling peg.

The best result in table 1 with respect to pursuing stable terms of trade is achieved by the strong-currency option. Table 2 suggests that this must be fully ascribed to the combination of rather small volatility - measured by the variance - and a relatively modest average change of the terms of trade under that system. Very remarkable is the decline of the terms of trade on the export side with both the crawling peg and managed floating systems, although these exchange-rate systems involve the largest appreciations of the guilder during the period. This is explained by the very high degree of sensitivity of the Netherlands' export price in guilders to exchange-rate changes in the econometric model that underlies the computations. The rate's influence may be somewhat overestimated, although one has to draw such a conclusion with caution. In a small, open economy the exchange rate does, in fact, have a considerable influence on the export price by its direct effect - as a result of attempts by exporters to offset incipient alterations of competitiveness - as well as by means of the indirect effect - through the import price and costs of production.

Finally, table 2 shows that, as is usually expected, the variance of official foreign-exchange market interventions is largest for the strong-currency option. The surprising thing is, however, that the crawling peg - which contains a fluctuation margin - shows much less intervention variability than the managed-floating system. The complete optimal time paths of these interventions are presented in figure 2. Leaving aside the pure floating system, the time paths show a large degree of similarity.

FIGURE 2
Optimal Official Interventions in the Foreign Exchange Market

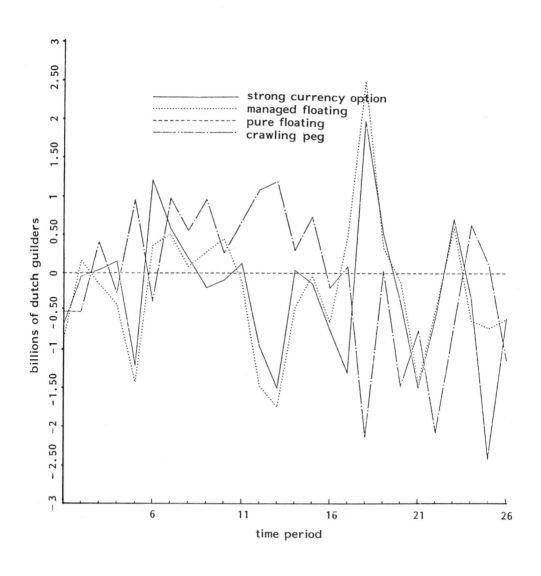

6. CONCLUDING REMARKS

In the previous search for a hierarchy of exchange-rate systems, a deliberate choice was made in favour of the application of optimal control techniques to a decision model. The main advantage of this approach is the possibility to consider simultaneously both the effects on various objectives and the control of more than one instrument. Moreover, various shocks of different natures may be simultaneously introduced in the analysis. By applying the approach to a time period which is rich in external economic shocks, the alternative policies are in fact implicity subjected to a test of robustness regarding such a mixture of shocks. Of course, each exogenous shock which an economy must cope with has its optimal exchange-rate system. Since, however, it cannot be changed frequently, as soon as a new shock of a different nature occurs, the robustness in question is important in practice. Consequently, in following the approach based on optimality, important features of partial analysis which are associated with alternative approaches are evaded. This is achieved, however, at the cost of a loss in potential to generalize the outcome of the analysis, because of the necessity to establish priorities for policy objectives and instruments.

Nevertheless, the approach provides an opportunity to counter-attack certain general conclusions. For instance, the statement: "We are better off as we are" with the present fluctuating exchange rates (see Meltzer (1984)), cannot be generally accepted. Employing an econometric model and a quantified loss function for the Netherlands, in the period 1970-76 a crawling peg exchange-rate system appears optimal among a limited set of systems. In addition to the crawling peg, the other systems which were included in the analysis are: managed floating, the so-called strong-currency option (comparable with the system reigning in the Netherlands during the period examined), and pure floating exchange rates. This sequence corresponds with the degree of optimality.

The outcome of the optimal policy under the system of the crawling peg distinguishes itself positively regarding the high mean and final level of economic activity, pursuing the desired balance on current account and, especially, the low rate of inflation and its stable development. In these respects, floating exchange rates produce, in contrast, bad effects. Another characteristic of the optimal crawling-peg regime is the large appreciation. Therefore, the differences in the effects which optimal policies under the varying exchange-rate systems exert on economic activity and hence on economic recovery is somewhat surprising. The quantitative significance of the nature of the exchange rate system for economic recovery is, however, remarkably slight and hardly exceeds two per cent. Moreover, the crawling peg does not score with respect to all aspects of economic activity. It does not, for instance, result in the most stable economic development. For the achievement of that objective managed floating has to be preferred.

In contrast to the effect on GNP, the influence of the exchange rate on the rate of inflation appeared to be of significance. For example, the strong guilder under the crawling-peg system reduced the annual inflation rate by over 2.5 per cent compared to the strong-currency option. These effects of the exchange rate on GNP and inflation support the stance of The Netherlands Bank in the seventies - advocated by Kessler (1981, p. 50) - that a devaluation of the guilder was not desirable in those years because it would have contributed little to employment, whereas it would have had the disadvantage of higher inflation. In fact, our results even point to a somewhat more extreme viewpoint.

The explanation of the, on the whole, only small effects of the choice of the exchange-rate system in the preceding analysis is two-fold. First - and possibly most important - in the period examined the Netherlands' economy was characterized by a complete price indexation of wages. It is well-known that in that case the effect of exchange-rate changes on economic growth is negligible in the longer-run. Indeed, in simulations with the model, the effect of an exchange-rate alteration appeared to be mainly short-term (see Jager and De Jong (1984)). As a result, its effect, taken as an average for the whole period, will be small. Second, by continuously considering the *optimal* policy corresponding to a particular exchange arrangement, not only are the external variables subject to change, but so is the entire set of instrumental variables. Differences between the exchange-rate arrangements in the influences of the external variables on the policy objectives can thereby be - partly - neutralized by a divergence in the optimal application of the other instrumental variables. This aspect is characteristic of the difference between a simulation study and the determination of the optimal policy. It also adds realism to allow, as the latter does, the remaining policy measures to undergo the consequences of a change in the exchange-rate arrangement.

Finally, it is useful to make some remarks about the relevance of the outcome of this analysis for policy making. The question whether a single country, assessing the alternative exchange-rate systems, pre- fers one of them has been approached here from the viewpoint of natio- nal isolation. Considerations concerning desired forms of international cooperation, already functioning international agreements, allowance for the interests of partner countries, or possible reactions by the rest of the world to the national choice of the optimal exchange-rate system were ignored. These limitations to the practical relevance of the present investigation can only be partly defended by referring to the smallness of the Netherlands. Likewise, the existence of a mixed form of ex- change-rate systems has been left out of consideration. Such a mixed form does currently exist for the guilder, with an adjustable-peg sys- tem in the EMS, the strong-currency option through the link with the Deutsche mark, as well as a floating regime for the EMS currencies against the outside world. This mixed form is extremely difficult to model.

These limitations of the current investigation, which, in fact, it has in common with all theoretical and empirical research, imply that its results certainly are not directly applicable in practice. They are, however, important material for making eventual policy choices.

The crawling-peg system that has emerged here as the optimal system raises suspicion in industrial countries. This emanates from the attendant so-called vicious circles of depreciation and inflation in the countries which applied the system in the past. This suspicion appears to be unjustified. These countries are not only characterized by the use of the crawling peg, but also by the fact that they belong to the group of less developed countries with often less stable and less powerful economic policies, and possibly different policy preferences. Moreover, the crawling-peg system shows more similarity with the adjustable peg than is generally recognized. It is, for example, significant that the

IMF, only recently, observed that the EMS may begin to assume the character of a crawling peg (International Monetary Fund (1983, p. 51)).

It is, indeed, justified to raise the objection against a crawling-peg system that markets can regularly expect with near-certainty that parity changes are imminent. It is wrong, however, that this will in all probability induce speculative capital flows which necessitate such efficiency-disturbing measures as the use of capital restrictions. If the fluctuation margin around the parity is small, with, for example, inter-vention points at 2.5 per cent distance as used in the present analysis, and if, for example, the parity is determined by the average actual exchange rates in the recent past, speculation will not be very profit-able. Of course, an important assumption is that economic policy is carried out in a convincing and orderly way. Is it not, in fact, this policy, however, that is also indispensable for a stable EMS and any other successful exchange-rate system with an adjustable peg?

APPENDIX I
A description of the submodel of international economic relations[1].

The budget constraint for the government is contained in equation (1.1)
of table 1.1. The financing of additional government expenditures, ΔG,
will take place through: increased borrowing in the capital market, ΔKG;
an expansion, in comparison with the preceding period, in the amount
of money-market financing, ΔMG; raising the level of tax receipts, ΔT;
the returns on the foreign assets which are obtained by new intervention, $(0.035 \Delta RES + 0.055 \Delta B)$; and increasing the size of "other"
government receipts, ΔOG.

The returns on foreign assets require some explanation. A distinction has been made between short- and longer-term investments in
foreign assets. The international monetary reserves are deemed to be
invested short term. Moreover, the possibility exists in this model that
the assets obtained through official exchange-market intervention are
invested for such a long time in national capital markets that they lose
their reserve function. In this way, monetary authorities can evade at
least a part of the opportunity costs of reserves. Consequently, with
respect to the determination of the optimal policy, the right-hand side
of equation (1.9) must be supplemented with the change in such a
longer-term investment, ΔB. It has been assumed that the returns
earned by the central bank through its investments accrue, via the
profit and loss account of the bank, to the government. This means
that these returns enter the political decision process. They are approximated by applying the optimal portfolio approach to both short-
term and longer-term investments of the monetary reserves. The
average returns for the period 1970-76 proved to be 3.5 per cent for
short-term, and 5.5 per cent for longer-term investments. This explains
why the increase in the returns on foreign assets is $0.035 \Delta RES + 0.055$
ΔB.

In the export equation (1.2) the coefficient of world trade, WH,
has not the perhaps expected value of one, because the equation is
formulated in first differences[2]. The relative-price effect occurs with
a lag extending five through eight quarters. The price level of the
competitors of Dutch exporters, PXC, is expressed in Dutch guilders,
as is the own export price, PX. The influence of the - effective -
exchange rate of the guilder, π, on PXC is shown in equation (1.4).
The inclusion of CAP in equation (1.2) reflects the impact of the pressure of demand on the supply-side of exports, whereby exports are
stimulated by overcapacity and its effects on the exporters' terms of
delivery. The interest rate appears, as an indicator of the costs of
trade credit, negatively to influence the size of international trade, as
can be seen in the import equation (1.5). Both the national product and
its price in relation to the import price have the theoretically expected
effects on the imports.

(1) For the list of symbols, their meaning and the sources of the data,
see Appendix II.
(2) An equation for the value of exports has been obtained with a
considerably higher coefficient of determination. This relationship,
however, makes the model unstable and was, for that reason, replaced.

It follows from equation (1.3) that an alteration in the exchange rate cannot simply be expressed by an equivalent relative change in the international terms of trade of a country. Theoretically such an approach would be acceptable when the assumption of completely elastic supply curves is made. For the Netherlands this assumption has to be rejected because of the significant effect of the exchange rate on the export prices in guilders. The *direct* effect of a devaluation of the guilder by 1 per cent point is, five quarters later, an increase of the Dutch export price in guilders by 0.34 per cent point. This outcome justifies the specification of the relation between the exchange rate on the one hand, and the Dutch import and export prices on the other. Of the cost-determining factors only the import price turned out to have an impact on the export price. The turbulent development in the prices of internationally traded goods since 1972 is represented by a dummy variable for the Dutch export price, PXDU. In the import price equation (1.6) the effect of the exchange rate seems to be somewhat exaggerated. The dummy variable, PMDU, follows the trend of world import prices starting with 1973.

Net private capital inflow, CA, for the Netherlands is explained in equation (1.7). The fact that the *change* in the domestic and foreign interest rates appeared to influence capital movements markedly better than their *levels* gives support to the stock as opposed to the flow – adjustment of international capital movements. The reaction of CA to changes in the interest rates – to the extent that a quarterly model can throw light on the matter – is unlagged. In these respects this model displays similarities with portfolio balance models[1].

The inclusion of the three terms following the interest rates in the right-hand side of equation (1.7) is an attempt to portray speculative capital movements. The parity, in later years the central rate, and subsequently the central rate in the framework of the so-called Snake arrangement, are, after having been transformed to an effective exchange rate, represented by π^*. In the event that the level of the actual effective exchange rate surpasses that of π^*, the value of the guilder as appraised by the market exceeds the average value desired by the monetary authorities. As this difference increases, the chance of a revaluation of the guilder rises. As a result, speculative capital inflow will exhibit the tendency to increase[2]. The significantly positive regression coefficient of $(\pi - \pi^*)$ is therefore theoretically sound. It will nevertheless make a difference whether, given the discrepancy between π and π^*, the value of the guilder is rising or falling. In the former case speculative capital inflows will be encouraged; this explains

(1) Genberg (1981) sharply distinguishes between perfect capital mobility, which he defines as an unlagged reaction of capital flows, and perfect substitutability. He shows in that article that – what is now well-known – in portfolio balance models there is a greater possibility of an *effective* intervention than in monetary models. The latter have the added characteristic of perfect substitutability.
(2) See Haberler (1977, p. 120): "It has become increasingly clear and by now should be common knowledge that the method of changing rates by occasional large jumps, the adjustable peg, made it easy and almost riskless for speculators to anticipate changes in the exchange rate".

the positive regression coefficient for the variable $(0.5\Delta\pi 1 + 0.5\Delta\pi 2)$ [1] In fact, it indicates the presence of so-called bandwagon behaviour [1]. In addition, the speculative capital flows may be affected by the development in the level of the country's monetary reserves. In the case of a relatively high value of the guilder on the exchange market as well as an increase in its trend, a fall in the stock of reserves will tend to cause a decline in speculative capital inflows. This is because the positive development in the value of the guilder will then have been realized, at least partially, through official exchange-market intervention in favour of the guilder. This diminishes the importance given to a strong or strengthening guilder. The significant positive regression coefficient for the variable $(0.5\,\Delta RES + 0.5\,\Delta RES1)$ in equation (1.7) is therefore understandable. Of course, the effects of $(\pi - \pi^*)$, $\Delta\pi$ and ΔRES can occur independently of each other. An increase of the reserves, for example, will increase the confidence in the future exchange rate of the guilder and so lead to a rise in capital inflows.

The variable CADU is a dummy variable. It reflects the changes over time, beginning in 1970, in the uncertainty about the future levels of the exchange rates in the world and in the openness of the Netherlands' capital market as well. These two features are of importance for variations in long- as well as short-term capital movements. The value of CADU is positively related to both of these features so that, given the strength of the guilder during this period, a positive association between CADU and CA could be expected. The specification of equation (1.7) is seen to agree with this pattern [2].

The permanent *ex post* equilibrium on the foreign-exchange market leads to equation (1.8) and reflects the intervention function of the monetary reserves. After substitution of the earlier mentioned behavioural equations for ΔX, ΔM, and CA in this equation, only π, π^*, ΔRES and ΔB are not yet classified as either endogenous or predetermined variables. Of these, only π is not an instrument of economic policy, so that the balance-of-payments identity in fact determines the exchange rate. As such, the present model of exchange-rate determination can be typified as a so-called balance-of-payments model (see Genberg (1981)) with, as appeared in the foregoing, elements of a portfolio-balance model. After having carried out the substitutions, the balance-of-payments equation shows that, following a disturbance in the equilibrium of the exchange market, the exchange rate depends in the short run on - the determinants of - net capital inflow and intervention policy. Only after a number of quarters have elapsed is there a reaction from the real sphere and its feed-back to the exchange rate.

(1) This effect is characterized by elastic expectations with respect to the exchange rate.
(2) The equation for capital inflows described here was by no means the best result on statistical grounds. The simulation results of the model appeared to be very sensitive to the specification of the equation for CA. In this regard equation (1.7) was superior.

Table 1.1 - Submodel of the international economic relations

$$\Delta G \equiv \Delta KG + \Delta MG + \Delta T + 0.035 \; \Delta RES + 0.055 \; \Delta B + \Delta OG \qquad (1.1)$$

$$\Delta X = 0.175 \; \Delta PX - 0.236 \left[0.125 \; (\Delta PX5 + \Delta PX6) + 0.25 \; \Delta PX7+ \right.$$
$$ (7.15) \qquad (2.89)$$
$$\left. + 0.5 \; \Delta PX8 \right] + 0.230 \left[0.125 \; (\Delta PXC5 + \Delta PXC6) + 0.25 \; \Delta PXC7+ \right.$$
$$ (2.65)$$
$$\left. + 0.5 \; \Delta PXC8 \right] + 0.572 \quad CAP2 + 0.247 \; \Delta WH - 0.658 \; S1 \qquad (1.2)$$
$$ (2.73) \qquad\qquad (2.88) \qquad\quad (2.75)$$

$$R^2 = 0.68; \; D.W. = 2.49; \; \rho = 0.56$$
$$(3.97)$$

$$\Delta PX = 0.712 \; (0.6 \; \Delta PM + 0.2 \quad PM1 + 0.2 \; \Delta PM2)$$
$$ (13.05)$$

$$-0.343 \; (0.25 \; \Delta\pi3 + 0.25 \; \Delta\pi4 + 0.5 \; \Delta\pi5) + 0.477 \; PXDU \qquad (1.3)$$
$$(2.31) \qquad\qquad\qquad\qquad\qquad (3.34)$$

$$R^2 = 0.97; \; D.W. = 2.01; \; \rho = 0.50$$
$$(3.47)$$

$$\Delta PXC = -1.112 \; \Delta\pi + 0.921 \; \Delta PXCM \qquad (1.4)$$
$$ (51.97) \qquad (63.59)$$

$$R^2 = 1.00; \; D.W. = 2.05; \; \rho = 0.75$$
$$(6.87)$$

$$\Delta M = 0.151 \; \Delta PM + 0.422 \; (0.5 \; \Delta YRB1 + 0.5 \; \Delta YRB2)$$
$$ (6.45) \qquad\quad (5.17)$$

$$-0.106 \quad (0.8 \; \Delta PM4 + 0.2 \; \Delta PM5) + 0.237 \; \cdot (0.8 \; \Delta \; PY4+$$
$$(3.83) \qquad\qquad\qquad\qquad (3.83)$$

$$+ 0.2 \; \Delta PY5) - 0.238 \; (0.6 \; \Delta R + 0.2 \; \Delta R1 + 0.2 \; \Delta R2)$$
$$ (2.67)$$

$$+ 1.217 \; S2 + 1.871 \; S4 + 0.903$$
$$(2.78) \qquad (4.30) \qquad (3.55)$$

$$R^2 = 0.81; \; D.W. = 2.02; \; \rho = -0.55$$
$$(4.02)$$

$$\Delta PM = 0.544\,\Delta PM1 - 0.430\,(0.3\,\Delta\pi2 + 0.7\,\Delta\pi3)$$
$$(9.86) \qquad\qquad (3.00)$$

$$-0.649\,(0.6\,\Delta\pi4 + 0.4\,\Delta\pi5) + 1.546\,PMDU + 0.273 \qquad\qquad (1.6)$$
$$(5.19) \qquad\qquad\qquad (11.37) \qquad\qquad (2.17)$$

$$R^2 = 0.97;\ D.W. = 2.11$$

$$CA = 1.462\,\Delta R - 0.999\,\Delta RE + 0.506\,(\pi-\pi*)$$
$$(8.86) \qquad (7.30) \qquad\quad (3.40)$$

$$+ 0.318\,(0.5\,\Delta\pi1 + 0.5\,\Delta\pi2) + 1.449\,(0.5\,\Delta RES +$$
$$(1.87) \qquad\qquad\qquad\qquad (6.24)$$

$$+ 0.5\,\Delta RES1) + 1.020\,CADU - 0.491\,S2 - 0.679\,S4$$
$$(3.37) \qquad\qquad (2.29) \qquad\quad (3.17)$$

$$- 2.839$$
$$(1.69) \qquad\qquad\qquad\qquad\qquad\qquad\qquad\qquad (1.7)$$

$$R^2 = 0.82;\ D.W. = 2.05;\ \rho = 0.93$$
$$(15.35)$$

$$\Delta X - \Delta M + \Delta PIT + CA - CA1 \equiv \Delta RES - \Delta RES1 + \Delta B - \Delta B1 \qquad\qquad (1.8)$$

$$\Delta\pi \equiv \pi - \pi1 \qquad\qquad (1.9)$$

$$LR \equiv \Delta X - \Delta M + \Delta PIT + LR1 \qquad\qquad (1.10)$$

APPENDIX II
List of symbols, sources and calculation methods

The symbols are listed in alphabetical order. A symbol preceded by " " indicates that first differences were used. A variable marked with an asterisk stands for its desired time path. The data have mainly been taken from the following sources: Central Bureau of Statistics, *Maand-schrift* (Monthly Bulletin), The Hague; Central Planning Bureau, *Centraal Economisch Plan 1978*, The Hague; The Netherlands Bank, *Kwartaalbericht* (Quarterly Bulletin), Amsterdam; and International Monetary Fund, *International Financial Statistics*, Washington, D.C. In the following these publications will be referred to as CBS, CPB, DNB and IMF, respectively. All stock and flow variables are in billions of guilders.

π Effective exchange rate of the guilder (quarterly average: 1970=100). Calculation for the period 1966-71: first the series for the nominal exchange rate was determined, where the rate in a particular quarter was set equal to the average of the rates with respect to the U.S. dollar at the end of the current quarter and that of the preceding quarter. By setting the rate obtained in this way for the first quarter of 1971 equal to the average effective rate for that quarter, the series is transformed with the effective rate as base. The source of the data till 1971, and the average effective rates since 1973, is the IMF. The average effective rates for the years 1971 and 1972 were taken from Rhomberg (1976).

π^* Desired effective exchange rate of the guilder (quarterly average). Calculation technique: first the series of desired *nominal* exchange rates was constructed. Up until the second quarter of 1971 this consists of the parity, and after December 1971 of the central rate of the guilder, expressed in U.S. dollars. After 1973 (II) the central rate of the guilder, expressed in German marks and resulting from the Snake arrangement, has been used. Source: DNB. Next, the resulting series has been transformed to the desired effective exchange rate by dividing the actual nominal exchange rate for each quarter by the desired nominal exchange rate, and then multiplying by the actual effective exchange rate of the guilder.

B   Volume of international monetary reserves efficiently invested so that the function of reserve asset is lost. Generated by applying the optimal control techniques.

CA   Net private capital inflow, including banking transactions. Source: DNB. For the years 1966 and 1967 the values are extracted from the Annual Reports for 1967 and 1968 of the Netherlands Bank.

CADU Dummy variable for the explanation of CA. During the period 1970-76, which can roughly be characterized as a time of a floating, or of expectations of a floating guilder with respect to the U.S. dollar, CADU has been given the value 2. In the years when the Netherlands' capital inflows were moderated through the temporary installation of the so-called "obligatiecircuit" (bond circuit) CADU has been set equal to 1, whereas in 1973, the year of turbulence for the exchange rate, CADU has been increased with 1.

CAP   Indicator for the size of unused capacity. Calculation: YRP - YR.

G   Nominal government expenditures. Source: DNB.

KG   Amount of the government's financial deficit covered by borrowing in the capital market. Source: DNB.

LR   Balance on current account (cash basis). Source: The Netherlands Bank, *Annual Report 1967* and *Annual Report 1968*, for the quarterly figures for 1966 through 1968; DNB for the other quarters.

M   Nominal imports of goods and services (cash basis). Source:DNB.

MG   Government's liquidity shortage. Source: DNB.

OG   "Other" government receipts minus the paper profits on international monetary reserves. Source of the "other" receipts: DNB.

PIT   Foreign net primary incomes and income transfers. Source: DNB.

PM   Import price index. Source for annual figures (1970=100): Central Bureau of Statistics, *Nationale Rekeningen (National Accounts)* This series has been converted to quarterly values[1].

PMDU Dummy variable for the explanation of PM. Based on the series of the change in the world import price. Source: IMF.

PX   Export price index. Source for annual data (1979=100): Central Bureau of Statistics, *Nationale Rekeningen (National Accounts)*. This series has been converted to quarterly figures[1].

PXC   Index of the price of competing world exports expressed in guilders (1970=100). This series has been supplied directly by the Central Planning Bureau.

PXCM Price index for competing world exports expressed in foreign currency. Calculated as: $PXCM = (PXC.\pi)/100$.

PXDU Dummy variable for explaining the behaviour of PX. Based on the series of the change in the world export price. Source: IMF.

PY   Price index for gross national product in market prices (1970=100). Calculated as: $100.Y/YR$.

(1) By means of the method developed by Doornbosch and Lisman (1968).

RE Interest rate on the foreign money market. Approximated by the net yield on three-month Euro-dollar deposits (percentage; average of the final month of the quarter). Source: DNB.

RES Stock of international monetary reserves corrected for the allocation of SDRs as well as for changes due to revaluations. Source: DNB.

R Interest rate on the domestic money market. Approximated by the rate for three-month loans to local authorities (percentage; average of the final month of the quarter). Source: DNB.

Si Dummy variable for the i-th quarter (i = 1, 2, 3, 4).

TG Government's financial deficit. Calculated as: KG + MG.

T Nominal tax receipts of the government. Source: DNB.

X Nominal exports of goods and services (cash basis). Source: DNB.

Y Nominal gross national product measured in market prices. The values were supplied directly by the Central Planning Bureau.

YB Nominal disposable income. Approximated by: Y - T.

YR Real gross national product measured in market prices (1970=100). The figures were supplied directly by the Central Planning Bureau.

YRB Real disposable income. Calculated as: 100.YB/PY.

YRP Indicator for YR in the case of full employment. Calculated by interpolation of the series for YR using the so-called "peak-to-peak" method.

REFERENCES

Akhtar, M. and Spence Hilton, R., "Effects of exchange rate uncertainty on German and U.S. trade", *Federal Reserve Bank of New York Quarterly Review*, Spring 1984, pp. 7-16.

Amman, H.M. and Jager, H., "Endogenous target values in the linear-quadratic control model; an extension and application", *Research Memorandum*,No. 8418, Department of Economics, Amsterdam, 1984.

Amman, H.M. and Jager, H., "Modeling a crawling peg exchange-rate system for the Dutch economy; an application of optimal control theory", *Research Memorandum*, no. 8515, Department of Economics, Amsterdam, 1985.

Bergsten, C.F. and Cline, W.R., "Trade policy in the 1980s", *Policy Analyses in International Economics*, No. 3, Washington, 1982.

Bergsten, C.F. and Williamson, J., "Exchange rates and trade policy", in Cline, W.R., (ed.), *Trade policy in the 1980s*, Washington, 1983, pp. 99-120.

Doornbosch, R. and Lisman, J.H., "Afleiding van kwartaalcijfers uit jaartotalen", (Derivation of quarterly data from yearly data), *Statistica Neerlandica*, Vol. 22, pp. 199-205.

Emminger, O., "The search for a more stable international monetary system", in Wallich, H.C., et al., *World money and national policies*, New York, 1983, pp. 17-33.

Friedlaender, A.F., "Macro policy goals in the postwar period; a study in revealed preference", *Quarterly Journal of Economics*, Vol. LXXXVII, 1973, pp. 25-43.

Genberg, H., "Effects of central bank intervention in the foreign exchange market", *IMF Staff Papers*, Vol. 28 (1981), pp. 451-476.

Grauwe, P. de, "What are the scope and limits of fruitful international monetary cooperation?", in von Furstenberg (ed.), G.M., *International money and credit: the policy rôles*, Washington, 1983, pp. 374-408.

Grauwe, P. de, and Fratianni, M., "Economic interdependence since the early seventies", *International Economics Research Paper*, No. 43, Centrum voor Economische Studiën, Leuven, 1984.

Group of Thirty, *The problems of exchange rates: a policy statement*, New York, 1982.

Haberler, G., "How important is control over international reserves?", in Mundell, R.A. and Polak, J.J., *The new international monetary system*, New York, 1977.

International Monetary Fund, *Annual Report 1983*, Washington,D.C.,1983.

Jager, H., *De behoefte aan internationale monetaire reserves als uit-vloeisel van optimale economische politiek* (The need for inter-national reserves consequent upon optimal economic policy), Dis-sertation, Groningen, 1981.

Jager, H., "Optimal exchange-rate policy in an open economy", *De Economist*, Vol. 130, 1982, pp. 228-263.

Jager, H., "Flexible exchange rates and national monetary policies: a comment", in L. Tsoukalis (1985).

Jager, H. and de Jong, E., "On export performance and export elastic-ities; a macro-economic approach", *De Economist*, Vol. 132, 1984, pp. 224-231.

Kenen, P.B., "Floats, glides and indicators: a comparison of methods for changing exchange rates", *Journal of International Economics*, Vol. 5, 1975, pp. 107-152.

Kessler, G.A. "De invloed van het Nederlandse monetaire beleid en wisselkoersbeleid op de ontwikkeling van de werkgelegenheid", *Maandschrift Economie*, Vol. 45, 1981, pp. 53-80.

Mayer, H., "The theory and practice of floating exchange rates and the rôle of official exchange-rate intervention", *BIS Economic Papers*, No. 5, Basle, 1982.

Meltzer, A.H., "Cures that are worse than the disease", *Financial Times*, August 22, 1984.

Morgan Guaranty, "The firm dollar", *World Financial Markets*, July 1983, pp. 1-13.

Pindyck, R.S., *Optimal planning for economic stabilization*, Amsterdam, 1973.

Shafer, J.R. and Loopesko, B.E., "Floating exchange rates after ten years", *Brookings Papers on Economic Activity I*, 1983, pp. 1-86.

Swoboda, A.K., "Exchange rate regimes and U.S.-European policy interdependence", *IMF Staff Papers*, Vol. 30, 1983, pp. 75-112.

Thygesen, N., "Exchange-rate experiences and policies of small coun-tries: some European examples of the 1970s", *Essays in Inter-national Finance*, No. 136, Princeton, 1979.

Thygesen, N., "Flexible exchange rates and national monetary policies", in Tsoukalis, L. (1985).

Tsoukalis, L. (ed.), Europe, America and the World Economy, Oxford and New York, 1985 (forthcoming).

Williamson, J., "The crawling peg in historical perspective", in Williamson, J. (ed.), *Exchange rates rules; the theory, per-formance and prospects of the crawling peg*, London and Basingstoke, 1981, pp. 3-30.

9. POLICIES AND RESPONSIBILITIES OF THE INTERNATIONAL MONETARY FUND: BACK TO BASICS

T. de Vries

1. INTRODUCTION

In spite of two major amendments to the Articles of Agreement of the International Monetary Fund (IMF), its rôle remains to a large degree defined by its purposes as set out in the original Article I. These purposes appear today in the amended Articles exactly as they were agreed at Bretton Woods and deserve to be quoted in full:

a) To promote international monetary cooperation through a permanent institution which provides the machinery for consultation and colla-boration on international monetary problems.

b) To facilitate the expansion and balanced growth of international trade, and to contribute thereby to the promotion and maintenance of high levels of employment and real income and to the development of the productive resources of all members as primary objectives of economic policy.

c) To promote exchange stability, to maintain orderly exchange arrange-ments among members, and to avoid competitive exchange deprecia-tion.

d) To assist in the establishment of a multilateral system of payments in respect of current transactions between members and in the elimina-tion of foreign exchange restrictions which hamper the growth of world trade.

e) To give confidence to members by making the general resources of the Fund temporarily available to them under adequate safeguards, thus providing them with opportunity to correct maladjustments in their balance of payments without resorting to measures destructive of national or international prosperity.

Monetary Conditions for Economic Recovery, ed. by C. van Ewijk and J.J. Klant

f) In accordance with the above, to shorten the duration and lessen the degree of disequilibrium in the international balances of payments of members.

In less legal language and with the addition of some interpretative phrases these purposes can also be summarized as follows:

a) The Fund must be a center for international monetary cooperation to deal with monetary problems that may arise within its field of action.
b) Members are obligated to maintain orderly exchange arrangements and avoid competitive exchange depreciation, but they are not bound (nor were they bound at Bretton Woods) to any particular exchange rate regime.
c) In collaboration with the Fund, members are expected to eliminate payments restrictions on *current* transactions.
d) The Fund shall provide members with temporary conditional credit to facilitate but not to avoid balance of payments adjustment.
e) The Fund has a rôle in the provision of international liquidity and it shall "meet the need, as and when it arises for a supplement to existing reserve assets". This objective appeared at the head of some twelve articles dealing with special drawing rights (SDRs) that were added to the existing ones in 1969 by the First Amendment[1].

Thus, the Fund is a highly specialized institution and this specialization has enabled it to remain an effective and businesslike organization, qualities not so common among international institutions. These same features have also enabled the Fund to remain free to a surprisingly large degree from purely political pressures. It should be noted the purposes do not include "saving the world", contrary to the apparent assumption of those who constantly call upon the Fund to deal with any unsolved international economic problem around since the Fund is such an efficient institution. Nor do the purposes include the provi-

(1) After the Second Amendment this objective appears, slightly redrafted, as Article XVIII, Section 1.

sion of long-term or development finance for which purpose the International Bank for Reconstruction and Development was specifically created.

I shall argue that a great deal of innovation and (additional) constructive activity by the Fund is possible well within the framework of its present purposes. For this reason I have added the words "Back to Basics" to the title of this paper.

2.   EXCHANGE ARRANGEMENTS

Section c) of the Fund's purposes quoted above in fact deals with exchange rates. It is noteworthy that this provision, dating from 1944, is fully applicable to the present situation.

Indeed, it is a mistake to describe the exchange rate regime agreed at Bretton Woods as one of fixed exchange rates. Exchange rates were to play an important rôle in the adjustment process. The system envisaged at Bretton Woods did contain elements of a doctrine as to how payments equilibrium was to be maintained. It was well analyzed by Marcus Fleming many years ago (see Fleming (1963, 1978)).

The new orthodoxy as established at Bretton Woods was the exact opposite of the old faith of the gold standard. Whereas under the gold standard manipulation of internal demand played a vital rôle in maintaining payments equilibrium, the essential element of the new doctrine was that national authorities were to be free to pursue purely domestic objectives, and in particular policies designed to maintain full employment without price inflation. The maintenance of external equilibrium was to be assured by three main instruments:

a) exchange rate adjustments (if different policy preferences had led to disequilibrium in external payments);

b) the use of exchange controls to regulate capital outflows, and

c) temporarily, during a transition period, restrictions on imports.

Indeed, in the late 1940s and early 1950s these three instruments were all used in order to maintain or restore external equilibrium.

Perhaps the importance of the rôle that exchange rate adjustment was to play can best be illustrated by a quote from Lord Keynes' speech in the House of Lords on the working of the proposed International Monetary Fund:

"In future, the external value of sterling shall conform to its internal value as set by our own domestic policies, and not the other way around" (see Keynes (1950)).

It would be hard to give a clearer expression to the predominance of domestic policies and to the vital rôle of the exchange rate in equilibrating payments between national economies that might pursue less than fully harmonized objectives.

The second major instrument was to be the restriction of capital outflows. It should be recalled that the post-war period was expected to be one in which the US capital markets would have an irresistable attraction for European investors. Instead of having to raise interest rates to prevent capital outflows, or to be forced to follow US domestic policies which were feared to be deflationary, the other industrial countries were allowed to shield themselves by the use of effective capital controls. Import controls, however, were thought of only as a temporary expedient of last resort. There are certain striking similarities between the preoccupations of 1944 and today's concerns.

In fact, however, the system developed quite differently from what was envisaged at Bretton Woods. As the European countries became aware of the inefficiencies produced by the restrictions on intra-European trade and began a process of dismantling them, the exchange control apparatus necessary to administer capital controls was also gradually dismantled. Moreover, instead of attracting capital, the United States became an exporter of capital and especially of official assistance in the form of Marshall aid. In these new circumstances, the distinction between controls on trade and controls on capital movements seemed less important, and capital controls were dismantled along with controls on the international flow of goods and services. This development was in clear contradiction with what had been envisaged at Bretton Woods, and it vitiated the mechanism that had been envisioned for the maintenance of payments equilibrium in some of its essential elements.

It was not until the early 1960s that it was discovered that in a world of free capital movements, the system envisaged at Bretton Woods could no longer work. The discovery was made on the occasion of the revaluation of the mark and the guilder in 1961. Since the small upward adjustments in the exchange rates were generally considered to be insufficient to correct the payments surpluses of these two countries, they resulted in large destabilizing capital movements. The official world was now squarely confronted with the problem created by the almost riskless opportunities for speculation offered by the combination of free capital movements and an exchange rate regime with as its central feature an "adjustable peg". This term together with a description of the flaw of a system combining these two elements appeared in writings by Meade dating back to 1951, but the difficulties had been already analyzed in 1940 by Graham (see Meade (1951); Graham (1940); Friedman (1953)).

Contrary to Meade, however, who had concluded that the way out of the difficulties was a system of "variable exchange rates", it became official policy to freeze exchange rates altogether. International payments equilibrium was henceforth to be maintained by means of the adjustment of domestic policies.

It is remarkable that the world, and Great Britain in particular, thus moved, shortly after the restoration of convertibility, to a system that in its essential elements was the exact opposite of what had been envisaged at Bretton Woods, and that what came to be called the "Bretton Woods exchange rate system" was in fact widely different from what had originally been agreed. Contrary to what Keynes had stated, in the 1960s the British authorities tried again through domestic restrictive policies to make the internal value of sterling conform to the external value that happened to have been set. But this "gold standard" policy was of course bound to fail, given the priorities of society in the 1960s.

The result was a series of crises. It was attempted to overcome each such crisis by financing rather than by adjustment, until the payments disequilibria had become so large that major exchange rate adjustments became unavoidable. As correctly foreseen by the authorities, however, discretionary exchange rate changes under conditions of free capital movements provoked insurmountable disturbances ending in the collapse of existing arrangements. The outcome was the floating of exchange rates between the world's major currencies after a period of profound confusion.

What is surprising with hindsight, is that it took almost a decade, namely from the first sterling crisis in 1964 until the general adoption of floating rates by the major countries in 1973, for this result to be reached.

Looking back over a much longer period, a basic tendency toward an increase in exchange rate flexibility can be noted. The gold standard of the years 1875-1914 was characterized by immutable exchange rates. In the system envisaged at Bretton Woods exchange rate changes played a significant rôle, but they were to be used only with the explicit approval of the international community as embodied in the IMF. In the post-1973 system it is hard to discern any guiding principle for the exchange rate movements among the major currencies.

The increase in exchange rate flexibility among the major currencies is the natural companion of the development of the nation state, and its increasing involvement with the national economy. Only small states, aware of the constraints on their sovereignty in view of their limited power, are now willing to give up national monetary autonomy in favour of fixed exchange rates with some major trading partner. The theory of the optimum currency area provides us with good reasons why the choice made between these two alternatives should come out differently for small (i.e., most) countries than for large ones.

In the long-run, one may argue, increasing interdependence is incompatible with exchange rate flexibility. That may be so. This conclusion has little practical value, however, if applied only to exchange rates. The same forces that increase interdependence also render the nation state inadequate as time progresses. Yet it would take a major shift in the way societies look at themselves and at the nation state, and fundamental changes in political organisation, before these forces also bring about exchange rate stability.

3. ELIMINATION OF PAYMENT RESTRICTIONS

Over the years the Fund has been diligent in the pursuit of the elimination of payments restrictions on current transactions. This purpose as well as the Fund's activity in this field has the objective of avoiding a return to the damaging exchange controls of the 1930s with their exploitation as a means of political domination and their harmful effect on economic welfare. The continued success of this Fund endeavour is certainly of great importance.

Yet, as briefly indicated above, it is my view that this process has gone too far, in that it has been extended to the almost complete liberalisation of capital transactions along with the current ones. This development has produced another striking reversal of the priorities established at Bretton Woods. Instead of the priority accorded there to the proper functioning of the goods markets at the expense of freedom for capital transfers, today capital movements are given priority, and goods markets have to function as best they can in light of the exchange rates that result. If this produces too large disequilibria in the goods markets, it is necessary to resort to "voluntary restraint" or other restrictive and protectionist measures. In my opinion this reordering of priorities is damaging to world welfare.

Could the predominant rôle of capital movements in the determination of exchange rates be remedied by greater surveillance so as to arrive at a harmonization of policy between the major countries? It is not immediately obvious that surveillance of general economic policies is the appropriate instrument for dealing with excessive capital flows. Nor is the experience with surveillance since 1960 very encouraging. Moreover, the value of surveillance is not always beyond question. At present, it is doubtful that the world would be better off if the US monetary authorities were prevailed upon to pursue an easier monetary policy without first having overcome the difficulties by way of a reduction of their budget deficit, and many other countries know these difficulties at first hand. Let it be noted in passing that the resulting dependence of the European countries on US monetary policies is due to their failure to unite into a federal state, a failure that has also produced a loss of meaningful European independence in most other important policy areas - economic, political, military, etcetera.

A more direct approach than the roundabout way of surveillance, and hence perhaps more promising, would be to focus attention on the appropriate regime for capital transfers. The original Articles approached this matter from the angle of the control of capital transfers, and they are very clear on the subject. Even after two amendments, Article VI, Section 1 states flatly:

"A member may not use the Fund's resources to meet a large or sustained outflow of capital...., and the Fund may request a member to exercise controls to prevent such use of the resources of the Fund. If, after receiving such a request, a member fails to exercise appropriate controls, the Fund may declare the member ineligible to use the resources of the Fund".

This is strong language indeed. In the first place, this Article, dating from 1944, clearly assumed that members, or at least members with a deficit in international payments, would be able to put into operation a system of effective controls to prevent the outflow of capital. In addition, the Fund had the right to request a member to exercise those controls in order to limit the capital outflows, and failure by the member to do so could result in a decision to prohibit any further use by the member of the resources of the Fund.

Clear as the provisions are, they were still not enough for the US authorities. At the time (1946), they believed, not without reason, that the United States would be the principal surplus country, and consequently would have to finance use of Fund resources by deficit countries. They also wished to make sure beyond any doubt that those resources would not be used to finance capital movements from Europe to the United States. Accordingly, the US Executive Director requested a formal interpretation of the Fund's Articles on the subject.

The interpretation requested was adopted by the Executive Directors on September 26, 1946, that is, almost immediately after the Fund had started its operations. It restated the same principle in other words:

"The .... authority to use the resources of the Fund is limited to.... temporary assistance in financing balance of payments deficits *on current account*" (Decision no. 72-1, reprinted inter alia in *Selected Decisions of the International Monetary Fund*, Washington: International Monetary Fund, 1976).

By mid 1969, however, world opinion on capital movements had changed, and the Executive Directors followed suit by "clarifying" that their previous interpretation, prohibiting the use of Fund resources for capital transfers, should now be taken to mean the opposite:

"The Executive Directors decide by way of clarification that decision No. 71-2 does not preclude the use of the Fund resources for capital transfers". (Decision no. 1238-(61/43), reprinted in *Selected Decisions*, op. cit.).

This "clarification" is less curious than it might seem at first sight. At a time when the industrial countries had in fact decided to adopt a system of fixed exchange rates and free capital movements, and were embarking on a major effort to make that system work by means of policy co-ordination, it did make sense for the Fund to support countries defending an existing exchange rate through domestic restrictive measures, and to make its resources also available to help such a country ward off attacks of speculative capital. We have here an example of the flexibility, in the pursuit of its basic objectives that the Fund has exhibited during most of its history, and of its capacity to adapt to changing circumstances, which is all part of the secret of its success.

Nevertheless, I submit that the time has now arrived for a re-evaluation of the regime for capital transfers that would be most beneficial to world economic welfare. The abolition of capital controls was among the major factors that made the exchange rate regime foreseen at Bretton Woods unworkable. Even more important, the predominant rôle of capital movements today in determining exchange rates between the world's major currencies is harmful. It leaves the monetary authorities helpless in the face of enormous flows of private capital. Intervention on the exchange markets can at best have a marginal influence as official liquidity is overwhelmed by private international liquidity.

Moreover, and certainly not least important, these uncontrolled private capital movements have, under the pressure of competition, resulted in widely excessive short-term credits to developing countries. The outcome is the debt crisis with which we are now saddled, and which will be with us for a number of years to come. Private capital movements have led to unsustainable economic expansion in LDCs and to investment in inappropriate directions, that must now be corrected by a painful and excessively deflationary adjustment process. Moreover excessive bank credit has even endangered the domestic monetary system of some of the major industrial countries, including the United

States, although a major and concerted effort has so far been successful in avoiding a banking crisis.

In view of these developments, it is surprising how little attention is being given to the question of an appropriate medium-term regime with respect to capital transfers. The experience to date hardly increases in an international capital market to produce anything approaching satisfactory results. It is often argued that private bankers are at least as able as officials to judge the creditworthiness of individual countries and their need for capital transfers. That argument misses the point, however. The objective of the private bankers is to maximize their private profits and not to ensure the proper working of the international monetary system, and it has become clear that the profit motive is not sufficient to ensure by itself the smooth functioning of the system.

This same argument is at the root of a fruitless discussion about whether present exchange rates are "right" or "wrong". Those who argue that they are right argue that present exchange rates produce market equilibrium. That argument implicitly assumes all capital transactions to be desirable. Those who are of the opinion that present exchange rates are wrong look mainly at current transactions. They are saying that current transactions plus some "desirable" amount of capital transfers are in disequilibrium. Rather than being an argument over exchange rates, this is an argument over what are appropriate and desirable capital transfers. It would help the international discussion if it were more clearly focussed on this central aspect of the question.

In fact, given their present crude instruments, monetary authorities are faced with an impossible choice. To meet the problem they have been forced to adopt an approach that shows some similarities with the nuclear stalemate. By means of a financial Balance of Terror they try to avoid both present collapse and future overlending. Obviously such a policy involves brinkmanship. On the one hand they must maintain the system at the brink of collapse. Banks must not be "bailed out". They must relearn the lesson of the inter-war period and suffer losses on their international credit portfolio so as to keep them from resuming the reckless lending of the 1970s as soon as the crisis is passed. On the other hand, the monetary authorities must, of course, avoid a banking crisis in the industrial world and also see to it that the developing countries do not collapse under a crushing and painful adjustment burden. At the same time, the threat of bankruptcy must continue to hang over these countries in order to provide an incentive for continuing the necessary but painful adjustment process.

The difficult task of the authorities, having to juggle with these various elements all at the same time is rendered hopeless by the experience from the past that, even if learned, the lesson will be again forgotten by the banks in a relatively short period. While in the first half of the post-war period international bank credit played a minor rôle, as banks still remembered the losses suffered in the 1930s on international credits granted in the 1920s, by the 1970s this lesson had been completely forgotten. Worse, the same cycle has been observed time and again over many centuries, and the following quote from a historical study may serve as a warning:

"As deposits poured in, it became increasingly difficult to find suitable investments... Rather than refuse deposits, the Medici succumbed to the temptation of seeking an outlet for surplus cash in making dangerous loans to princes. This policy proved to be their undoing as it had caused the ruin of the Peruzzi in the fourteenth century and later brought the Fuggers to the brink of bankruptcy. It seems that there was a general weakness.... to drift from private banking into government finance. Nearly always the results were catastrophic" (see De Roover (1948)).

What is striking is the persistence over many centuries of cycles of overextension of credit and ruin, and the equally persistent belief that "sovereign" borrowers were safer whereas in fact their sovereign power made it easier for them to avoid repayment. A policy of Balance of Terror seems no more likely to succeed in international finance than it did in domestic monetary management, where different methods were adopted in the end.

To remedy this situation Dr. H.J. Witteveen, former Managing Director of the International Monetary Fund, has proposed measures that would both encourage a resumption of international bank lending, but contain features to avoid excess lending (see Witteveen (1983)). To encourage continued international bank lending in present circumstances, he proposes that the Fund be enabled to set up an insurance facility for those bank loans it considers necessary for the success of agreed adjustment programs. The enthusiasm of the banks to make such insured loans is to be regulated by varying the percentage of the loans to be insured and the premium that the banks would pay for this protection.

At the same time, excessive international bank lending is to be avoided by a cooperative effort of the central banks in the main industrial countries amongst themselves, but also involving the Fund, because the effort would affect most member countries of the IMF. This collective action would be two-pronged. First, solvency requirements are to be imposed on the basis of a consolidated balance sheet of the major banks active in international lending (which all have headquarters in the major industrial countries). Second, reserve requirements are to be imposed on all deposits, including Euro-deposits, used to finance or created by this international lending. Their function would be to eliminate or reduce the competitive advantage of Euro-transactions in so far as they escape national regulation at present. They are, however, also to be an instrument to stimulate or restrain international bank lending by a technique well-known from national monetary policy. I believe that this or similar proposals deserve close attention, although they are as yet far from operational.

It should be noted that this proposal differs fundamentally from the many schemes to have some international institution to take over past credits that have gone sour. All these schemes have the basic flaw that they relieve the banks of the burden of past mistakes so that they are free to make new ones. It must also be stated that by recommending Witteveen's proposal for study, my personal position is closer to his than to that of Polak, who has criticized the proposal on the ground that its objectives could be better achieved by "the control of money creation in the main financial centers" (see Polak (1985)). Perhaps, however, their disagreement is more apparent than real as a cooperative effort of the monetary authorities of the main industrial countries is a central feature of the Witteveen approach.

4. TEMPORARY CONDITIONAL FUND CREDIT

So far I have perhaps dealt more with our international monetary system than with the operations of the Fund. The reason is that the rôle of the Fund in most matters discussed so far is essentially a marginal one. A more accurate and more constructive way of making the same point is to note that in these matters the Fund has functioned as a center for international monetary cooperation as envisaged by the Founding Fathers. Discussions on these questions have taken place largely among the monetary authorities of the Fund's members. These discussions have often taken place in one of the Fund's organs, and the Fund has played a crucial rôle in these discussions, not least by the perceptive analytical work of its highly qualified staff. Yet, the Fund's effective operational rôle in most of these areas has been limited by the very nature of these problems.

When we come to the temporary conditional credit that the Fund extends to its members, we enter the heart of its operational activities. We also encounter a great deal of criticism.

Let me first deal with the criticism, which I consider to be in error. It has been suggested that the Fund takes advantage of the balance of payments difficulties of its members to impose harsh adjustment programs on needy countries. This way of putting the matter seems to imply that a country would have the option to carry on without adjustment, if only it could get by without money from the Fund (see Polak (1984)). This is not the case, however. The reason that a country turns to the Fund is that its economic position has become unsustainable. Basic adjustment measures are therefore necessary. Credit from the Fund simply allows the country concerned more time for this adjustment effort so as to make it less painful. The need for adjustment is the result of this country's economic position; it does not follow from any arbitrary decision in favour of harsh principles by the Fund, its major members, or anybody else.

Since 1982 the Fund has moved even further in the direction of ensuring adequate finance for countries implementing reasonable adjustment programs. When the Fund found that its own resources were insufficient to allow adequate time for a reasonable adjustment program to become effective, it cast itself in the rôle of coordinator of balance of payments assistance by a variety of other lenders: commercial banks, export credit guarantee agencies, aid donors, the World Bank, etcetera. In view of the existence of the Balance of Terror described above, the

Fund has for the past two years been put in a position where it could, and in many cases has, prescribed to the various groups of lenders just mentioned how much fresh money each should provide to arrive at the total necessary to finance a reasonable adjustment program. These lenders have been willing to put up the additional credits because the alternative was courting the risk and the blame of causing an international banking crisis.

The extraordinary power in international finance that has thus fallen to the Fund is the consequence of inadequate official control over international lending. In this light, proposals such as that by Witteveen are quite modest. As so often in international monetary affairs, the refusal to adopt relatively modest courses of action because they are considered too radical, in the end leads to crises and to the adoption of far more radical solutions. It is less than convincing to argue in essence that efforts at controling international capital transfers by a cooperative effort are overly ambitious and unnecessary because the Managing Director of the Fund is already determining the amount each group of creditors should lend to particular countries. As has been noted, this power has fallen to him directly as the consequence of the existence of the "Balance of Terror" in international finance, and it is therefore unlikely to last.

Contrary to its public image, the Fund has thus considerably softened the harshness of the adjustment process that otherwise would of necessity have resulted from the cessation of international bank lending. This does not mean, however, that the resulting adjustment process is not painful. Decisions have been made in the past by lenders and borrowers alike on the basis of the expectation of continued rapid economic expansion and negative real interest rates. As actual developments have been very different, many investment decisions have turned out to be unjustified in the new circumstances. So far the economic costs of these past mistakes have been shifted largely to the borrowers. These borrowers have only been able to bear those costs with a supportable degree of discomfort because Fund programs have helped them to eliminate a measure of economic waste, and to define more effective macroeconomic policies.

In designing these programs, the Fund has looked exclusively at finding the right balance between a desirable and effective adjustment path and the amount of finance it could reasonably expect to put together in the manner described above. It has not tried to vary the degree of adjustment it has recommended to individual countries with one eye on the situation in that country and another eye on the level of world activity, and rightly so. If world demand needs to be stimulated, the place to do it would be in those industrial countries that have reasonable control over their economic policies, and certainly not in the countries which the Fund is helping to attain such control. This is what has happened in fact, for the much maligned US budget deficit has had at least one important favourable aspect: it has helped the world to overcome in part the recession which the need for and the resistance against fundamental structural adjustment had brought about. Keynesian budgetary stimulation has been applied where it was most effective, namely in the United States.

The Fund is thus thoroughly engaged in carrying out its central rôle, namely promoting an appropriate balance between adjustment and financing in and for those countries where the economic position has become unsustainable. This was the central operational rôle laid down for it in the Articles of Agreement at Bretton Woods, and it is striking that after much discussion of international monetary reform the Fund has reverted to that central rôle, and on a scale and in a manner that would have been inconceivable only a few years ago.

All this activity does not mean, of course, that there are no problems with regard to temporary conditional credit by the Fund. Given the importance that this rôle has acquired the opposite is the case. One difficult problem facing the Fund is its attitude towards its poorest members that have in fact become long-term debtors of the Fund, as each repayment of a previous credit is financed, and even overfinanced, by credit in connection with a successor program. These countries, many of them African, are too poor to repay the Fund, nor is there any conceivable short-term adjustment program that would make such repayment possible. On the other hand, Fund credits are financed through the monetary reserves that other members keep on deposit with the Fund, and such long-term credits are in clear conflict with the Fund's financial structure, and indeed with its purposes.

5.   THE SDR

As noted in the Introduction, in one area the Fund and its member countries have tried to move beyond the tasks laid down at Bretton Woods, although not beyond the tasks envisaged for the Fund by Lord Keynes, one of its Founding Fathers. I refer, of course, to the creation and management by the Fund of an international reserve asset: the SDR.

At its inception, the SDR can be said to have been created to reinforce the gold-dollar exchange standard which had developed spontaneously in the two decades after World War II. By the middle of the 1960s, it became a predominant point of view that this system was reaching its safe limits in the creation of international liquidity. In 1964, rising foreign exchange reserves held in dollars (that is US liabilities to foreign Central Banks) equalled the value of the declining US gold stock at about US$15 billion. From there on, it was thought that the United States could not continue to provide the system with additional foreign exchange reserves in the form of dollar balances without becoming prone to the risk of a sudden massive demand for the conversion of dollars into gold. As the only existing primary reserve asset into which conversion could take place, namely gold, became insufficient, it had to be supplemented by a second, internationally created, primary reserve asset.

The SDR was to meet the demand for primary reserve assets in two ways. First, through a general allocation of SDRs, all monetary authorities received additional primary reserve assets directly. At the same time and more important, an allocation provided the United States with an additional reserve asset with which to meet the demand for conversion of dollar balances. In fact, a number of requests for conversion of dollars was met by the US authorities by providing SDRs.

The abandonment, however, of predictable and conservative domestic policies by President Johnson, as he continued his domestic programs without raising taxes to finance the Vietnam war, led to a large additional supply of dollars at the same time that preferences shifted in favour of holding more conservatively managed currencies. It had long been recognized that a currency system geared to a reserve center can only function as long as the center pursues conservative and generally approved financial policies. The abandonment of that stance by the United States was another major factor in the downfall of the gold-dollar exchange standard.

But such was (and is) the economic power of the United States, that the fundamental change in the reserve system which now occurred took a very different form from what had generally been expected. The United States severed the link between the international monetary system and gold by refusing to prevent the gold price from rising through further sales from its gold stock. The result was that, at a much higher level, the gold price became subject to volatile and un-predictable fluctuations. As a consequence, gold has now become unable to function as a usable reserve asset.

The outcome of this development was, in the first place, that the international reserve system became more firmly based on the dollar than ever before. Although the D-mark and the yen now play a modest rôle as reserve currencies, the dollar has clearly become the predomi-nant reserve asset, and one on which the system is centered. But a system centered on the dollar alone no longer needs a primary reserve asset to reinforce it. Thus, the basic purpose for which the SDR was created has disappeared and the question has arisen what, if any, its rôle must be in international monetary relations.

A further complication is the gradual discovery that there is a real limit to the willingness of central banks to hold more than a certain proportion of their monetary reserves in claims on the Fund, at least in the form these claims have at present (see Polak (1984)). This con-straint applies to the sum of the two types of claims held by a member of the Fund: SDRs plus what are called "Reserve Positions in the Fund" (RPFs) that accrue to surplus countries as the natural result of the granting of monetary credit by the Fund to debtor members.

There appear to be a number of reasons for this constraint. A first reason is that dollar reserves are anonymous whereas SDRs and RFPs are public. If a currency is under pressure, it is possible for issuing authorities to support it without market knowledge of the fact, or at least of the amount. The use of SDRs, on the contrary, is public knowledge and may lead to an additional loss of confidence in the currency. The problem is compounded if the country would want to use its RPFs through a drawing on the Fund.

A second difficulty is that the Fund requires the existence of a "payments need" for the proper use of claims on the Fund. No matter how often the Fund assures its members that it will apply this test flexibly, its existence nevertheless constitutes a psychological barrier. This latter point is related to the third and perhaps most important aspect, namely that SDRs are not real "money". In order to intervene in financial markets, SDRs have first to be converted into real money, such as dollars, pounds, marks, in which transactions in private markets are conducted. This finding, however, also points toward an important improvement in SDRs that might increase its attractiveness to monetary authorities.

When the SDR was created, it was thought wise to limit its circulation to official institutions, almost exclusively central banks. It now turns out that, in order to be viable in the future, the liquidity of the SDR and its "money-ness", may have to be assured by tranforming it into an asset in which private transactions also take place. In addition to the increased liquidity and anonimity thus provided, it would also make official intervention in currency markets directly with SDRs both possible and practical. This may not be a new idea, although writing in Dutch I pleaded in favour of it already in 1974. Yet the time may now be ripe for renewed study of such action. It might ease a constraint on the financial activities of the Fund produced by the manner in which it is financed: from the reserves of member countries.

6.   SUMMARY AND CONCLUSIONS

While the Fund should continue to operate within the framework of its basic purposes that have served it well over the years, additional constructive action is possible and desirable within that setting.

Apart from domestic developments, exchange rate arrangements have changed a number of times in the post-war period under the pressure of the liberalisation and then the intensification of international capital movements. At present, capital movements are clearly the predominant force determining exchange rates. If the results are considered to be unsatisfactory, improvement must be sought by focusing attention directly on ways to guide international capital transfers rather than seeking to do so by the roundabout way of surveillance over general economic policies. During the past two decades, surveillance has not been a success.

Guidance over capital transfers is even more clearly required in the field of bank credit to developing countries. Its absence has produced a serious debt problem, a near banking crisis, and an excessively painful adjustment process in the debtor countries. For want of better instruments, the monetary authorities, including the Fund, are trying to steer the system by means of a Balance of Terror: debtor countries are kept in a state of near-bankruptcy so as to push them toward continued adjustment, but their precarious state also forces the banks to grant fresh credits so as to avoid breakdown. Through brinkmanship the authorities try to avoid both present collapse and future overlending.

The experience with domestic monetary management over the centuries lead to the conclusion that this effort is unlikely to be successful in the long run. Better policy instruments have been adopted in the domestic system, and have recently been proposed for international monetary arrangements.

Within the existing framework, Fund action has been substantial and constructive. Contrary to popular misunderstanding, the Fund has stretched out and moderated the burden of adjustment. Adjustment is necessary, not because the Fund or anybody else says so, but because the economic position of the country has become unsustainable. A Fund program cum credit does not impose adjustment; it reduces the degree of adjustment that would otherwise come about without the Fund credit. This is even more true as the Fund has cast itself in the rôle of coordinator of balance of payments credit, prompting other groups of lenders into granting fresh credit in conjunction with agreement on a Fund credit arrangement.

With the near disappearance of the monetary rôle of gold, the dollar moved to the center of the international reserve system in the early 1970s. An almost purely dollar-centered system has no need for a primary reserve asset, and there is no clear rôle for the SDR in present arrangements, although matters may change in the future. As a result of the suspension of the convertibility of the dollar and the ending of the gold-dollar standard, the SDR, along with gold, lost its central position in the system.

As neither a dollar system nor a multi-currency system is likely to be permanent, attention should be given by the Fund to increase the liquidity and to improve the monetary properties of the SDR by promoting its private use also.

REFERENCES

Fleming, J.M. (1963), "Developments in the International Payment System", *Staff Papers*, International Monetary Fund, November.

Fleming, J.M. (1978), *Essay on Economic Policy*, New York.

Graham, F.D. (1940), "Achilles Heels in Monetary Standards", *American Economic Review*, March.

Graham, F.D. (1953), "The Case for Flexible Exchange Rates", in Friedman, M., *Essays in Positive Economics*, Chicago.

Keynes, J.M. (1944), Speech on May 23, 1944; reprinted under the title "The International Monetary Fund" in Harris, S.E. (ed.), *The New Economics*, New York, 1950.

Meade, J.E. (1951), *The Balance of Payments*, London.

Meade, J.E. (1955), "The Case for Variable Exchange Rates", *The Three Banks Review*, September.

Polak, J.J. (1982), "The Present Status of the International Monetary System", mimeo.

Polak, J.J. (1985), "The Rôle of the Fund", in *Problems of the International Monetary System*, Federal Reserve Bank of Boston.

Roover, R. de (1948), *The Medici Bank*, New York.

Witteveen, H.J. (1983), "Developing a New International Monetary System - The Long Term View", The 1983 Per Jacobson Lecture, Washington.

PART III

MONETARY CONDITIONS FOR ECONOMIC RECOVERY

10.   LESSONS OF THE MONETARIST EXPERIMENT

N. Kaldor

1.   INTRODUCTION

The great revival of "monetarism" in the 1970s, culminating in the adoption of the strict prescriptions of the monetarist creed by a number of Western Governments at the turn of the decade – particularly by President Reagan's administration in the U.S. and Mrs. Thatcher's in Great Britain – will, I am sure, go down in history as one of the most curious episodes, comparable only to the periodic outbreaks of mass hysteria (such as the witch hunts) of the Middle Ages. Indeed I know of no other instance where an utterly false doctrine concerning the causation of economic events had such a sweeping success in a matter of a few years without any attempt to place it in the framework of accepted theory concerning the manner of operation of economic forces in a market economy.

The central assertion of monetarism – assiduously propagated for a number of years by a single American economist, Professor Milton Friedman of Chicago – is that an excessive increase in the supply of money, caused by the decisions of the note-issuing authority, the Central Bank, was the main, if not the sole, cause of inflation; that the cyclical fluctuations of the economy are reflections of the irregularities and aberrations with which the money supply is increased by the monetary authority, who are responsible also for distortions in the structure of production caused by imperfect anticipation of the delayed effects of increases in the money supply on prices. Since on account of unstable and highly variable "time lags" it is hopeless to expect that the monetary authorities can prevent such instabilities by well-timed measures (or compensate for them by well-timed counter-measures), the only safe rule to follow is to secure a modest and stable rate of increase in the rate of growth of the money stock which by itself will

Monetary Conditions for Economic Recovery, ed. by C. van Ewijk and J.J. Klant
© 1985, Martinus Nijhoff Publishers, Dordrecht. All rights reserved.

serve to stabilize the value of money and gradually eliminate cyclical instabilities.

2. THE EVOLUTION OF MONEY

The basic error, which was widespread long before Friedman and the new monetarism, lies in the assumption which regards the money supply as the *source* of the demand for goods and services. Money was invented at a fairly early stage of human development – it was an essential by-product of the development of a social economy, which meant specialisation of individual "agents" and the division of labour, with its concomitant, the emergence of markets which provided for regular exchanges of the goods produced by one person as against goods produced by others. The use of an intermediary "medium of exchange" made it very much easier to exchange things between partici-pants especially in circumstances where the number of different kinds of goods and services which the typical market participant bought to satisfy his own needs were far more numerous than the number of things which he produced and offered for sale; and where there were numerous buyers and sellers of each commodity competing with one another. The advantages of "indirect exchange" through a universally accepted medium of exchange must have become obvious at a very primitive stage of evolution, and the qualities needed for a suitable medium – things in general demand and stable in exchange value, durable, and for the sake of comfort, also of a high value in relation to bulk (this was the main advantage of precious metals as against oxen or animal skins – each of which is known to have been used as money) marked out the commodities suitable for use as an exchange medium; there was also the advantage of using only one or at most a few com-modities for the purpose which made market transactions much less complicated. The use of a commodity as money meant that there was an extra demand for it, since some of it was always held for purposes of exchange, apart from its other uses.

The demand for money, from the very beginning, was a *reflection* of the demand for commodities, and not the source of that demand. And the value of the money commodity depended, in the longer run at least, on its costs of production, in the same way as the demand for other commodities. With the expansion of the general level of production, the value of monetary transactions through the purchases and sales of goods and services expanded *pari passu*, which made it profitable to expand the production of the money commodity in line with commodities in general. From the very beginning therefore the increase in supply of money in circulation was a response to increased demand and not an autonomous event, though occasionally the supply of the money commodity ran ahead of the increase in the supply of other commodities – as with the gold discovered in the new Spanish colonies of the 16th century – when money could be said to have exerted an autonomous influence on the demand for goods and services. It did so because those who first came into the possession of the new gold were thereby personally enriched, and thus became the source of additional demand for goods and services. But the converse of this proposition was equally true: where the increase in the supply of the money commodity lagged behind, this placed obstacles on economic expansion which historically were gradually overcome with the successive introduction of money substitutes.

This latter development was closely associated with the development of banking. Originally goldsmiths (who possessed strong rooms for the safe keeping of gold and other valuables) developed the facility of accepting gold for safe keeping, and issued deposit certificates to the owners. The latter found it convenient to make payments by means of these certificates, thereby saving the time and trouble of taking gold coins out of the strong room only to have them re-deposited by the recipient of the payment who was likely to have had much the same incentive of keeping valuables deposited for safe keeping. The next step in the evolution towards a credit money system was when the gold-smiths found it convenient to lend money, as well as to accept money on deposit for safe keeping. For the purpose of lending they had to issue their own promissory notes to pay cash to the *bearer* (as distinct from a named depositor) on demand; with this latter development the gold-smiths became bankers, i.e. financial intermediaries between lenders and borrowers. Since real money (gold) was only required on specific occasions (i.e. for making payments abroad or when the nature of the contract specifically provided for payment in cash) the banks found that the amount of such notes issued to borrowers came to exceed many times the amount of gold deposited in their vaults by their lenders – though the total amount they owed to the lenders was always larger than the total amount lent to the borrowers. The apparent contradiction between the formal solvency of the banks where the volume of credits granted to borrowers was compared with their total obligation to their depositors, and their apparent insolvency when the value of the promissory notes issued was compared with the amount of gold held for their encashment was not properly understood for a surprisingly long period, and gave rise to prolonged controversies between those (like Edwin Cannan) who firmly believed in "cloak-room banking" and those who believed that by issuing pieces of paper which came to serve as a circulating medium the banks were "creating credit" which meant an effective enlargement of the money supply.

Yet the essential function of banks in the creation of "finance" (or credit) was well understood by Adam Smith, who, in his long chapter on Money in Book 2 of the *Wealth of Nations*, regarded branch-banking as a most important invention for the enrichment of society. He described how, as a result of the finance which banks were able to place at the disposal of producers, the real income of Scotland doubled or trebled in a remarkably short time. Expressed in Keynesian terms, the "finance" provided by banks made it possible to increase investments ahead of income or savings, and to provide the savings counterpart of the investment out of the additional incomes, generated by a multiplier process by additional spending.

Since the notes issued by *some* banks were found more acceptable than those of others, giving rise to periodic payments crises and uncertainty, it was sooner or later everywhere found necessary to concentrate the right of issuing banknotes in the hands of a single institution [1], such rights being circumscribed by reserve requirements of

---

(1) The Bank of England was granted the monopoly of the right of issuing notes by a joint stock company in England in 1709, and most European countries granted such a monopoly of the right to issue notes to a bank which became the "central bank" – i.e. the bank which kept the reserves of all other banks. In the U.S. the Federal Reserve Banks were given the monopoly to issue banknotes in the present century.

some form, etc. These banknotes, in the course of the present century, became the *ultimate form* of money since gold convertibility was abandoned in most countries either as a result of the First World War or of the economic crisis after 1929. However, just as gold coins gave way to banknotes to current accounts with the clearing banks, which proved a safer and more convenient way of holding money than cash in the form of banknotes, and to transfer money between persons through the agency of cheques. And for much the same reason which led to the creation of money through credits granted by the banks in the form of the banks' promissory notes, the granting of bank credit led to the creation of money in the form of chequing deposits which came to exceed manifold the amount of banknotes in the vaults of the banks (or, what comes to the same, of credits with the central bank) in existence. This "credit money" in the form of either non-interest bearing chequing accounts of of interest-bearing deposits which are not directly available as a medium of payment, but which could hardly be left out of account in measuring the quantity of "money" in circulation (if only because of the ease with which deposits of one kind can be converted into deposits of the other kind). Moreover, deposits of the clearing banks have close substitutes in other, easily transferable and capitalcertain forms of holding wealth such as deposits with building societies, Treasury Bills or short-term bonds (bonds with near-dates of maturity), travellers cheques, and, most of all, deposits in the Eurocurrency markets (the total value of which latter has been estimated to have risen from 39 billion U.S. dollars to 1.35 trillion dollars, or by 3,353 per cent between 1965 and November 1981 (estimates given in the New York Herald Tribune's *Special Supplement on Euromarkets*, November, 1981). The latest "money substitutes" consist of credit cards which came into use after World War II, and which are now estimated to account for 90 per cent of payments in the more expensive hotels and restaurants.

3. MONEY SUPPLY AND DEMAND IN A MODERN ECONOMY

3.1. The Monetarist View

In the light of the above, the main contention - and indeed, the *sine-qua-non* - of monetarism that the money supply of each "economy" is exogenously determined by the monetary authority of the "economy" concerned [1] may be questioned from the start. Monetarists, following Milton Friedman, assume that the monetary authority determines the so-called "monetary base" (or "high-powered money" to use Friedman's expression) which is nothing else but the amount of banknotes issued which at any one time are partly in the hands of the public and partly in the hands of the banks, whether in the form of vault-cash or of deposits with the central bank, whilst either legally enforceable rules or conventions determine an established ratio between this "base money" and of all other forms of money. Hence the "monetary authority" ultimately determines the supply of money in all forms. It does so partly by active measures such as "open market operations" by which the central bank buys or sells government securities in exchange for its own notes, and partly by passive measures, the re-discounting of short term paper consisting of public or private debt, where it seeks to achieve its objective as regards the money supply by varying its own rate of re-discount. The further assumption that the (inverted) pyramid of bankmoney bears a stable relationship to the monetary base is supposed to be ensured by the banks' rationing credit so as to prevent their liabilities from becoming larger (or rising faster) than the legal or prudential reserve ratio permit. It is admitted, however, that each "economy" characterised by the possession of a separate currency must be wholly autonomous, which means that the central bank is not under any obligation to maintain its exchange rate, at a predetermined relationship with other exchange rates (as was the case under the pre-1914 gold standard or the Bretton Woods system), but that it allows its exchange rate to fluctuate freely so as to achieve a balance in the foreign exchange market without central bank intervention. (The possibility that payments, whether among the same nationals or between different nationals is effected in other currencies or through transfers between extra-territorial bank accounts has not to my knowledge, been explicitly considered).

---

(1) The monetary authority is the note issuing central bank, which may or may not be acting with the consent or under the advice of the Government of the country concerned.

While the first and most important credo of monetarism is that the supply of money is always exogenous [1] the second and almost equally important credo is that the public's *demand* for money, as a proportion of income is a stable one, not much influenced by changes of interest rates and other factors (see for a critical appraisal of the latter assertions Hendry and Ericsson (1983)).

Given the fact that the demand for money represents a stable function of incomes (or expenditures) Friedman and his associates conclude that any increase in the supply of money, however, brought about (including, e.g. that caused by open market operations which lead to the substitution of cash for short-term Government debt in the hands of discount houses or other financial institutions) will imply that the supply of money will *exceed* the demand at the prevailing level of incomes (people will "find themselves" with more money than they wish to hold) and this defect will be remedied, and can only be remedied, by an increase in expenditures which will raise incomes sufficiently to eliminate the excess of supply over the demand for money.

3.2. Commodity Money and Credit Money

As a description of what happens in a modern economy, and as a piece of reasoning applied to situations where money consists of "credit-money" brought about by the creation of public or private debt, this is a fallacious piece of reasoning, an illegitimate application of the original propositions of the quantity theory of money which (by its originators at any rate) were applied to situations in which money consisted of commodities, such as gold or silver, where the *total quantity in existence* could be regarded as exogenously given at any one time as a heritage of the past; and where sudden and unexpected increases in supply could occur (such as those following the Spanish conquest of the Inca empire), the absorption of which necessitated a fall in the value of

---

(1) Friedman at one stage considered that this need not necessarily be the case, but that it has mostly been the case in the past, as a matter of fact, (see Friedman (1969), 266-284) though in his latest book (Friedman and Schwartz (1982)) the exogeneity of the money supply is taken for granted without any discussion or argument.

money-commodity relatively to other commodities. Until that happened, *someone* was always holding more gold than he desired, and since all the gold which is anywhere must be somewhere, the total quantity of gold to be held by *all* money-users was independent of the demand for it. The only way supply could be brought into conformity, and kept in conformity, with demand was through changes in the value of the commodity used as money.

However, the same reasoning cannot be applied to cases where money was not a commodity like gold or oxen, but a piece of paper (banknotes) or simply a book-keeping entry in the account of banks. The rules relevant to the creation of "credit-money" are not of the same kind as those relevant to the production of gold or similar commodities. Credit money comes into existence, not as result of mining but of the granting of bank credit to borrowers who use it (in the majority of cases) to finance expenditures of a non-recurrent kind - such as those involved in the enlargement of stocks carried by manufactureres or traders or their replacement at higher prices, or the purchase of plant and machinery, etc.. The new credit first appears as an addition to the balances held by the borrowers. As the money is spent on wages, the purchase of materials, etc., the same addition will appear in the balances of the recipients, except insofar as there are leakages into imports or taxation. We may suppose that some part of the additional receipts will be saved, which may be reflected in an increase in savings deposits. The same thing is repeated when the money is disposed of by the second and third recipients.

To the extent that the second, third, recipients, and so on, find that they have more than enough money in hand, they will apply the difference to the repayment of bank loans, and thereby extinguish the "excess supply" of money.

Could we then suppose that the additional credit of £100 brings about an "excess supply" of money in an analogous manner to that created by the discovery of new gold? If the original borrower did not need £100 he would have borrowed less - say, £80 - and left the remainder as an unutilized borrowing facility. If the subsequent recipients find that they have more money in hand than they need, it is they who will repay some of their bank loans. Again, the "excess money" is extinguished through loan repayment. If the second recipient is a net creditor to the bank, his bank balance will be enlarged; and if he finds that it is now too large he will transfer some of it to interest-bearing savings deposits or apply it to the purchase of financial assets of some other kind. This means that in *the sense required* by monetarist theory an excess in the supply of money cannot come into existence; and if it did, it would be automatically extinguished through the repayment of bank indebtedness either by the original borrower or by others.

The vital difference in the *modus operandi* of the two kinds of money, commodity money and credit money, was not perceived (as far as I know) by any of the "schools" of economic theory. The original inventors of the quantity theory of money in the 18th Century, such as David Hume, were naturally thinking of the supply of gold as determing the amount of money in circulation, and the same remained true of the writers in the 19th Century, such as Walras and Marshall, who wrote at a time when paper money was a far more important element in monetary circulation. They did not think, however, that this called for any fundamental revision of the traditional theories [1]. None of them questioned the assumption that the quantity of money, however defined, is an exogenous variable. The same was true of Irving Fisher, who in 1911 presented the authoritative modern version of the quantity theory (see Fisher (1911)), together with the well-known equation, $MV=PT$. He regarded the variations in the quantity of money as the main cause of fluctuations in prices. The same was true of Keynes (see Keynes (1923)), who advocated a "managed currency" in preference to a return to the gold standard, mainly in order to secure a more stable money supply and thus avoid the effects of the vagaries of gold on the price level. The causal chain running from money to prices was never

(1) Walras was clearly troubled by the complication due to credit money and the use of the "clearing house" for offsetting claims and liabilities. In the end he sought refuge in the notion that while paper money makes the total quantity of money larger than it would be otherwise, it will always be in a fixed proportionate relationship to "real money", and once this is established the effective amount of money in circulation, while larger, will function in much the same way as if only "real money" existed.

questioned; and the exogenous character of the money supply was something Keynes continued to believe in even when his new theory of effective demand gave a wholly new explanation of how the demand for goods and services is determined. Side by side with the multiplier equation $Y = (1/(1-k))I$ which gives the core of the new theory, he retained traces of his old beliefs in the liquidity preference equation, $M=L(Y,r)$, where the *demand* for money is assumed to vary with the rate of interest as well as the level of money incomes, but the *supply* of money was treated as an exogenous constant in the same way as in the quantity theory. This formulation puts the whole burden of adjustment following upon changes in profit expectations, investment, etc. on the velocity of circulation, which was assumed (tacitly rather than explicitly) to vary to whatever extent was necessary to reconcile the change in demand brought about by Keynesian factors with the change in the level of expenditure defined according to Fisher.

Milton Friedman first thought of testing the Keynesian hypothesis by comparing the movements in total money income (or expenditure) with the corresponding movements of the quantity of money. He took the *absence* of any correlation between M and Y as an empirical test of the Keynesian theory - which is only another way of saying that changes in V (the velocity of circulation) induced by changes in the rate of interest, proved sufficient to validate changes in demand originating in changes in investment or in the propensity to consume [1].

Much to his (initial) surprise he found that historically the correlation was not between Y (or the GDP) and V, but between Y and M; changes in money income were strongly correlated with changes in the quantity of money in circulation, normally with a (highly variable) time lag. If our main proposition is correct, and the changes in the money

(1) At one stage economists of both the Keynesian and anti-Keynesian persuasion appeared to be in agreement that the validity of the Keynesian theory hangs on an empirical issue - the interest sensitivity of the velocity of circulation. This entirely depended on the assumption that M is an exogenous constant. If, as is argued in this paper, M is endogenous and varies with the individual's demand for cash, the Keynesian theory would be refuted (not confirmed) by the absence of correlation between M and Y.

supply arise in consequence of changes in the demand for goods and services, we would expect, in the course of the investment cycle, increases in the amount of money in circulation to precede increases in investment: the finance for a particular investment project has to be assembled first, before the actual expenditure is incurred.

3.3. Implications for Monetary Policy

The main conclusion of this analysis is that the behaviour and the significance of changes in the money supply will be quite different according as we consider a commodity money economy or a credit money economy. In the latter case changes in the money supply are always consequences, not causes, of changes in the money value of daily transactions, or in the national income, etc.. This does not mean that what is commonly regarded as "monetary policy" is futile or ineffective; it means that the monetary instruments operate by a circuitous route – by changing the level of economic activity and thereby the *demand* for money. Any change in the money supply is consequential on the change in demand, and not the other way round.

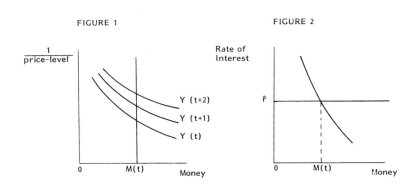

FIGURE 1

FIGURE 2

The difference between the two situations could best be shown by two simple diagrams, the one relating to the classical situation of a pure commodity money economy, and the other to the modern situation of a credit money economy. In Figure 1 the value of money (the inverse of the price level) is shown on the vertical axis while the quantity of money is shown on a horizontal axis at a given time t as an exogenous constant. In Figure 2 the demand for money is shown in the same way, but the supply of money is not an exogenous constant – at a *given* rate of interest it is capable of being expanded or contracted indefinitely.

In Figure 1, $Y(t)$, $Y(t+1)$, etc. represent the public's demand curves for holding money; on strict quantity theory grounds, these curves should be rectangular hyperbolae, indicating that prices will vary in inverse proportion to the quantity of money, so that the amount of money held in terms of real purchasing power is invariant to prices. In the case of Figure 2 the forward falling demand curve represents increasing amounts of real purchasing power held in the form of money with lower rates of interest on account of liquidity preference. The advantage of holding wealth in the form of money is liquidity – the ability to apply purchasing power in any direction, and the cost of liquidity is the sacrifice of income which the same purchasing power might have earned if invested in less liquid forms [1].

By varying the rate of interest the monetary authority can un-doubtedly exert an influence on economic activity, and even a bigger influence on the foreign exchange markets, through speculative inflows and outflows. But there is no evidence to show that these are important objectives of economic policy which could not be equally well attained (and with far better prognostication of its effects) by fiscal policy. The announcement of a target rate of increases for the "money supply" whether attained or not, does not make any difference to the future movement of either output or inflation, except insofar as it is taken as

---

(1) At one stage "liquidity preference" was regarded as the essential factor which distinguished Keynesian theory from pre-Keynesian theories – since it loosened the tie between the level of effective demand and the level of expenditure as determined by monetary factors. All this, however, depended on the assumption of the quantity of money being determined irrespective of all the other factors which determined the demand for goods and services. If we regard money as an endoge-nous factor, liquidity preference and the assumption of interest-elas-ticity of the demand for money ceases to be of any importance.

a "guide-line" in wage negotiations [1].

4. MONETARIST POLICY IN THEORY AND PRACTICE

4.1. Experiences with Monetarist Policy Prescriptions: the Pre "New Monetarism" Period

However, the burden of contention of the monetarists was the very opposite. It is the rate of increase in the money supply (in one or other of the many definitions of "money") which alone causes an excessive increase in the demand for goods and services (excessive *relative to* the potential availabilities) and therefore a stabilization policy ought not to be based on the Keynesian techniques of forecasting the rise in demand "under the existing policies" (from the forecast changes in investment or the budgetary deficit, the balance of payments, savings propensities, etc.) and compare it with an optimal path, based on the forecast improvement in productivity, private investment, external demand, etc.. On Friedman's view all this is both unnecessary and, taken in isolation, ineffective because

(a) the economy is fully self-adjusting and tends to produce the optimal output on its own, unless it is prevented from doing so by Government interference; and

(b) the actual course of the economy will follow the optimal path, so long as the "money supply", which is fully under the control of the Central Bank, is made to increase at the optimal rate[2].

(1) There are countries, such as Germany, where the memories of the great inflation of 1922-23 are still very vivid, and where the popular view tends to attribute the inflation to the printing of a lot of paper money which soon became worthless, and regards this as the cause, and not just a symptom, of what occurred. In such circumstances the monetary guidelines issued by the German Bundesbank may serve as a useful indication of how far wage increases could be carried without causing inflation.
(2) Friedman and the monetarists do not recognise that inflation could prevail without excessive demand, owing to the excessive rise in costs (mainly wages) which arise on account of the struggle between different classes to secure a larger share of the cake.

Improbable as it may sound, this extraordinary proposition was firmly believed in at the turn of the last decade in a number of important countries simultaneously – by Mr. Volcker, the Chairman of the Federal Reserve, by Mrs. Thatcher and her close personal advisers in England, and by leading figures in a number of other countries. Its outward expression was the setting of "targets" for the increase in money supply in a large number of countries and, at least for a time, to regard the realisation of these targets (by open-market operations, changes in interest rates, and, in some countries, by quantitative controls on the increase in bank credit supported by budgetary measures both on the revenue side and the expenditure side) as the first priority of policy.

By these measures "monetarist" Governments and central bankers managed to reduce the effective demand for goods and services below their potential considerably, which in turn *may* have caused a slowdown in the increase of the amount of money people wished to hold.

However, experience has soon demonstrated that the central bank has no *direct control* over the amount of its banknotes in circulation. The reason for this is that the Bank cannot refuse payments to its own creditors by refusing to honour cheques drawn on itself by the account holders, and if it wishes to avoid major crises in the banking and financial system it cannot close the "discount window", i.e., it cannot refuse to re-discount eligible bills on the ground that it is only willing to issue new money up to a certain daily maximum. Central banks are extremely sensitive to the danger of bank failures which can easily escalate. To an extent which is rarely admitted in public, central banks regard the maintenance of the credit pyramid – the solvency of the banking system – as their most important function, which takes precedence over economic objectives if these appear to be in conflict.

Traditionally, the core of central banking policy consisted of protecting the reserves (in gold or reserve currencies) through the instrument of changes in the Bank Rate. Ostensibly, such changes served the purpose of keeping the balance of payments with foreign countries on an even keel – a loss of reserves was taken as evidence of an unfavourable balance, and *vice versa*. The policy worked in the sense that even moderate changes in short-term interest rates (relatively to other financial centres) sufficed to reverse the trend in the movement in reserves. But until the new monetarism came into fashion stabilizing the quantity of money in circulation, as distinct from stabilizing the volume of international reserves, was not regarded as a primary objective.

In the last five years or so all this has changed. A number of countries adopted monetarist policies with the objective of stabilizing the economy (and, in the view of some, of increasing its operational efficiency) by regulating the amount of money in circulation. There is no time here to give even an outline of a comprehensive survey: two examples must suffice.

4.2. The British Experience with New Monetarism

The first relates to Britain where monetarism was first adopted by Dennis Healey, under a Labour Government, sometime in 1977. However, since its methods and objectives have never been made explicit, it is best to begin with the monetarist policies of the present Government, which came into office in May 1979. The first year of the policy was a disastrous failure. The money supply, as defined by "sterling M3" [1], which was planned to rise by 7-11 per cent, had actually risen by 22 per cent; both the money supply and the price level rose twice as fast under the new monetarist regime than they did under the five years of the previous Labour Government [2]. This was attributed, with extreme naiveté, to the lack of confidence of the public in the Government's "earnestness" in carrying out its policies. Hence in the second year the Government adopted a "medium term strategy" which provided that the annual change of the money stock, the public sector borrowing requirement and the rate of increase in the price level, were to be gradually

(1) This is the broader definition of money comprising both demand deposits and time deposits of the clearing banks.
(2) The cause of this was their failure to recognize (in true monetarist fashion) that prices can rise on account of a rise in costs and not only the pressure of demand. Their first Budget was deflationary in terms of the pressure of demand but strongly inflationary in its effects on prices on account of the switch from direct to indirect taxation, the rise in mortgage rates, charges for school meals, etc.

and steadily reduced over a four-year period. It was never explained why public belief in the seriousness of the Government's intentions should operate as a stabilizing instrument, and why a four-year plan should be taken so seriously. Anyhow, the performance in the second and third years was not much better than that of the first year – the money supply targets had to be repeatedly "re-based" to start from a higher level. In the meantime the "supporting policies" of tax increases and expenditure cuts, and allowing the £ to become extremely over-valued, meant that unemployment kept on growing, and industrial production shrinking rapidly.

The level of import prices was greatly moderated by the rise in the exchange value of the £, whilst North Sea oil coming on stream brought with it a large surplus on current account. As a result of all this by the end of the fourth year the Government could claim to have succeeded in bringing down inflation from the 8.5 per cent rate which they inherited in May 1979 and the 22 per cent attained in August 1980 (at the end of their first year in office), to 4 per cent a year in the year from mid-1983 to mid-1984. This latter result was largely due, however, to the rise in unemployment by 2 million (from 1 million to 3 million) and the consequential fall in the size of wage settlements, as well as an annual rise in industrial productivity due to the closure and disappearance of the least efficient tail of industry. These factors however have by now exhausted their effects and a renewal of the upward trend in the inflation rate is anticipated. Over the period as a whole total real consumption increased by 5 per cent. But there was a 9.5 per cent fall in the total number of employees in employment and a 13 per cent fall in the output of manufacturing industries. Gross in-vestment in the manufacturing industries fell by 42 per cent, that in plant and machinery alone, by 33 per cent. This is a far worse record than that of the Great Depression of 1929-32.

(In all this it was the coincidence of the sudden large turn-around in the balance of payments due to oil with the deflationary policies of the Government which had the most unfortunate consequences. In order to take full advantage of oil as an additional source of income, amoun-ting to 6-7% of the GDP and 20% of imports, internal demand needed to be expanded sufficiently to allow the foreign importers of oil (mainly

the countries of the EEC) to pay for oil by exports (mainly of manufactures) without such exports exerting an adverse effect on domestic
output. But the actual policies followed were the very opposite, so that
the benefit of oil, in terms of the GDP, was offset by the induced
additional shrinkage of manufacturing output and employment).

4.3. The American Experience with the New Monetarism

The other example I wish to mention is that of the United States of
America. Here the Federal Reserve traditionally followed much the same
kind of policies as European central banks, operating mainly through
short-term interest rates and engaging in open market operations so as
to ensure that actual rates conformed to the official re-discount rate. In
addition, the Federal Reserve maintained tighter controls on its member
banks through the institution of variable minimum reserve requirements.
But there was no attempt to regulate the *quantity* of money other than
through the instrument of interest rates and changes in minimum reserve requirements.

However, in the monetarists' view all this was the wrong policy for
securing stability of prices. To stabilize the economy and to avoid
inflation what is needed first of all is to secure a *steady growth in the
money supply*, not a steady rate of interest. Hence the "new" policy of
the Federal Reserve, formally announced by Mr. Volcker, the Chairman
of the Federal Reserve Board, on October 6, 1979, was to secure a slow
and steady growth of the monetary aggregates M1 and M2 by varying
the reserves available to the banking system through open market
operations, *irrespective* of the accompanying movements in the rates of
interest. From that day on dramatic changes started to happen which
were quite different from those expected. The money supply failed to
grow at a smooth and steady rate; its behaviour exhibited a series of
wriggles. The rate of interest and the rate of inflation, though both
were very high at the start, soared to unprecedented heights in a very
short time. By March 1980 the rate of interest rose to 18.6 per cent
and the rate of inflation to 15.2 per cent (in annual terms), and a little
later both were over 20 per cent - which had never occurred before in
the United States since the Civil War, whether in peace-time or in
war-time. And there was a mushroom-like growth in new forms of

making payments and new instruments for circumventing the Fed's policy – through the invention of money substitutes of all kinds, like "NOW" accounts and money market funds, the transfer of business to non-member banks or to branches of foreign banks, and so on. The Fed's reply to all this was that the failures in its declared policies were all due to "loopholes" in the existing system which must be closed. Congress obliged their friends in the Fed very quickly, passing the Monetary Control Act of 1980, supplemented by invoking the International Banking Act and the Credit Control Act. These extended minimum reserve requirements to all deposit-taking institutions, whether or not they were member banks of the Fed, as well as to branches of foreign banks in the U.S.. But none of this helped, as the British Radcliffe Committee foretold would happen twenty-two years earlier, when it said that the extension and multiplication of controls through a wider spread of regulated institutions would only mean that new forms of financial intermediaries and of transactions will appear which will cause the situation continually "to slip from under the grip" of the authorities.

The American monetarist experiment was a terrible failure, as was publicly admitted by Friedman and Meltzer in 1982, though they insisted that it was the fault of the authorities in not being able to run a monetarist policy properly – not the fault of basic theory. Short of the old Chicago plan for 100 per cent reserves, there was certainly no way in which the authorities could have stopped the banks inducing the public to exchange more of their currency notes for deposits and thereby enlarge the lending power of the banks. After a year and a half of continued failures and a chaotic volatility of everything – interest rates, exchange rates, inflation rates – the experiment was abandoned and the system returned, in effect, to the traditional policy of regulating interest rates but with a more deflationary stance; partly, I presume, to offset the inflationary force of excessive federal deficits – and thereby cause the rest of the world to suffer (or benefit, as the case may be) from the consequences of an overvalued dollar.

In retrospect none of this would have happened if the Fed had studied and understood the analysis and prescription of the British Radcliffe Committee in 1959, according to which central banks should not really be concernecd with the money supply as such - it is the regulation of interest rates, and not of the quantity of money, which in the words of the Report "is the centre-piece of monetary action".

5. EVALUATING THE NEW MONETARIST POLICY

In Britain "monetarism" has not been formally abandoned (as it has recently been in Chile) but it is *vieux jeu*. Nobody watches the money supply figures any longer with any interest, and Ministers, though professing complete consistency in their policies, are increasingly forgetful about money, and increasingly emphatic about the need to moderate the excessive rise in wages - something which is quite contrary to Milton Friedman's philosophy. The economy has been slowly recovering since the middle of 1982, though the foreign trade position in manufactures continued to deteriorate. Britain, for the first time for centuries, became a net importer of manufactured goods. Her share in world exports in manufactures, which was on a slowly rising trend up to 1979, declined by nearly 20 per cent in 1980-84. Unemployment, at 13.5 per cent of the labour force, is higher than that of any other developed industrial country. There is nothing to set against these losses in terms of greater mobility between industries, or in the field of quality and product innovation which would enable one to say that the monetarist experiment brought some improvements as well as imposing large losses of output relative to Britain's enlarged potential. In the United States, on the other hand, the continuation of a strict monetary policy conducted through a policy of very high interest rates, was far more than offset by the expansionary effects of the very large deficit in the Federal Budget, so that real GNP rose by nearly 10 per cent between the first quarter of 1983 and the first half of 1984, and unemployment fell from 10.2 per cent to 7.6 per cent over the same period.

The U.S. and U.K. experiments in monetarism have thus left Friedman and the monetarists in an intellectually highly embarrassing position. Friedman has admitted that as far as the United Kingdom is concerned, the money supply is *not* exogenously determined by the monetary authorities but he attributed this to the "gross incompetence" of the Bank of England. Later he implied the same about his own country. However, this puts an entirely new complexion on monetarism. It was nowhere stated in the writings of Friedman or any of his followers that the quantity theory of money *only* holds in countries where the monetary authorities are sufficiently "competent" to regulate the money supply. If the Bank of England is so incompetent that it cannot do so, how can we be sure that the Bank of Chile or of Argentina or Mexico – to take only the highly inflationary countries – are so competent, or rather so competently incompetent, as to make it possible to assert that the inflation of these countries was the *consequence* of the deliberate action of their central banks in flooding these countries with money? How indeed can we be sure that any Central Bank – not excluding even the German Bundesbank or the Swiss Bank – are sufficiently competent to be able to treat their money supplies as exogenously determined? And what happens if they are not? Surely we need a general theory of money and prices which is capable of embracing the cases of countries with "incompetent" central banks, such as Britain and the United States.

REFERENCES

Fisher, I. (1911), *The Purchasing Power of Money*.

Friedman, M. (1969), *The Optimum Quantity of Money and Other Essays*, Chicago.

Friedman, M. and Schwartz, A.J. (1982), *Monetary Trends in the United States and the United Kingdom, their Relation to Income, Prices, and Interest Rates, 1867-1975*, Chicago.

Hendry, D.F. and Ericsson, N.R. (1983), "Assertion without Empirical Basis: an Econometric Appraisal of Friedman and Schwartz", Bank of England Panel of Academic Consultants, Panel Paper no. 22, *Bank of England*, October.

Keynes, J.M. (1923), *Tract on Monetary Reform*, London.

11. THE SIGNIFICANCE OF RECENT EXPERIENCE WITH MONETARY POLICY IN SHAPING FUTURE ECONOMIC POLICY

P. Korteweg

1. INTRODUCTION

The first problem in discussing the recent experience with monetary policy is to decide how recent is "recent". I would like to concentrate on the past two or three years but, in order to put these most recent developments in perspective, I shall begin by going slightly further back in time, to 1977. Let me briefly explain why.

Most economic analyses begin with either the first or the second oil crisis, the reason for which is of course the enormous rise in the price of energy. For many firms, however, and in particular those which invest, money and capital are essential "raw materials", just like energy. Prior to 1977 the real rate of interest (using Fisher's definition) was low or even negative and the rate of inflation very high. Thereafter the reverse was increasingly the case. In 1977 for the first time money and capital were no longer cheap in the Netherlands. By "cheap" I mean that the interest rate was hardly sufficient to compensate for the inflation loss. I would argue that monetary and fiscal policies played an important part in this change. Before looking at more recent developments I should like to review briefly several important trends and events.

2. MONEY AND INFLATION

By early 1977 there was such an ample supply of money and the inflation rate was so high that the Nederlandsche Bank decided to impose credit ceilings. This compelled banks and other credit institutions either to put a brake on credit expansion, in particular where lending for investment in real estate was concerned, or to fund additional loans by capital market borrowing or by an increase in other

Monetary Conditions for Economic Recovery, ed. by C. van Ewijk and J.J. Klant

TABLE 1

Monetary growth and inflation (in %)

	M1	M2	Pc
1972-76	11.5	15	9
1977-81	5	5	5.5
1982-84	8	8.5	4

Note: For 1984 it is assumed that the annual growth rate of M1 (cash balances + demand deposits) is 4% and that M2 (M1 + near money) will grow by 7% in accordance with recent figures. Consumer prices (Pc) are assumed to rise in 1984 by 3.5% similar to the estimate of the Central Planning Bureau.

long-term liabilities. This slowed down money creation and inaugurated a period marked by lower rates of growth in the money supply and less inflation. Table 1 clearly shows the slow-down in the rate of monetary expansion in the period of credit control (1977-81), partially under the influence of the deterioration of the current account in 1977-80. Inflation also fell sharply. To some extent developments in the Netherlands paralleled trends in a number of other western countries, but in other respects they were diametrically opposed to them. For example, in the period 1976-79 inflation was reduced to less than half in the Netherlands while it doubled in the same period in the United States (from 5.5% to 11.5%).

3.   THE INTEREST RATE AND GOVERNMENT DEBT

The rate of interest was apparently unaffected by this drop in inflation. After reaching a low point in 1977 it began to rise rapidly. This was particularly true of the Fisherian real rate of interest, defined here ex-post as the long-term nominal interest rate minus the actual rate of change of the consumer price level. Obviously, the high real rate of interest in the Netherlands is not unrelated to the rate in other countries. Still, part of it, as was the case with inflation, may justifiably be called "made in Holland". I am referring in particular to the fact that budgetary discipline in the Netherlands has not kept pace with monetary discipline. In 1977 the long-term public debt, at almost 90 billion guilders, was roughly equal to the total money supply (M2). By

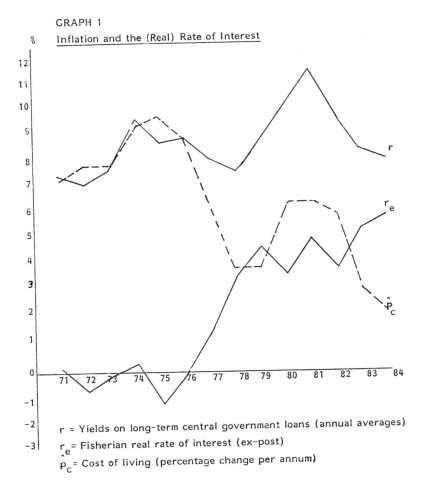

GRAPH 1

% Inflation and the (Real) Rate of Interest

r = Yields on long-term central government loans (annual averages)

r_e = Fisherian real rate of interest (ex-post)

$\hat{P}_c$ = Cost of living (percentage change per annum)

the end of 1983 this debt was approximately 1.5 times as large as total money supply. The scarcity of money relative to public sector debt has therefore significantly increased and this inevitably led to higher real interest rates being desired by investors. Table 2 shows that the growth of public debt increasingly outstripped the growth of the money supply. As is generally known this situation is not unique for the Netherlands. Although economic reality cannot be captured in a couple of simple tables, it will be helpful to bear these trends in mind as I go on to examine recent monetary experience in greater detail. Specifically, I want to make a number of observations regarding the interrelationships between monetary and budgetary policies.

266

TABLE 2

Growth of long term public debt, domestic money supply and the real
rate of interest (in %)

	1 growth rate of public debt	2 growth rate of M1	3=1-2 difference	4 real rate of interest
1972-76	9	11.5	-2.5	-0.5
1977-81	12.5	5	7.5	+4
1982-84	17	8	9	+5

Note: Public debt is the total of long term central government debt and
long term debt of local governments. From table 1 it is clear that
choosing M2 instead of M1 will not alter the conclusion.

4.   BUDGETARY RESTRAINT AND MONETARY MODERATION

The policy of curbing public expenditure did not lead to a sharp
decline in the rate of growth of this expenditure until after 1982, while
it was only after 1983 that for the first time an actual reduction in the
ratio of public spending to national income occurred. Pessimists never
thought this was possible: in their view the deflationary effect of public
spending cuts would affect national income so severely that as a result
public spending relative to national income would increase rather than
decrease. My feeling is that the rôle of monetary policy in this was
neither irrelevant nor easy. On the one hand, it increased the chances
of success of cutting public expenditure and, on the other hand, it was
itself frustrated by the large budget deficits and balanceof-payments
surpluses. I would now like to explore these two aspects somewhat
further.

Since 1982 government policy has aimed at correcting the structure
of expenditure, which is very unbalanced at present, by reducing the
share of consumption and increasing the share of investment in national
income. The reduction of public expenditure has an important rôle to
play in the realisation of this aim, for four reasons. First, high levels
of public expenditure have resulted in a high consumption ratio since to
a considerable extent this expenditure finances consumption. Obviously,
the remedy is to reverse this trend. Second, the financing of this

expenditure, through increased borrowing as well as through increased taxation, negatively affected private investment. The incidence of the increased tax and social security burden was shifted towards the business sector, reducing profits and making new investments less attractive. Here also the obvious remedy is to reverse this trend. Third, reducing the share of public spending in national income and thereby the burden of fiscal and social taxes will moderate wage costs and thus encourage investments. Fourth, and finally, there is the political conviction that the majority of investment decisions are the prerogative of business rather than of the government. Thus, spending cuts affecting consumption were not to be compensated by government investment. Of course this entails certain risks, but leaving something to someone else always involves an element of risk. Now, of course, the shift from consumption to investment would not succeed if the business sector, the motor of the economy, failed to function. Then the operation would indeed become risky. A motor without oil will get jammed when you try to shift from reverse to first gear. I apologise for this rather mechanical methaphor, but my point is this: it is precisely because the authorities refrained from imposing on the private sector, and in particular on industry, a tight monetary policy, that the policy of reducing public expenditure can bear fruit. I would not dare to disappoint the reader by ignoring the "MV=PT" identity. This identity demonstrates that as long as the product of M and V keeps growing, nominal national income cannot fall. As long as this is the case - and it is - a reduction in

TABLE 3

Growth of net national income, money growth and income velocity of money (in %)

	Y	=	M1	+	V
1978	7.5		5		2.5
1979	6		3		3
1980	6		6		0
1981	4.5		-2.5		7
1982	4		10		-6
1983	2.5		10		-7.5

individual components of demand, like in public expenditures, cannot result in a drop in total demand. Which is exactly what the authorities envisaged. This process can also be explained as follows. The graph below shows the combinations of inflation and economic growth over the past few years, which were located, of course, on both the macroeconomic supply and demand curves (see also Korteweg (1978)). None of us exactly knows where these curves lie. But we do know that the supply curves will be upward-sloping and the demand curves downward-sloping. The graph demonstrates that probably no drop in total demand has occurred since 1982. Given the course of events since 1982 it is

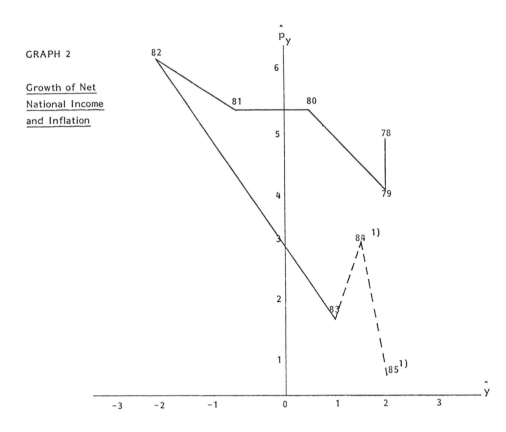

GRAPH 2

Growth of Net
National Income
and Inflation

$\hat{y}$ = Percentage change per annum in net national income (volume)

$\hat{p}_y$ = Net national income deflator

1) Estimates by the Central Planning Bureau

implausible that the demand curve shifted to the left during this period. It is rather more plausible to assume that the points we observe from 1982 onwards lie on the same or virtually the same demand curve. Due in part to the decline in production costs (labour costs and interest payments) the macroeconomic supply curve could shift to the right. Partly because monetary policy was not too tight, prices could rise faster than costs, so that business profits increased. This prevented the demand curve from shifting to the left, which would have happened if monetary policy had been too tight. Economic growth probably would then have been impaired by the much debated phenomenon of a shortfall of demand. In that case each guilder saved would indeed mean a guilder lost in terms of total demand.

The graph also shows that renewed economic growth was accompanied by a much lower rate of inflation. Certain observers see a danger in this. In a recent article on the government Budget Memorandum in the journal "Economische Statistische Berichten" Professor Ritzen, for instance, commented:

"This policy may go sour because of the decline in inflation. In the Macroeconomic Forecast for 1985 inflation is estimated at 1.5% (assuming an exchange rate of ƒ3 to the dollar), which comes dangerously close to deflation".

I do not share this view. I consider it quite unlikely that the currently ample supply of money and liquidity ratio which is high by historical standards will bring a combination of real contraction and a fall in inflation. Price stability is one of the unanimously declared goals of economic policy. Now that this goal is within reach one cannot say that the policy is wrong. On the contrary, the approaching price stability is in fact one of the most positive developments of the past few years.

5. MONETARY POLICY: LIMITATIONS

Now I would like to take a look at how the imbalance in the economy have restricted the room for manoeuver of monetary policy. Private demand for bank credit has been very low during the past few years, primarily because of the relatively low demand for investment funds. The contractive impact this had on monetary expansion was, however,

TABLE 4

Liquidity creation (in billions of guilders)

changes in stocks of the money
creating institutions (banks and central bank)

		1981	1982	1983	July 1983 June 1984
I	credits	13.9	10.2	11.8	11.7
	of which				
	a) to the private sector	(10.8)	(5.6)	(6.7)	(7.6)
	b) to the government	(3.1)	(4.6)	(5.1)	(4.1)
II	net foreign assets	4.4	4.5	4.5	11.1
III	long term liabilities				
	(increase = -)	-11.6	-4.0	-2.3	-10.1
IV	treasury account at the central bank (increase = -) plus short term government debt with nonbank-residents	0.7	-0.7	0.7	-4.0
V	others	-1.8	-0.6	-2.1	0.6
VI	domestic liquidity (M2)	5.6	9.4	12.6	9.3
	growth (in %)	(5.3)	(8.4)	(10.4)	(6.6)
VII	near money	7.2	2.3	5.5	7.1
VIII	money supply (M1)(VI-VII)	-1.6	7.1	7.1	2.2
	growth (in %)	(-2.4)	(9.9)	(10.1)	(2.7)

Source: Table 2.1 and 3.1 Annual Report and Quarterly Report, De
Nederlandsche Bank.
Note: Net foreign assets (item II) includes net purchases of foreign
securities.

more than offset by other factors. In the first place the low rate of investment contributed to a sizeable surplus on the current account of
the balance of payments. This surplus was not cancelled out by extra
capital outflows, with the result that there was a high national liquidity
surplus. Secondly, the enormous increase in the supply of government
debt in combination with the depressed state of private demand for
bank credit created an unusual appetite for it on the part of the banks
and other financial institutions leading indirectly to monetary financing
of the government deficit. Table 4 summarizes monetary developments
since 1981. The monetary authorities were far from indifferent to the
high rate of monetary expansion in 1982 and 1983: the fear of inflation,
a weakening of the guilder and higher interest rates resulting from this

growth was by no means misplaced when one considers that the cumulative growth of nominal national income in the two years mentioned was
6.3%, while the cumulative growth of the money supply (M1) was 20%.
We, and that applies to the Nederlandsche Bank as well, were definitely
somewhat nervous each time we received the monthly growth figures.
Some monetary flexibility was alright, but a situation similar to that in
the mid-1970s, which I described earlier, would have been dangerous.
The fact is, however, that, while the dangers were recognised, there
was almost nothing that could be done about it. Any restriction on
monetary expansion would have entailed measures to curb either domestic money creation or the flow of funds from abroad. Each of these
options entailed a dilemma.

6.   MONETARY POLICY: DILEMMA'S

The first dilemma arose in connection with domestic credit policy.
Given the economic situation, restrictions on credit to an already depressed private sector would have been draconian indeed. Besides, as
this type of credit accounted for only a very small proportion of the
total, it would have been impossible to avoid imposing restrictions on
credit to the public sector. The public sector would then, however,
have had to fund its deficit in some other way and this would also have
had monetary consequences. The alternative of compelling banks to
finance their credit operations with long-term funds would have caused
a rise in the long-term interest rate and was therefore equally un-
appealing. Moreover it would have slowed down the capital outflow,
thereby counteracting the monetary contraction aimed at.

There was thus no good alternative to the policy pursued. It was
particularly fortunate that the rising dollar did not necessitate a domestic monetary contraction. Circumstances make it less likely now that
a strong dollar will accelerate inflation. In the recent past wage indexation has been less strict. Also, international commodity prices are
currently under downward pressure. In 1981 circumstances were less
favourable and they forced monetary authorities to take strong action
against the rising dollar. The Bundesbank suddenly raised its bank
rate from 9% to 12% and the Nederlandsche Bank was forced to take
similar measures to maintain the exchange rate of the guilder. Since

then the strongly improved inflationary outlook has allowed the Bundesbank to assume a much more permissive attitude towards the dollar appreciation. While the Bundesbank continued to intervene in the foreign exchange market, monetary expansion in Germany was not allowed to become too tight. This has been of considerable help to the Dutch authorities in their efforts to promote economic recovery: thanks in part to this the interest rate dropped and exports held up well when domestic demand stagnated.

The second dilemma would have occurred if we had tried to stem the liquidity flows from abroad. A real appreciation of the guilder would have helped to reduce the surplus on the current account and thus also the inflow of liquidity. Given our relatively low inflation rate such a real appreciation could only be attained by revaluing the guilder, once or several times, vis-à-vis all other EMS-currencies. That course of action, however, was undesirable because it would not have solved the problem of too low investments, which is the basic factor behind our current account surpluses.

In sum, it can be concluded that the dilemma's which confronted monetary policy in the recent past and made its proper conduct considerably more difficult, stem directly from our highly unbalanced government budget and structure of expenditure.

7. THE CURRENT SHAPING OF MONETARY POLICY

The situation of recent years has been unique in post-war history, nor can I think of any parallel before the war: a policy of public expenditure cuts being applied in an economy marked by severe structural imbalance at a time of strong monetary expansion and a rapidly depreciating guilder vis-à-vis the dollar. In cases like this one must rely heavily on fundamental principles and common sense.

The first remark I want to make is that it is being increasingly realized that it is useless in the long-term for central banks to try to suppress the dollar exchange rate in the exchange markets with interventions unless these are accompanied by a corresponding adjustment in domestic monetary and fiscal policy. The dollar appreciation resulted from the monetary restraint the Fed has been pursuing in the recent past in combination with an increased credit demand in the US. The increased credit demand is due to the strong economic recovery as well as to the federal government's budget deficit, which has grown rapidly in recent years contrary to the trend in a number of other industrial countries. This fundamental process cannot be countered with official interventions and, indeed, monetary authorities refrained from attempting to do so. What interventions took place were directed towards restoring orderly market conditions. Also monetary authorities in Europe, as was pointed out above, resorted to a lesser extent than before to monetary restraint in order to defend their currencies against the dollar.

A second remark concerns our reaction to a sizeable decline in the velocity of circulation of money where this is caused by a persistent rather than a temporary deterioration in the economy. We all know, I hope, that we should not deviate from the structurally desired rate of monetary expansion in the event of a temporary slump. The situation over the past few years, however, has involved major adjustments in a deep recession. I am convinced that it was the right course of action under these circumstances to allow the large decline in the velocity of circulation to be accompanied by a relatively easy supply of money.

8. THE FUTURE SHAPING OF MONETARY POLICY

I would like to follow these reflections by an exploration of the tasks which face us as, monetary authorities in an open economy. The scenario for 1982 and 1983 which I outlined still partially applies today. I say partially because there are signs of changes for the better. Economic growth is picking up, thanks in part to a recovery in investment. The growth in the money supply has slowed down somewhat and the imbalances are becoming less pronounced. All efforts must now be directed to sustaining the recovery and this calls for more than simply an appropriate monetary policy. We need a flexible labour market, entrepreneurial enthusiasm for innovating investment, and a lower tax and social security burden. I realize that the contributions of budgetary and monetary policies should not stand alone, but I know that they are indispensable. Low inflation and low interest rates are essential for a lasting economic recovery. As I mentioned in my introduction, the drop in inflation in the Netherlands was not accompanied by a pro-

TABLE 5

Long term interest rates and inflation in some countries (in %)

	long term interest rate (a)					% change in cost of living index (b)					(c) = (a) - (b)				
	70/79	80	81	82	83	70/79	80	81	82	83	70/79	80	81	82	83
USA	7.2	11.4	13.7	12.9	11.3	7	13.5	10.5	6	3	0	-2	3	7	8.5
Japan	7.4	8.4	8.2	8.0	7.8	9	8	5	2.5	2	-1.5	0.5	3	5.5	6
BRD	8.0	8.5	10.4	9.0	7.9	5	5.5	6	5.5	3	3	3	4.5	3.5	5
France	9.8	13.8	16.3	16.0	14.4	9	13.5	13.5	12	9.5	1	0.5	3	4	5
UK	12.0	13.8	14.7	12.9	10.8	12.5	18	12	8.5	4.5	-0.5	-4	2.5	4.5	6.5
Italy	10.1	15.3	19.4	20.2	18.3	12.5	22	19	16.5	15	-2.5	-6.5	0.5	3.5	3.5
Netherlands	8.3	10.2	11.6	9.9	8.5	7	6.5	6.5	6	3	1.5	3.5	5	4	5.5
Belgium	8.7	12.2	13.8	13.4	11.8	7.5	6.5	7.5	8.5	7.5	1	5.5	6.5	5	4.5

Note: for 70/79 a period average is calculated

portionate decline in interest rates. The table below shows that this experience was not unique to the Netherlands.

Let me discuss factors which are more or less important to the level of interest rates and I will, whenever feasible, suggest ways in which I think they may be brought down.

First, the increasing scarcity of capital reflected in the real interest rates shown in column three of table 5 is a worldwide phenomenon. It is to be found in countries with large budget deficits (such as the United States and the Netherlands), but also in countries with only small deficits (West Germany and the United Kingdom). At an earlier point I mentioned how the strong dollar benefits our exports. Now, however, I must mention a major drawback of the economic influence that the USA wields over the Old World. The large budget deficit and the strong economic expansion in the USA have pushed up interest rates outside the USA as well. In view of our own inability to practise budgetary discipline we are hardly in a position to reproach the Americans severely, so I shall not pursue this point. It is not fruitful to complain about something that is beyond your control; it is far better if we ourselves follow the advice virtually everyone gives the Americans. Restricting public sector demand for capital will have precisely the same effect in Europe as on the other side of the Atlantic, namely an improvement of the ratio of money to public debt and thus lower interest rates.

Second, we are all aware that most banks around the world have many debtors on their books whose financial standing is not exactly unimpeachable. Many of these are Latin American countries, but the banks cannot always rely on the creditworthiness of Western debtor countries either. Banks thus felt compelled to make considerable bad-loan provisions in order not to endanger their own solvency. It seems fair to say that the business volume of the banks, as measured by their voluntary lending operations, has declined substantially. The banks therefore had to obtain their reserves primarily by larger interest rate margins and thus by higher interest rates. Competition with other financial institutions is the limiting factor here (for an illustration of the importance of this competition, see Advokaat (1984)). In this article he argues, for example, that it is difficult to achieve differentiation in tariffs within the banking system because it is "plagued by commercialism of an intensity that spoils the markets that everyone attempts to attract the maximum volume of funds at the lowest price"). As debt rescheduling progresses and financial competition intensifies, the interest rate margins and hence interest rates themselves will fall; I am not pessimistic about that.

Third, now and then one still encounters the view that interest rates can be brought down by means of easy monetary policy. Experience since 1977 tells quite a different story. There may have been a time when the central banks could deceive the financial markets with easy monetary policy and thereby artificially bring about a reduction in real interest rates. Since the 1970s this is no longer possible. The expansionary monetary policy of the recent past demonstrates that once more. I attribute only a minor rôle to central banks in the determination of the real rate of interest (see Korteweg (1984)). I have remarked that the central banks are caught in a double "quantity trap": a restrictive money supply causes interest rates to rise and an excessive monetary expansion also produces high interest rates, but now because of inflationary expectations. This quantity trap will prevent the authorities from successfully pursuing an activist monetary policy. By way of a conclusion I shall therefore outline the form which monetary policy should take in future.

10. CONCLUSIONS

As the economy is brought back under control, in other words as structural imbalances disappear, we should increasingly take notice of the fact that money can play only a limited rôle. Dr. M. Lusser, member of the Board of Directors of the Swiss Central Bank recently expressed this idea as follows (see Lusser (1984)):

"Wir müssen uns, erstens, eingestehen, dass wir über die genauen Wirkungszusammenhänge der Geldpolitik immer noch zu wenig wissen, um eine konjunkturelle Feinsteuerung der Wirtschaft mit Erfolg durchzuführen. Geldpolitischer Massnahmen können bei falscher Dosierung oder bei einer Fehleinschätzung der Wirkungs- verzögerung aber rasch prozyklisch wirken".

The real significance which I attach to monetary policy is that it can create the stability necessary for lasting economic growth. No more and no less. Monetary policy cannot create any permanent extra supply of goods and services. In this respect I would say that "money does not matter". Preference should be given to a stable long-term monetary growth which finances the structural growth of productive capacity and which takes account of any identifiable trend changes in the income velocity of money. In our open economy which is a full member of the EMS this means that the monetary authorities should pursue a money stock policy aimed at financing the structural growth of the demand for money entirely by liquidity creation from domestic sources, and a money market policy aimed at ensuring that private capital flows will largely offset current account imbalances. Whatever our differences in analysis and opinion, it is on these practical rules of conduct of monetary policy that I am sure Professor Kessler and I will be in complete agreement.

REFERENCES

Advokaat, H.G. (1984), "De grenzen der kredietverlening", NIBE.

Lusser, M. (1984), "Die Grenzen der Geldpolitik in einer offener Volks-wirtschaft", lecture at the International Bankers Club, October.

Korteweg, P. (1978), "De stagnatie van de jaren zeventig, feiten en verklaringen", in *Pre-advies voor de Vereniging voor de Staat-huishoudkunde*, Leiden.

Korteweg, P. (1984), "Does ample money creation stimulate economic recovery" in Korteweg, P., *Financial and Monetary Policy Studies*, Deventer.

12. MONETARY CONDITIONS FOR ECONOMIC RECOVERY; THE DUTCH PERSPECTIVE

G.A. Kessler

1. INTRODUCTION

I will deal with the monetary policy problems of a small country which is a member of the EMS, and which has a very open economy and a still rapidly growing population of 18 years and older. By international standards, this small country has a high unemployment level, a large public sector borrowing requirement, a substantial surplus on the current account of the balance of payments and a low rate of inflation.

Apart from these and other objective characteristics of the Dutch situation which have to be taken into account in the analysis of the monetary policy perspective, there is also a more subjective fact to consider. I am referring to the circumstance that nearly 40 years ago, long before other countries began to pay serious attention to monetary factors, a monetary approach was evolved by the Netherlands Bank which has had a major impact on monetary policy and which even today forms the basis for much of monetary theory and practice in the Netherlands. As I myself was actively involved in the elaboration of this approach, it obviously has greatly influenced my thinking about the monetary policy perspective. Naturally, this thinking is also interwoven with my personal idiosyncrasies and my own estimation of opportunities and risks. This means that my assessment need not necessarily concur with that of the central bank.

2. THE INFLUENCE OF MONETARY FACTORS IN A CLOSED ECONOMY

Before going specifically into the monetary aspects of economic recovery in the Netherlands, it seems appropriate to give a brief outline of the monetary approach underlying my analysis. I will begin by leaving external relationships out of consideration.

Monetary Conditions for Economic Recovery, ed. by C. van Ewijk and J.J. Klant

The influence of monetary factors on the outcome of the economic process lies in the circumstance that the intermediary rôle of money in the exchange of goods, services and financial assets not only has immeasurable advantages for the economy in terms of efficiency, but also provides the monetary latitude for disturbances to arise with regard to the circular flow of the economy and the value of the money. Within these disturbances, a distinction can be made between in- flationary disturbances in the form of price inflation and/or a cyclical overheating of the economy and deflationary disturbances in the form of price deflation and/or cyclical underutilization of production capacity.

Economic agents hold money because of the certainty it provides with respect to ability to pay and stability of value. This demand for money has a positive relationship with the volume of transactions. At the macro-economic level, national income (GNP) generally provides an appropriate measure for these transactions. The demand for money shows a negative relationship with the excess of capital market rates over interest payable on deposits (the interest rate on liquid assets). The reason is that this interest rate differential represents the oppor- tunity costs ensuing from keeping wealth in the form of money instead of capital market investments.

The monetary latitude referred to consists of the fact that eco- nomic agents can make use of money-creating credit, as well as of the possibility for economic agents to activate existing cash balances, i.e. to reduce the size of their money holdings relative to transactions (GNP). The latter can take place under the influence of an increase in capital market rates (in other words an interest-rate induced decline in the demand for money), but it can also happen more spontaneously, for instance as a consequence of a change in cyclical prospects. Financing by means of money creation and/or activation can be termed inflationary financing.

Inflationary disturbances generate an increase in the nominal value of transactions, thus leading to an increase in the demand for money. These disturbances use up monetary latitude and are therefore, gener- ally speaking, impossible without inflationary financing. Since the desirable non-inflationary processes of economic growth and the un- desirable inflationary disturbances have in common that the demand for money increases, monetary policy is essentially concerned with bringing about the right dosage of monetary latitude. One of the problems a-rising here is that inflationary and deflationary disturbances may con-cur, as they can do notably when price inflation is accompanied by a cyclical deflationary interruption of the circular flow of the economy.

The economic agents' monetary financing dispositions in the form of the creation / activation of money, or the annihilation / inactivation of money, may be regarded as, respectively, inflationary or deflationary monetary impulses which may be included as exogenous variables in a model attempting to describe the influence of monetary factors on the outcome of the economic process.

In an extremely simplified model, of which the outward appearance is in line with the quantity theory, the interest rate mechanism is left out of consideration, and the interest-rate induced changes in the demand for money are therefore regarded as a monetary impulse. In the more comprehensive IS/LM model, on the other hand, the interest rate forms a crucial endogenous variable which acts as a "bridging variable" for the influence which monetary impulses (shifts of the LM curve) exert on the development of national income. Apart from monetary impulses, a rôle is also played in this model by budgetary or expendi-ture impluses (shifts in the IS curve). Although the IS/LM model does not do justice to the complexity of the monetary transmission mecha-nism, it must, from a didactical viewpoint, be considered of great importance because it brings out two aspects, viz. the indirect char-acter of the monetary transmission mechanism and the importance of, amongst other things, non-monetary factors and instruments for the outcome of the macro-economic process.

More generally formulated, the indirect influence of monetary factors ensues from the influence which the external financing climate has on the spending and investment decisions of economic agents. Expenditure and investment can be financed either internally or ex-ternally. Internally generated financing is done from income earned in the same period. In the case of external financing, recourse is had to credit or to financial assets. The external financing climate is reflected by the availablity and the price of external finance. The "milder" this climate, the smaller the reluctance of economic agents to undertake expenditure or investment which, in the absence of internally generated finance, must be financed externally. Since market rates also function as opportunity costs for internally generated finance, this is another route along which they can exert an influence on the volume of expenditure.

The availability and the price of external finance form separate elements of the external financing climate. The absence of full price competition in many financial markets may lead to divergences between movements in market rates and developments with regard to the availability of funds. This is especially true of, for example, the market for bank credit, which may furthermore be subject to quantitative restrictions imposed by the monetary authorities.

Divergences between price movements and availability can also be the result of "spontaneous" changes - i.e. changes that are not attributable to developments in national income or market rates - in the demand for money. I am referring notably to the influence which cyclical conditions and expectations about future interest rate movements can exert on the demand for money. Thus it is possible under recessionary cyclical conditions that, despite a major easing of liquidity conditions, there is still no significant decline in interest rates. Under these circumstances, however, the (potential) availability of external finance does increase.

Finally, allowance must be made for the fact that the interest rate sensitivity of the demand for money relates to the $excess$ of capital market rates over interest on liquid assets. This means that a rise in the latter can push up all interest rates without necessarily being attended by a limitation of the availability of external finance.

The reasons, set out above, why, in the monetary transmission process attention must be given to the availability and the price of external finance as separate elements of the external financing climate gain importance when the quantitative concept of liquidity is expanded to include not only money but also certain forms of near money. In the Netherlands, this broader definition was already adopted in the early 1950s. This was because short-term financial assets, which institutionally can at short notice be converted into newly created money without many costs or much risk of loss and which are held by the general public out of liquidity preference, must from a monetary point of view be equated with money. Although the borderline between near money and securities is not very pronounced, the expansion of the quantitative concept of liquidity can contribute materially to the exactitude and the degree of realism of the monetary analysis as a basis for a policy which is aimed at the most effective control over monetary latitude. The exact delimitation remains a question of policy efficacy which must - also in connection with the emergence of financial innovations - be given never-wavering attention.

It goes without saying that the significance of the interest rate on liquid assets increases when a wider concept of liquidity is chosen, as it now also includes the interest rate for near money. It is the excess of long-term or capital market rates over the interest rate on liquid assets (or money market rates) which must, in principle, be "explainable" in terms of, on the one hand, the ease of liquidity conditions - as may be reflected by the national liquidity ratio, i.e. the relationship between the money supply, including near money, and national income - and, on the other hand, the "intensity" of liquidity preference[1]. Simple scatter diagrams of the development of the interest rate differential and the national liquidity ratio show that the intensity of liquidity preference may be subject to sudden and violent fluctuations. This can be due not only to the above-mentioned influence of the trade cycle on the demand for liquidity, but also to the influence of expectations about future interest rate movements already mentioned. It is notably this latter factor which explains why, under certain circumstances, an inverted interest rate structure (with short-term interest rates being higher than long-term rates) can arise.

The foregoing may, of course, not lead to the conclusion that non-monetary factors do not affect the interest rate level. Their influence does make itself felt, however, via the relationships outlined in the previous section. The same is true of the influence of inflationary

---

(1) The implication is that when money market rates go up capital market rates will tend to follow even without a tightening of liquidity conditions or a rise in liquidity preference.

expectations. There is no question of such expectations having a direct effect on nominal interest rate movements. After all, inflationary expectations have no impact on the choice of whether to keep wealth in the form of liquid assets or in nominally fixed investments: inflation affects the real value of both equally strongly. It is, of course, possible that the expectation of (increasing) inflation can feed through to interest rates indirectly, i.e. via the expectation that interest rates will rise (and thus stock prices go down) and the consequent increase in the demand for liquidity. This expectation of higher interest rates arises, however, from an anticipation of a tightening of the money supply and/or a rise of the interest rate on liquid assets induced or permitted by the monetary authorities in view of (intensified) inflation. Experience in many countries shows that this "expectation mechanism" can, depending on the policy actually pursued by the authorities, be so weak that in times of high inflation very low or even negative real interest rates may prevail.

Returning to the monetary transmission process whose indirect character I have sketched above, it must be emphasized that, contrary to the beliefs of some economists, there are insufficient grounds to assume that, apart from the influence of the price and availability of external finance – which can also be seen as the influence of a substitution effect – other effects, such as wealth effects and "direct" effects play an important rôle in monetary transmission. That an increase in the volume of money causes an increase in the "relevant" wealth of economic agents and thus influences the volume of expenditure via wealth effects has been rightly contested in literature. The arguments put forward in support of this hypothesis are too far-fetched to lay claim to any relevancy. It is undoubtedly true that interest-rate induced changes in the market value of negotiable investment objects may affect consumer spending. This (indirect) effect is, however, part of the interest rate mechanism. The allegation that there is a "direct" mechanism apart from substitution and wealth effects is in my opinion unfounded, as the basis for such a mechanism remains entirely obscure. The above holds, a fortiori, for the influence of monetary expansion on the rate of price increase. Pricing in the goods market and the labour market is subject to supply and demand conditions which doubtless feel the influence of the external financing climate; there is, however, no question of an underlying direct influence emanating from the rate of monetary expansion.

The only mechanism with a more direct character is that of the expectations raised. It is undeniably conceivable that the rate of monetary expansion raises expectations which affect the goods, labour and foreign exchange markets. Yet it must be pointed out once again that these expectations are anticipatory in character and can therefore not be viewed apart from an assumed underlying transmission process. This process has no direct effects. Raised expectations which conflict with the underlying process are not longlived and cannot therefore provide a basis for the efficacy of monetary policy. On the contrary, they can have a destabilizing effect. The views put forward by some monetarists that the expectations of the aggregate economic agents are "rational" because they are based on correct information about the intentions of Government policy and on correct qualitative and quantitative insight, also shared by the Government, into the monetary transmission process are far away from reality and can consequently not provide any basis for the policy to be pursued.

In summary, it may be finally noted that the indirect effect of monetary factors on expenditure and investment decisions implies that for an easing of monetary latitude to be effective, there should at least potentially be expenditure and investment *intentions*. As concerns portfolio investment this is probably nearly always the case. The process of portfolio selection can be reactivated time and again. With regard to consumption and capital investment the situation is different. It is conceivable that the circumstances are such (e.g. stagnation in real income developments, unfavorable prospects with regard to profitability and sales) that an easing of external financing conditions has only a very slight effect on expenditure. Generally speaking, this effect will be greater as the economy is structurally healthier and more dynamic. In this connection it must be concluded that the influence of monetary factors (and, with them, of monetary policy) on the outcome of the economic process is more conditioning than causative in nature.

3. MONETARY FACTORS IN TRANSACTIONS WITH OTHER COUNTRIES

Via the price and the availability of external finance the monetary latitude inherent in the economy, of course, also exercises an influence on expenditure and investment abroad, in other words, on the import of goods and services and on the export of capital. In the case of imports, it is usually best in macro-economic analysis to regard them as a sequel of total national expenditure. That is why attention should be directed first of all at capital transactions.

Just as national external financing conditions and especially national interest rates as a cost factor affect capital exports these rates as a yield factor also influence capital imports. Conversely, foreign interest rates are a cost factor affecting capital imports, and a yield factor influencing capital exports. Thus *net* capital transactions are determined to a major extent not only by underlying factors such as the surplus or deficit of savings at home and abroad and cyclical prospects, but also by the spread between financing conditions at home and financing conditions abroad. This is, of course, true first of all of the most interest-rate sensitive part of capital transactions. Capital transactions with a more structural character, however, such as equity investments, are also susceptible to the influence of the price and especially the availability of external finance at home and abroad.

It is of great monetary importance that, when viewed by itself, the balance of external current and capital transactions undertaken by the non-monetary domestic sectors leads to an increase (in the case of a surplus) or a decrease (in the case of a deficit) in the combined money holdings of these sectors. In principle, reverse liquidity movements take place abroad simultaneously[1]. The balance-of-payments outcome referred to here, which because of its *monetary* character can be termed the *monetary* balance-of-payments outcome, thus leads to international liquidity movements which affect liquidity conditions both domestically and abroad. It thus forms a very important channel

---

(1) This symmetry is broken insofar as capital imports have the character of credit granted by foreign *banks*.

through which domestic monetary impulses can make themselves felt abroad, and foreign monetary impulses can affect the domestic situation.

This constellation forms the basis for what is termed the monetary approach to the balance of payments and for the automatic tendency towards equilibrium which the balance of payments to some extent has. If the domestic monetary impulses correspond with the increase in the demand for money ensuing from the rise in national income, and if there is no disequilibrating monetary influence from abroad, a monetary balance-of-payments deficit can generate its own counterforces: the outflow of liquidity will lead to monetary tightening, which can bring about a reduction in capital exports and an increase in capital imports via an increase in intérest rates. This process of financial adjustment will, in principle, persist until monetary equilibrium has been restored to the balance of payments.

It is not only the non-monetary sectors (public authorities, the personal and business sector, and the institutional investors), but also the banks who participate, actively or otherwise, in external capital transactions such as lending and placing or receiving deposits. The foreign exchange market is in overall equilibrium if, at the prevailing exchange rate, the balance of the banks' capital transactions is equal and contrary to the monetary balance-of-payments outcome. The latter is thus spontaneously reflected in a change in the net foreign asset position of the banking system. If there is no such spontaneous equi- librium in the foreign exchange market, the exchange rate of the na- tional currency will, barring foreign exchange interventions by the central bank, rise (in the case of a surplus) or fall (in the case of a deficit). Under a system of fixed exchange rates, the central bank has committed itself to intervene in the foreign exchange market whenever the exchange rate threatens to deviate vis-à-vis any other participant by more than a specific margin from "parity".

Just as the monetary balance-of-payments outcome influences the liquidity holdings of the "general public", thus the foreign exchange interventions of the central bank exercise an influence on the liquidity (or more precisely: the cash position) of the banks. This, too, can exert an equilibrating influence. In the case of foreign exchange sales by the central bank, the ensuing tightening of the banks' cash position can make money market rates go up, so that - via various processes which are beyond the scope of this paper[1] - the development of the net foreign asset position of the banking system undergoes a change (smaller rise, greater decrease) which restores equilibrium in the foreign exchange market. Mutatis mutandis, the same goes for foreign exchange purchases. The balancing function of the central banks' monetary reserves is thus taken over by the net foreign assets of the banking system.

Instead of leaving the influencing of the banks' cash position and money market rates to the "automatic pilot" of the obligatory foreign exchange interventions, the central bank can, of course, also bring influence to bear through its money market instruments.

It goes without saying that exchange rate changes are also a mechanism to bring about equilibrium in the foreign exchange market. In a system of fixed exchange rates, this mechanism plays a rôle only within the agreed narrow margins. Nevertheless it can, especially in the case of disequilibria which are considered to be temporary, be so effective that the intervention limits are not reached and balancing actually takes place entirely through a change in net foreign assets. How this works exactly need not be discussed here. Suffice it to say that the prevalence of *stabilizing* expectations of exchange rate changes, based on unshaken confidence in the maintenance of the parity, plays and essential rôle in this connection[2].

Under a system of floating exchange rates it is also the *stabilizing* expectations of changes in exchange rates which enable the foreign exchange market to find exchange rate equilibrium at short notice[3].

(1) The change in the preparedness of non-banks to bear foreign exchange risks plays an essential rôle in this connection.
(2) Together with a change in the preparedness of non-banks to bear foreign exchange risks.
(3) A change in the exchange rate can, of course, also exert a more basically equilibrating influence, for example, on the current account of the balance of payments via a change in the competitive position. This influence, however, sometimes exhibits a considerable time-lag, while in the short-term it can even have a contrary effect (J-curve effect).

As, however, there is no fixed point in the form of a "parity" under this system, and great uncertainty can arise about the equilibrium exchange rate in the longer term, there may have to be a considerable measure of overshooting before exchange rate movements subside. This means that a system of free floating is generally marked by a considerable degree of instability - unless this is prevented by (coordination of) monetary policies.

It is important to emphasize that under a free floating system, there is no question of the monetary balance-of-payments outcome being practically nil all the time, so that there would be no international monetary influence in this respect. Changes in the net foreign asset position of the banking system are after all still possible, even under a free floating system. Attempts to achieve greater exchange rate stability by means of interventions in the foreign exchange market (managed floating) will, in general, add to the chances of major monetary balance-of-payments surpluses or deficits. Furthermore, in a climate marked by exchange rate uncertainty these interventions can, if they are excessive, have a destabilizing effect.

To maintain a sufficient degree of exchange rate stability under a system of floating exchange rates, a much more important instrument is money market policy directed at developments in the foreign exchange market[1]. As already described net foreign assets of the banking system can be stimulated to perform a balancing function by means of influencing the cash position of the banks. It goes without saying, however, that it is impossible in the longer term to prevent persistent monetary balance-of-payments disequilibria from feeding through to exchange rate movements. As market doubts on the tenability of the exchange rate grow, the difference between money market rates at home and abroad, which is necessary to maintain equilibrium in the foreign exchange market,will have to become greater. The tensions and problems (such as a possible inverted interest rate structure) ensuing

(1) In the Netherlands this part of monetary policy is sometimes called monetary policy in the narrow sense, to distinguish it from monetary policy in the broad sense, which is aimed at influencing the development of the monetary aggregates.

notably for the deficit country may eventually increase to such an extent that the more fundamental forces affecting the foreign exchange market (such as a disadvantageous difference in the rate of inflation) must be accommodated by allowing exchange rate adjustments.

4.   MONETARY NORMS

As set out above monetary policy is essentialy concerned with the right dosage of monetary latitude.   In an open economy, this latitude affects both domestic cyclical conditions and the outcome of the balance of payments. In this connection it is primarily national expenditure and external capital transactions which play a rôle as intermediary macro-economic variables.

The domestic cyclical conditions have a volume aspect (degree of capacity utilization; employment) and a price aspect (development with regard to the value of money). Since each of these aspects is of major importance and since it is by no means certain that the link existing between them (the Phillips curve) eventually allows a satisfactory degree of capacity utilization to concur spontaneously with a satis-factory stability of the value of money, it follows that there is a need not only for monetary policy, but also, in principle, for another policy instrument to influence the macro-economic process. Monetary policy may attempt to stifle the inflationary process by withholding the necessary monetary latitude from the economy, but the ensuing monet-ary tightening will, in the first instance, be at the expense of effective demand and thus of employment. It is only via disturbing the circular flow of the economy that the rate of inflation can be brought down, and it is highly questionable whether and to what extent a recovery of employment can be brought about in the long run on the basis of monetary policy alone without being accompanied by a revival of infla-tion. This policy dilemma cannot be solved by budgetary policy as the latter, like monetary policy, makes its macro-economic influence felt notably through the level of national expenditure.

It is in the field of wage determination that there is a logical need for an additional possibility to influence the outcome of the economic process. Which form this should take need not be discussed here. It need not necessarily be based on dirigist competencies on the part of the public authorities. Central consultations with intelligent persuasion and the preparedness of the employers' and employees' organizations to make allowance for the outcome of these consultations can be of major importance to ensure the necessary discipline and thus to avoid a situation in which this discipline has to be brought about by monetary means at the cost of employment and growth. In this connection the issue is not just the attainment of a satisfactory cyclical development, but also the ability to ensure that in a structural sense as well (competitive position, industrial profitability) the conditions for a balanced economic development are met.

As far as external transactions are concerned, the monetary balance-of-payments outcome and the need for intervention or exchange rate movements in the foreign exchange market are generally major policy concerns. The structure of the monetary balance-of-payments outcome too (i.e. the shares of current and capital transactions) is an obvious policy concern from the national point of view and an imperative policy concern when viewed internationally. The outcome of the current account of the balance of payments is the result of the cyclical situation at home and abroad, as well as of a complexity of factors which together can be termed the competitive position.

In view of the foregoing, a distinction can be made, within the framework of a model for international policy coordination, between three categories of balance-of-payments disturbances, viz. cyclical, financial and fundamental disturbances.

In the case of *cyclical disturbances*, the volume of national expenditure deviates from the norm which can be derived from production capacity, the "normal" degree of capacity utilization and the (internationally accepted) balance-of-payments target for the current account. These disturbances can be combatted with the instruments of demand management, viz. monetary policy and budgetary policy. The trading partners of countries faced with such disturbances are confronted - for so long as the disturbances persist - with the policy dilemma that targets regarding the degree of capacity utilization and the balance of payments cannot be realized simultaneously. Under these circumstances a counter-cyclical policy and maintenance of exchange rate stability seem the most compatible with optimum international policy coordination.

In the case of *financial disturbances*, external capital transactions are insufficiently attuned to current transactions corresponding with the balance-of-payments target. Monetary policy is the most obvious instrument to eliminate these disturbances (financial adjustment). As it is especially the interest rate differentials and not the interest rate levels which exert an influence on capital transactions, this gives rise to another problem of international policy co-ordination. Furthermore, it must be taken into account that monetary policy has an impact not only on capital transactions, but also on national spending and thus on cyclical conditions. This means, in principle, that it may be necessary to employ budgetary policy as well if cyclical equilibrium is to be maintained (the problem of the monetary budgetary policy mix).

A *fundamental disturbance* is a situation where the competitive position is either too weak or too strong to attain the (internationally accepted) target set for the outcome on the current account of the balance of payments under "normal" cyclical conditions at home and abroad. As in the case of a cyclical disturbance originating abroad, the policy dilemma arises that the targets with regard to the degree of capacity utilization and the balance of payments cannot be achieved simultaneously by means of demand management instruments. In this case the solution must be sought in an adjustment of the relative cost level vis-à-vis other countries. Wage and exchange rate policy (where money market policy has to play a rôle) are the appropriate ways of achieving such a cost adjustment. It is obvious that international policy co-ordination is of major importance in this matter[1].

The above outline of macro-economic policy problems regarding domestic and external equilibrium shows that monetary policy is concerned with various macro-economic objectives (value of money, employment, current account of the balance of payments, monetary balance-of-payments outcome, developments in the foreign exchange market),

(1) Under a system of fixed exchange rates such coordination is, by definition, ensured as far as the exchange rate target is concerned; changes in intervention limits are possible only under international agreement.

that these objectives may not be compatible, and that thus an important rôle has to be played by other macro-economic policy instruments as well in a policy effort which is more internationally co-ordinated. The question is what the criteria should be, under these circumstances, for the right dosage of monetary latitude. As pointed out earlier, monetary latitude consists in the possibility for inflationary financing by making use of newly created money or by dishoarding of (i.e. activation of) existing money balances. Since the possibilities for activation are restricted by the size of the money supply it is self-evident to regard the problem of the dosage of monetary latitude in the first instance as that of the dosage of the increase in the money supply.

As the availability of external finance need not necessarily be reflected by interest rate movements, the latter do not form a reliable indicator for the assessment of the desirable rate of growth for money supply. The "equilibrium rate of interest" necessary for cyclical equilibrium is a very uncertain and changeable variable, which can, furthermore, deviate from the interest rate level necessary for balance-of-payments equilibrium. The postulate that the growth rate of the money supply should be attuned to the "spontaneous" increase in the demand for liquidity (with monetary equilibrium ensuing) also provides little policy support since everything turns on the meaning given to the concept spontaneous.

A more operational approach is that where attention is given to the national liquidity ratio and where consequently the question is asked whether and to what extent the increase in the money supply should keep pace with the rise in national income. Numerous policy considerations can play a rôle here.

(a) Insofar as there is an unacceptable rate of price increase, it is for monetary policy to help break the inflationary spiral by not including the inflationary component of the increase in the demand for liquidity in the allowable growth of the money supply. If a monetary tightening brought about in this manner leads to a recessionary disturbance of the economy, this must be attributed to the failure of income policy to influence the process of wage and price determination.

(b) If there is a danger of cyclical overheating, the growth of the money supply should also be smaller than the increase in the demand for liquidity ensuing from developments with regard to national income. This is all the more so because the emergence of a spontaneous cyclical activation of liquidity must also be taken into consideration.

(c) In the reverse situation, it can be said that under recessionary circumstances or – more in general – in times when industry spontaneously increases its liquidity holdings, a rise in the national liquidity ratio may be justifiable. In order, however, to maintain a sufficient degree of monetary controllability, care will have to be taken that the ratio does not rise excessively.

(d) In the longer term, the assesment of the acceptability of movements in the liquidity ratio must also take into account the possible long-term or structural nature of changes in the relative size of the demand for liquidity, such as, for example, the influence of changes in the relationship between national income and transactions (the so-called differentiation factor) and changes in the distribution of national income over the various categories of households as well as the influence of income or transaction elasticities of the demand for liquidity which deviate from 1. There is, generally, still much uncertainty on this matter. Furthermore, it can make a difference on which quantitative liquidity concept the assessment is based. It is, to some extent, true that an income elasticity of the demand for liquidity which lies in the vicinity of 1 may be regarded as an indication that liquidity considerations play a major rôle and that the relevant financial asset should therefore be considered part of the money supply.

(e) Finally, in an open economy, concern for the balance-of-payment position is a very important matter, which cannot be ignored by monetary policy. In the case of a monetary balance-of-payments deficit there is an outflow of liquidity. Such an outflow can persist only if it is compensated for by liquidity creation from domestic sources. It is, generally speaking. for monetary policy not to allow such a development. Thus, a process of financial adjustment is set in motion, which can, via monetary tightening (a decline of the liquidity ratio) and an increase in the interest rate level compared with other countries, lead to restoration of monetary balance-of-payments equilibrium. Under such a policy it is no longer the total increase in the domestic money supply, but the increase from domestic sources (domestic liquidity creation) which is attuned to the accepted development in national income. Except in the case where monetary tightening must be considered desirable also for domestic reasons (inflationary price increases, cyclical overheating) the recovery of external equilibrium could to a certain degree be at the expense of domestic equilibrium. Depending on the underlying situation, it will be the other instruments – viz. those of budgetary policy and those regarding the competitive position (income policy, exchange rate policy) – which will have to help provide the basis for a general recovery of equilibrium.

The foregoing is, mutatis mutandis, also true of a monetary balance-of-payments surplus. In this case the attunement of domestic liquidity creation to the accepted development of national income leads to monetary easing (a rise in the liquidity ratio) which can contribute to external equilibrium via a decrease in interest rates, but which may detract from domestic equilibrium.

(f) It is of course not always necessary for monetary policy to give priority to the restoration of external equilibrium. It can sometimes be justifiable to compensate for monetary balance-of-payments disequilibria which are considered temporary, via monetary means (e.g. through the public authorities' borrowing policy) and to avert the consequences for the foreign exchange market entirely via money market policy. From the viewpoint of maintaining a sufficient degree of confidence in the national currency such a policy choice can be made sooner in the case of a monetary balance-of-payments surplus than in this case of a monetary balance-of-payments deficit.

5. MONETARY INSTRUMENTS

In the foregoing discussion control over the volume of domestic liquidity creation stands out as the most essential element of monetary policy. This implies that the monetary authorities are faced with the task of exercising an influence on the financing behaviour leading to liquidity creation. If, as is the case in the Netherlands, short-term financial claims on the public authorities are considered to be near money, these liquidity creating ways of financing can be classified as follows:

(a) central government recourse to short-term credit, whether or not supplied by the banking system, such as Treasury paper and short-term cash loans;

(b) local authority recourse to short-term credit, whether or not supplied by the banking system, such as short-term cash loans;

(c) long-term bank lending to the public authorities (such as the granting of long-term cash loans), short- and long-term bank lending to the private sector (such as the granting of personal loans, industrial credit and mortgages) and banking investments in securities (such as the purchase of bonds issued by the public authorities or the private sector), but only insofar as the gross expansion of the banks' domestic lending operations ensuing from these activities exceeds the growth in *long-term* domestic liabilities (i.e. liabilities which, from the creditor's point of view, do not have the character of money or near money).

It goes without saying that the primary responsibility for the liquidity creation as meant under (a) lies with the central government. The latter can also exercise control over local authority recourse to liquidity creation, for example by fixing a ceiling for short-term debt, as is the case in the Netherlands.

The comprehensive nature of the liquidity creation referred to under (c) makes it clear that it is generally not expedient to make a distinction by borrower in order to subject the latter to norms or guidelines; the central bank's monetary supervision is directed at the banking system. In exercising its supervision, the Bank may attempt to influence the behaviour of the banking system via an indirect method, viz. via the market mechanism; it can also try to safeguard the monetary outcome of this behaviour in a more direct manner.

In the indirect method of credit restriction, the framework within which the banks' portfolio selection is made is manipulated, although the banks retain their freedom of choice. Open market transactions, foreign exchange swaps, obligatory cash reserves related to the moneys entrusted to the banks, rediscount ceilings and special loans form the most important instruments by means of which the cash or liquidity position of the banking system can be controlled. Together with the official rates for the central bank's credit facilities, this line of action can exert a decisive influence on how money market rates come about and thus on the banks' lending rates. The interest rate mechanism plays a major rôle in the portfolio selection process which determines the monetary outcome of banking activities because, among other things, a rise in interest rates can bring about a reduction in the *demand* for credit.

A major point on which there is still much uncertainty is whether, apart from via interest rates, a clearly *independent* importance must be assigned in this process to the quantitative cash or liquidity relationships within the banking system. The base money approach is founded on this premise, but it has been shown that this approach, whose more mechanistic versions are totally in conflict with the principles of the portfolio selection process, does not apply at all for many countries, including the Netherlands. The complications ensuing from external capital transactions of the banks are just one of many factors to be kept in mind.

The multisectoral nature of the portfolio selection process even makes it uncertain whether a rise in money market rates induced within the framework of a restrictive monetary policy will always contribute to a reduction of the rate of monetary expansion. So long as capital market rates have not followed suit to a sufficient degree, near money becomes relatively more attractive. The ensuing increase in the demand for liquidity could lead to a positive response of the endogenous process of liquidity creation.

In the case of more direct forms of credit restriction, the endogenous character of the process of liquidity creation is to some extent undermined. The system applied in the Netherlands in the years 1977–81 entailed that the volume of the net monetary expansion referred to in the beginning of this paragraph under (c) was tested by a norm for each credit institution; if the norm was exceeded, non-interestbearing cash reserves had to be maintained. This norm, which showed the maximum allowable monetary expansion in the surveillance period, was expressed as a percentage (which was, in principle, equal for all credit institutions) of the starting position of the net monetary operations (gross monetary assets minus long-term liabilities). The normative element of the regulation was strengthened by the stipulation that the maintenance of a non-interest-bearing cash reserve does not relieve a credit institution from the obligation to prevent frequent and substantial overstepping of the limits.

It is conceivable that even without this normative or dirigist element, a regulation which has direct consequences for individual credit institutions as regards their rate of monetary expansion, could be more effective than purely indirect methods of monetary control. It might be possible, for example, to give the central bank, in consultation with the credit institutions, the power to oblige individual credit institutions to maintain non-interest-bearing cash reserves related to the volume of net monetary expansion recorded by such institutions in a moving 12-month period. If aggregate monetary expansion were considered to be becoming excessive the Central Bank, by raising the percentage of this cash reserve requirement, could bring about an effective inducement for the individual banks to reduce their contribution to money creation.

The major importance of being able to make use of more direct forms of credit restriction is that there is less danger for monetary policy to land in a situation where a choice must be made between policy objectives which cannot be realized simultaneously. Indirect credit restrictions push money market rates up, thus inevitably exercising an influence on the foreign exchange market. In this way conflicts may arise between policy targets relating to the control of the rate of monetary expansion and those directed at the exchange rate and the position of the foreign exchange market. The actual situation in most countries is that, in the absence of the possibility to make use of a more direct form of credit restriction, monetary policy has at its disposal only one instrument to perform two typically monetary policy tasks. The instrument of direct restrictions could meet the case and thus also be of great help to achieve a better international coordination of monetary policy.

Of course, this does not mean that if direct restrictions are imposed interest rates will not go up, nor that a conflict with external policy targets could never arise. The increase in interest rates expected to ensue from direct restrictions is smaller, however, and relates not so much to money market rates as to capital market rates, as well as, possibly, to the banks' lending rates. A conflict with objectives regarding the foreign exchange market need not immediately arise. There remains a certain scope for money market policy to take this external aspect into account.

The external policy targets do not, of course, relate solely to the foreign exchange market. Monetary balance-of-payments equilibrium (via financial adjustment) is - certainly in the longer term - another weighty target. In this respect, even when it is possible to employ direct restrictions, a conflict of policies cannot always be avoided. The increase in capital market rates can lead to an inflow of capital which may not only partially undo the intended restrictive effect on monetary conditions, but may also make it increasingly difficult for money market policy to ensure adequate equilibrium in the foreign exchange market. Under such conditions, the only basically correct policy reaction is a change in the mix with budgetary policy with the latter, as an instrument of demand management, taking over part of the domestic task of monetary policy. This will permit interest rates to decrease somewhat, and will bring about better compatibility of external and domestic policy targets.

6. GENERAL ECONOMIC CONDITIONS FOR ECONOMIC RECOVERY IN THE NETHERLANDS

As I have already stressed (section 2.) the effect of monetary policy on the outcome of the economic process is generally of a conditioning rather than of a causative nature. Other macro-economic instruments, are required as well to set the economic process on the right course. Using such instruments conditions other than monetary ones must also be fulfilled which are of paramount importance for economic recovery.

In a Western economy, characterized by the operation of the market mechanism, proper coordination of the various policy instruments can only be achieved if they are directed towards the simultaneous fulfilment of the basic conditions which are to be considered essential for the proper functioning of the market sector in particular. Ofcourse, government policy does also reflect political preferences. It is, however, essential that the basic conditions are not neglected. This is especially true for the contribution of monetary policy. Here lies a forceful justification for a highly independent position of the central bank.

Amongst the conditions outside the purely monetary sphere which are important to economic recovery in the Netherlands, three closely interrelated conditions exist as regards the determination of factor wages, viz.:

(a) the prevention, to the extent possible, of a price-push effect of labour costs;

(b) the improvement of profitability in industry;

(c) the strengthening of the competitive position.

The first aim serves the stability of the value of money which is of major importance for a balanced, credible and socially acceptable economic development. It also, however, helps to achieve the two other aims. After all, wage increases in excess of productivity erode profitability if prices remain stable, while, if profitability is maintained (and, consequently, price increases do occur) there is a danger of impairment of the competitive position

Although recent years have seen an improvement in industrial profitability, as regards both factor income and, to an even greater extent, disposable income (taxation, investment subsidies), a major further improvement must yet be viewed as a necessary condition for a sustained revival of investment, which is essential for economic recovery. The requirement of a further strengthening of the competitive position stems in part from the consideration that, in an open economy such as that of the Netherlands, the growth of exports invariably provides indispensable locomotive power for more rapid and more sustained economic growth. The still large surplus on the current account of the balance of payments (a good 4 per cent of national income in 1984) is in part - difficult to quantify exactly - due to domestic cyclical factors (stagnating consumption and housebuilding; underutilization of production capacity in the sectors producing for the domestic market), and must hence not be seen as an indication of an already sufficiently strong competitive position.

The moderation of wage developments, which will continue to be necessary in the years ahead, will place a heavy burden on the consultations between employers' organizations and trade unions, both at the central level and at the level of sectors of industries, as well as on the "guidance" which the Government may provide in this respect. To assume that the "market forces" will "automatically" lead to a satisfactory outcome would be short-sighted.

In connection with the observations made about the development of wage costs, it is necessary to discuss the objective regarding the external value of the guilder as reflected in the exchange rates. The Netherlands' membership of the EMS is a given political fact, which is accepted as such. The major interest which a small open economy such as that of the Netherlands has in maximum stability of exchange rate relationships with its principal trading partners and in the observance by these partners of the necessary policy discipline as a basis for policy co-ordination, constitutes the economic rationale for this political decision.

Within this framework, the factual orientation towards the Deutsche mark reflects a deliberate policy choice. Amongst the EMS partners, the Federal Republic of Germany exhibits the greatest policy discipline and generally the most vigorous economic development. This is reflected in the course of the domestic and the external value of the German currency. Thus, in the recent past, the orientation towards the Deutsche mark was instrumental in achieving a substantial mitigation of the inflationary nature of the external "climate" affecting the Netherlands economy. More in general, it provided and continues to provide welcome support for the Netherlands' own policy discipline. Moreover, the maintenance, through money market policy, of a strong position within the EMS – a precondition for a continued link with the Deutsche mark, even in the event of a future realignment – bolsters confidence in the guilder, permitting both money market rates and capital market rates to move at lower levels than would be possible in the absence of such confidence.

It is clear in this regard that this relative decrease in interest rates forms part of the influence – existing in principle – which international differences in rates of inflation may have, through exchange rate expectations, on international interest rate differentials. The exchange rate policy as outlined above can help this relationship to have its full effect, so that the real interest rate levels, despite a lower rate of inflation, may come to be not higher and in time possibly even lower than those abroad.

The foregoing means that, practically speaking, the movements in the external value of the guilder must be regarded for the Netherlands economy as an exogenous variable, being the result of the movements in the Deutsche mark/dollar rate and the movements in the exchange rates of all other currencies, including non-EMS ones, against the US dollar. Although within the EMS consultations can be held about the exchange rate movements of the dollar and although the money market and intervention policies pursued by Germany's EMS partners may have some effect, the possibility for the Netherlands to influence the external value of the guilder, while maintaining the stable relationship with the Deutsche mark, is nevertheless negligible. For the policy aimed at strengthening the competitive position, this means that the movements in the guilder's effective exchange rate must be regarded as an exogenous variable. The effective appreciation of the guilder has thus provided an additional incentive to moderate costs, fully in line with the disciplinary action of the external regime chosen. It is undeniably true that a sudden acceleration of this effective appreciation – as might occur if the overvaluation of the dollar, as it currently exists from a point of view of fundamental adjustment, were to end – could adversely affect the competitive position in the short run. In the longer term, however, this need not frustrate the policy aimed at strengthening the competitive position, the less so as the required additional moderation of costs need not imply a real burden, since the value of the currency also undergoes the effects of appreciation.

Amongst the measures to improve and protect supply side conditions a reduction and better control over public sector expenditure constitutes a crucial element of policy efforts to achieve economic recovery. This concern about the size of the public sector must be distinguished sharply from the desirability of reducing the public sector borrowing requirement. There can be no doubt about the fact that the size of the borrowing requirement is substantially in excess of the private sector's savings surplus under conditions of balanced expansion. Also it is indisputable that if the borrowing requirement is allowed to continue at its present level and interest rates do not come down, the public sector's interest charges will show a very sharp increase, far in excess of the rise in national income. The level at which in time interest charges will stabilize in proportion to national income could be a very high one, especially if interest rates were to continue to exceed the percentage increase in national income. That could seriously and for a long time aggravate the problem of curbing the public sector's expenditure.

Yet, it must not be concluded from the foregoing that economic recovery demands that the borrowing requirement should be reduced as rapidly as possible. The timing and the pace of this reduction must constitute a major policy consideration, as it is necessary to allow for yet another – in principle very important – condition for economic recovery: the existence of an adequate measure of domestic cyclical equilibrium in the sense of a satisfactory degree of capacity utilization and attractive and sufficiently diversified sales prospects.

As regards the cyclical situation (in 1984-85) one can speak of export led growth. There is a vigorous expansion of exports in excess of the growth rate of world trade. There also is some revival of investment in export oriented industry. A major overall increase in industry's investment ratio, as would be necessary for an important and sustained revival of the economy, is, however, not yet discernible. There is lack of any significant growth in most other categories of national expenditure such as personal consumption, housebuilding and public sector expenditure on goods and services. This, no doubt, has much to do with the endeavours to reduce the very high borrowing requirement of the public sector. Real disposable labour income and transfer income per head has been continuously on the decline during the last five years. Under the prevailing circumstances the expansion of industrial output has remained rather meagre and employment has hardly risen despite attempts to redistribute existing jobs. For the future the extent to which taxes and social premiums are reduced to the benefit of real disposable labour income is clearly a very important policy issue.

7. MONETARY CONDITIONS FOR ECONOMIC RECOVERY IN THE
    NETHERLANDS

As far as monetary developments are concerned, the position as it
emerges from the data about the recent past may be characterized as
follows:

- The public sector has succeeded fully, or more than fully, in
  covering its high borrowing requirement in the capital market. Consequently, the money creation attributable to the public sector is nil
  or even negative.
- On the other hand external transactions yield a substantial inflow of
  money (monetary balance-of-payments surplus) consequent on the fact
  that the large surplus on the current account of the balance of
  payments is only partly offset by net capital exports by the non-
  monetary sectors. Subscriptions by non-residents to public sector
  issues also play a rôle here.
- Money creation by the banking system resulting from lending and
  capital market investments not financed from long-term funds has
  been free from restrictions since 1981. In order to permit prompt
  action if necessary, a special reporting system has been maintained,
  but this has no curbing effect. The actual volume of the money
  creation in question, has in recent years, expressed as a percentage
  of the domestic money supply, exceeded the growth rate of national
  income by a considerable margin. Of late, domestic private money
  creation has slowed down considerably.
- These factors combined caused the national liquidity ratio to increase
  sharply in 1982 and 1983, after the slight increases already recorded
  in 1980 and 1981. The easing of liquidity was mainly concentrated in
  industry. In 1984 the upward movement of the national liquidity ratio
  has slowed down.
- Owing in part to the money market policy suited to the needs of the
  currency in the foreign exchange market, money market rates have
  moved at a level slightly above German money market rates.
- Since 1982 capital market rates have moved at a level well above
  money market rates. Consequently, the *structure* of interest rates in
  the Netherlands has shown a pattern which can be considered normal.
- In spite of the rise in the liquidity ratio capital market rates came

down only slightly and much less than the reduction in the inflation rate. (This rate probably falling to below 2 per cent in 1985). There was thus a further rise in long term *real* interest rates which certainly did not contribute to the investment climate of industry.

Turning to the question of current monetary policy, I want to concentrate on two issues which to a certain extent are mutually opposed. The first is whether there are still opportunities left for domestic monetary policy to contribute to a reduction in interest rates. Such a reduction could be of importance both to reduce the public sector's interest charges and to encourage a vigorous and sustained revival of industrial investment. The second issue is whether, in view of the development of liquidity conditions, restrictions should be imposed on the volume of domestic money creation. I shall discuss these two questions in some detail.

With regard to the level of interest rate, I have to emphasize first of all that, given the foreign exchange market objective of money market policy, money market rates and, hence, generally the bank's lending rate[1] cannot be influenced for domestic policy purposes. Factors exogenous to policy, such as interest rate movements abroad, together with the size of the monetary balance-of-payments surplus determine the moving market interest rate level at which the desired position of the foreign exchange market is achieved.

We, furthermore, have to note that there are at present no restrictions on the volume of money creation by the banking system. This creation is thus entirely in the nature of an endogenous variable. It follows that the only way for monetary policy possibly to bring about a domestically produced downward pressure on (long term) interest rates lies in an increase in money creation (or a decrease in liquidity annihilation) by the public sector. To that end, the public sector would have to cover its borrowing requirement to a lesser extent from capital market funds. The question is, however, whether it would be advisable to bring about an increase in the volume of domestic liquidity creation

(1) The bank's lending rate is traditionally linked to the Netherlands Bank's discount on promissory notes through a surcharge. If money market rates are higher, the banks can apply an additional surcharge.

in this way. It will be clear that for this to be advisable an obvious condition has to be met: the change in the financing behaviour should not have a *negative* influence on the confidence of foreign investors and money market agents. Taking this confidence factor into account I think that the existence of a large monetary balance of payments surplus can be seen as a indication that there may indeed be some scope for monetary policy to be directed at a downward pressure on interest rates. The monetary balance of payments surplus suggests that the financial adjustment to external conditions is incomplete. A greater volume of domestic money creation could, in principle, cause interest rates to fall to such an extent relative to other countries that monetary balance-of-payments equilibrium is restored through an increase in net capital exports.

By how much interest rates could fall and how large the money creation by the public sector would have to be is difficult to say in advance. The interest rate sensitivity of external capital transactions and the financing behaviour of industry and of the banking system are too uncertain to allow prediction. All we can say is that in principle, when monetary balance-of-payments equilibrium has been achieved and is being maintained, long-term interest rates may stabilize at a slightly lower level compared with the present "imbalanced" situation and the liquidity ratio at a slightly higher level. Parallel to this the volume of domestic liquidity creation would become just so much larger as to offset the cessation of the inflow of money from abroad.

I now, however, have to add a word of caution. Under present conditions there may exist some hesitation about whether it would be wise to attach decisive significance to the norm of monetary balance-of-payments equilibrium and to gear the financing behaviour of the public sector completely to this objective. An important consideration is that allowing monetary financing by the public sector could impair the political feasibility of bringing about the necessary policy changes to regain control over public expenditure. In addition, there is the fact that the national liquidity ratio has already risen substantially over the past few years. Allowing a further easing of liquidity conditions for the sake of a reduction of capital market rates could aggravate the problem of maintaining adequate monetary controllability.

Furthermore, it has to be acknowledged that the reduction in the overall level of interest rates to be attained by better financial adjustment of the balance of payments may well be rather marginal, since it cannot be excluded that money market rates would have to rise somewhat in order to keep the foreign exchange market in a satisfactory equilibrium. In view of these considerations I conclude that it would appear wise that a policy change to achieve better financial adjustment of the balance of payments should not, for the time being, go beyond such a limitation of the volume of public sector borrowing in the capital market that *annihilation* of liquidity by the public sector is prevented. The norm of monetarily *neutral* financing by the public sector, which is important not least for reasons of policy psychology, can thus be maintained.

I now come to the second question which I raised: in view of the development of liquidity conditions, should restrictions be imposed on the volume of domestic money creation? It is a fact that the liquidity ratio has risen considerably over the past few years. There is as yet little certainty about the occurrence of any long-term or structural changes in the relative volume of the demand for money. It is, however, beyond doubt that the sharp increase in the liquidity ratio has at least in part to be interpreted as an increase in the inflationary potential existing within the Dutch economy in the form of money and near money balances which can be run down in the future. At present these margins of liquidity, which have arisen in industry in particular, do not, of course, constitute an impediment to economic recovery. On the contrary, ample availability of external finance can aid the "climate" which must lead to the sorely needed revival of investment. It is very possible that the balances accumulated within industry are already in part "finance balances" intended for the financing of planned investments or investments of which the possibility is at least envisaged. For as long as these investments have not yet taken place and industry's demand for liquid assets consequently continues, an attempt by the monetary authorities to reduce the national liquidity ratio (for instance via even further increased capital market borrowing by the public sector) could only lead to a detrimental increase in capital market rates. At the same time, there would be even less financial adjustment to external conditions; the monetary balance-of-payments surplus would become larger still.

Some observers hold the view that the high public sector borrowing requirement, although financed with long term funds, must in an indirect way – namely because public sector bonds are purchased by non-residents and by the banking system – be held responsible for the easing of liquidity conditions. I do not share this view. In my opinion it fails to give adequate weight to the endogenous nature of the inflow of money from abroad and the money creation by the banking system and to the effect which has been exerted in this respect by the increase in the demand for money. A reduction in the public sector borrowing requirement will not by itself automatically help to bring down the national liquidity ratio.

A spontaneous redress of liquidity conditions could, however, occur if industry were to use its accumulated liquid assets for the financing of additional investments. It is conceivable that, in that situation, recourse to money creation would barely increase and that the growth of national income would lead to a rise in the demand for transactions balances which would "absorb" the activated liquid assets. The liquidity ratio would then come down. Of course, this possibility does not mean that there will never be circumstances under which monetary policy has an active rôle to play. The accumulation of an inflationary potential in the form of unused liquid assets is a matter for concern, because, though conceivable, it is not *certain* that the "discharge" of this potential will not in due course have an undesired inflationary impact on the economic process.

For as long as the domestic economy is still considerably removed from the danger zone of overheating and the course of costs and prices is satisfactory, whilst the balance-of-payments yields monetary equilibrium or even a surplus, it is possible to acquiesce in the easing of liquidity conditions. This, however, changes if developments in one or more of these respects become less reassuring. In that event, it could become necessary to ensure that domestic money creation does not exceed the rise in the demand for money imputable solely to the *volume* component of the increase in national income. If, in addition, a spontaneous running-down of cash balances accumulated earlier were to be expected, maximum permissible domestic money creation would have to be even lower.

8. CONCLUDING REMARKS

It would, of course, lead me too far to discuss the various situations with which the monetary authorities may be confronted when monitoring the process of economic recovery. The important thing is to acknowledge that monetary policy, although vital for the correct monetary conditioning of economic recovery, is by no means all-powerful. Its effect on the course of costs and prices is indirect; the use of monetary methods to combat inflation may result in an impairment of the circular flow of the economy. This responsibility should, however, not be evaded when there is no other way of restoring the necessary discipline with regard to wage and price determination.

There also are the constraints imposed by the open character of the Dutch economy. If a tightening of monetary conditions results in an undesired inflow of money from abroad, monetary policy has reached its limit in terms of what it can achieve for domestic equilibrium.

Furthermore it is important to stress that Dutch experience has shown conclusively that in order to control the volume of liquidity creation by the banking system, only a form of direct restrictions will do. Under the system of direct restrictions which has been used in the Netherlands a ceiling was established for monetary expansion of each individual credit institution. It is clear, however, that such a system cannot be operated on a permanent basis since competition between credit institutions would then become well-nigh impossible. For the instrument of direct monetary control to be available all the time a form will have to be found which does not interfere with interbank competition. In the foregoing discussion (see section 5.) a suggestion for such a system has already been put forward. In my opinion it would be a good thing if such a non-dirigist system of direct monetary control were to be developed since, from the point of view of internatinal coordination of monetary policy, there also appears to be an urgent need to have this instrument available. This brings me to some observations with respect to the international context.

The very openness of the Dutch economy obviously gives great weight to the international context in which economic recovery will have to be achieved. This is especially true for a country that has chosen for export-led growth. An international backslide into stagnation or, to put it in more general terms, an abnormal instability of international conditions would create serious impediments to recovery. Unfortunately the international outlook is not yet quite reassuring.

Export-led growth is, by definition, possible only in a few countries, viz. only by virtue of a much greater expansion of expenditure in other countries. The greatest support for economic activity abroad was and is provided by the USA where the policy pursued led to very powerful budgetary expenditure impulses, which despite the upsurge in economic activity, found their expression in a further increase and continuing high level of the public sector's financial deficit. In these circumstances, the responsibility of keeping a tight rein on economic expansion, which is very important from the point of view of stable economic growth, came to rest wholly on American monetary policy.

This American policy mix is to a large extent responsible for a level of most international interest rates which in view of the cyclical conditions and the slowing down of inflation has to be called high and for an exchange rate of the US dollar which in view of the huge deficit on the current account of the US balance of payments has to be labelled as overvalued. The heavy domestic task assigned to American monetary policy did not permit acount to be taken of external considerations. In the absence of more direct forms of credit restriction, American money market rates fell much less than the rate of inflation after 1981. This interest rate thus became so attractive to foreign depositors and other short-term investors that, despite the increasing deficit on the current account of the balance of payments and the lack of financial adjustment in long-term capital movements, the US dollar underwent a considerable appreciation in most foreign exchange markets. In turn, this appreciation and the expectations thus aroused of further appreciation increased the attraction of the US dollar even further. In these circumstances, most other countries had little room to evade the magnetism of American money market rates.

It is, of course, not my intention to examine these developments here in greater detail. They have been mentioned only to make clear that the international economic situation, even if we confine ourselves to the Western world, is still far from balanced. The inappropriate budgetary policy stance in the USA makes the cyclical prospects highly uncertain. In view of the huge deficit on the current account of the American balance of payments, the US dollar is clearly overvalued. The high level of interest rates consequent on the American policy mix, works against a lasting economic recovery in the Western world and the position of developing countries.

Dutch monetary authorities can do little or nothing to give protection against international instability. They should continue to build on stable exchange rate relations with the DM and to perform their modest and yet essential task at home to the best of their ability so that at least in their own field conditions for a sustained economic recovery are fulfilled as much as possible. They furthermore have continuously to stand in for better international policy co-ordination. International acceptance of the view that monetary policy should always also be directed at internationally co-ordinated external objectives and that for the achievement of domestic objectives another monetary instrument which functions in a more direct way has to be developed, would in my opinion constitute a great step forward.

13. MONETARY CONDITIONS FOR ECONOMIC RECOVERY: THE INTERNATIONAL PERSPECTIVE

E. van Lennep

1. INTRODUCTION

After the long recession which followed the second oil price rise, recovery is now under way in most major OECD countries. Its extent has varied from country to country: while a rapid growth of output and a substantial reduction in unemployment have already been experienced in the United States, growth rates in Europe have so far been more modest and insufficient to bring down unemployment. While the present outlook is generally favourable, there remains concern, particularly outside North America, that the recovery may prove to be fragile, partly due to pervasive obstacles to structural adjustments. Equally, especially in the United States, there is some concern that the recovery may be proceeding too rapidly, threatening a reacceleration of inflation. The task confronting policy makers in the present conjuncture is to ensure that neither of these developments becomes a reality and that a period of sustained recovery ensues. Today I would like to talk about the contribution monetary policy can make in this respect.

Let me define at the outset what I take to be the "ultimate goals" of monetary policy since, to a large extent, this will be the general theme of my contribution. The consensus we have arrived at in OECD economies is that it is counter-productive to pursue policies which accommodate inflation. This view gained favour in the late 1970s and crystallised particularly after the second oil price shock. Monetary policy should thus aim to provide a stable environment for private economic activity by reducing inflation to a low rate, possibly zero, and keeping it there. This will not, by itself, generate a sustainable recovery. Complementary policies, in the form of fiscal measures to reduce structural budget deficits and structural policies to enhance the

Monetary Conditions for Economic Recovery, ed. by C. van Ewijk and J.J. Klant
© *1985, Martinus Nijhoff Publishers, Dordrecht. All rights reserved.*

flexibility and efficiency of markets within the private sector must also be carried out. However, a steady, non-inflationary monetary policy should contribute to the sustainability of the recovery, once under way, as it would obviate the need for a future credit squeeze which, as so often in the past, has brought the expansion to an end.

The theme which I intend to develop today is not based on pure conjecture. It is based on a careful analysis of previous recoveries in the OECD area. It incorporates a plea to learn the lessons of past mistakes in the conduct of monetary policy. For this reason I intend to take some time to review the pattern of monetary policy in previous recoveries. Subsequently I will draw some implications for the conduct of monetary policy at the present conjuncture, and I will attempt to identify what additional ingredients may also be necessary if a sustainable recovery is to ensue.

2. THE STANCE OF MONETARY POLICY IN THE PRESENT AND PAST RECOVERIES

The charts A and B illustrate the stance of monetary policy during the early stages of previous cycles and during the present recovery for eleven OECD countries (the seven largest, Belgium, Denmark, the Netherlands and Switzerland). The behaviour of a number of indicators for each country is displayed over the period 1967-83, and the periods of recovery and expansion are denoted by the shaded areas. Although situations have differed from cycle to cycle and from country to country, a comparative survey of the charts suggests that there has been a general pattern since the 1960s. Monetary policy has often provided too much support during the early stages of recoveries and/or provided it for too long. Delays in restraining demand have often forced the authorities to impose or to acquiesce in steep rises in interest rates, but this has not prevented accelerations in inflation which have made expansions of activity unsustainable. The following points emerge from the charts:

(a) Previous cycles often displayed accelerations of monetary growth in early stages or continued high rates of monetary growth following an acceleration in the late stages of previous cycles. After some two years the acceleration has tended to stop and, in some cases, to be partially reversed for a time. In short, monetary growth has often been stimulatory early in the cycle and then moved to a more restrictive stance after recovery was clearly under way. During the current recovery there have been notable monetary accelerations in the United States, Canada, Denmark and to a lesser extent, the Netherlands.

(b) Short-term interest rates corroborate the impression given by the monetary aggregates. In the early stages of recoveries interest rates have usually been low, and in many cases falling. Frequently, however, one to three years into a recovery they have risen sharply, often in conjunction with monetary decelerations. The steepness and suddenness of many of the increases in interest rates, however, suggest that they were imposed only when pressures, either from inflation or weak exchange rates, mounted to such an extent that they then forced a policy reaction. It is likely that had monetary growth been restrained at an earlier stage, the necessary increases in interest rates could have been smaller and less abrupt.

(c) In the United States both short and long-term real interest rates are currently far higher than during previous recoveries or at any other stage of previous cycles except the end of the most recent one. This is not, however, the case in most other countries. Only in the Netherlands do they stand out as especially high by historical standards, particularly at the long end. In France, the United Kingdom and Canada real long-term rates can be said to be above levels of previous recoveries, but not by large amounts. Elsewhere, present levels of real interest rates are not out of line with past experience at this stage of the cycle. While they are in many cases higher than during recoveries in the early and mid-1970s they are generally comparable to levels prevailing at the beginning of the expansion of the late 1960s.

The overall conjunctural situation near cyclical troughs is summarized in table 1. While the severity of the recent recession has no precedent in the post-war period when measured in terms of unemployment, this is not the case when measured in terms of production. The recessions of the late 1960s and early 1970s were comparatively mild, but this was not true of the slump which followed the first oil price

316

TABLE 1

Conjunctural Situation near through of Past and Present Cycles

	Late 1960s downturn			Early 1970s downturn		
	Output fall in recession (a)	Associated fall in the inflation rate (b)	Recovery begins (c)	Output fall in recession (a)	Associated fall in the inflation rate (b)	Recovery begins (c)
	(%)	(percentage points)		(%)	(percentage points)	
United States	1.8	1.2	July 67	6.8	3.5	Nov. 70
Japan	–	3.5	Sept.68	3.0	5.3	Jan. 72
Germany	9.6	4.1	May 67	5.4	1.0	Dec. 71
France	–	0.5	Oct. 67	2.0	1.8	May 71
United Kingdom	3.5	4.2	Aug. 67	3.2	4.5	Feb. 72
Italy	–	2.0	Mar. 68	13.1	0.8	Apr. 72
Canada	–	1.3	Feb. 68	2.7	3.8	Oct. 70
Belgium	2.1	3.7	Apr. 67	7.1	1.3	May 71
Denmark	n.a.	n.a.	n.a.	n.a.	2.6	Q2.71
Netherlands	3.2	4.5	May 67	2.9	1.1	Dec. 71
Switzerland	1.0	4.2	Q1.68	1.4	0.7	Q2.72

	Mid-1970s downturn			Recent downturn		
	Output fall in recession (a)	Associated fall in the inflation rate (b)	Recovery begins (c)	Output fall in recession (a)	Associated fall in the inflation rate (b)	Recovery begins (c)
	(%)	(percentage points)		(%)	(percentage points)	
United States	15.4	7.4	Mar. 75	12.3	12.3	Nov. 82
Japan	19.5	24.0	Mar. 75	3.9	8.3	Feb. 83
Germany	10.8	5.5	July 75	9.8	4.3	Dec. 82
France	14.7	6.1	May 75	10.1	5.5	
United Kingdom	10.8	19.5	Aug. 75	15.5	18.2	May. 81
Italy	17.5	15.3	May 75	16.6	8.1	June 83
Canada	9.6	6.9	Oct. 75	17.6	7.9	Dec. 82
Belgium	15.6	12.6	Aug. 75	16.3	2.6	Dec. 82
Deneark	20.3	12.5	Mar. 75	12.5	8.3	Oct. 82
Netherlands	8.5	7.7	Aug. 75	14.3	5.0	Aug. 82
Switzerland	18.2	11.0	Q1.75	9.2	6.1	Q4.82

– Negligible

n.a. not available

a. Industrial Productions for all countries except Denmark; manufacturing sales for Denmark. The figures in the table show the difference between the highest output level associated with the previous expansion and the lowest output level associated with the downturn.

b. The inflation rate is defined as the change in the consumer price index compared to twelve months earlier. The figures in the table show the difference between the highest inflation rate associated with the previoss expansion and the lowest inflation rate associated with the downturn.

c. Cyclical turning points designated by OECD Secretariat using phase-average trend method of separating trend from cycle.

rise. With the exception of Canada, and to a lesser extent the United Kingdom and the Netherlands, all countries considered here experienced, at that time, a fall in production which was comparable to, or much greater than, that which has occurred in the recent cycle. A similar pattern is observable with respect to inflation. All countries experienced declines during each of the last four recessions. While the falls in the late 1960s and early 1970s were in many cases modest, reductions from the high rates experienced during the mid-1970s and more recently were very substantial. In some countries, notably the United States, the recent fall in inflation has exceeded that of the mid-1970s. However, in other countries, notably Japan, where the peak inflation rate during the mid-1970s was much higher than in 1980, reductions during the mid-1970s were greater than those experienced recently. While we are conscious of the need to achieve reductions in the unprecedentedly high level of unemployment, particularly in Europe, we must remember that in 1975 the outlook for output and employment appeared equally disturbing, and, in many countries, the progress against inflation just as impressive, as they do today. Furthermore, despite the impressive gains of recent years inflation still remains around 5 per cent or higher in most countries. We should therefore be wary of providing too much stimulus to the economy on the grounds that inflation has been permanently defeated.

One further notable aspect of the present economic situation is the extent to which the cycles in individual countries have become synchronized. The upswing which started in 1967 in the OECD area as a whole began in individual countries at various times covering an 18 month span, while during the following cycle 20 months elapsed between the first and last countries' recoveries. During the expansion which preceded the first oil price rise and the recession which followed it, cyclical situations became more closely aligned and individual upturns during the mid-1970s began within a nine-month span. While recovery began in the United Kingdom considerably earlier than elsewhere and it is not clearly evident in France, cyclical positions in the other nine countries remain highly synchronized. Eight entered the expansion phase between August 1982 and February 1983, a six-month span, and the nineth (Italy) began a recovery only four months later, in June

1983. As international trade linkages reinforce domestic developments when cyclical movements become synchronized internationally, this may be a signal for caution. Inflationary pressures during 1973-74 and 1979-80, and deflationary pressures during the subsequent recessions, were alike strengthened by this international linkage, and a danger exists that this may recur.

Two further features concerning the cyclical behaviour of inflation stand out and these are summarized in table 2. First, the correspondence between cyclical troughs in output and associated troughs in inflation is weak. In a few cases, notably around 1967, trough rates of inflation occurred near or even before cyclical turning points, so that inflation began to rise as soon as the economy recovered. However, in many cases during the early-1970s upswing, and in all cases during the mid-1970s expansion, inflation continued falling well after recovery had begun. Second, while the speed with which inflation responded to recovery varied, all these recent cyclical expansions resulted in accelerations. Although oil price rises played a rôle during the 1970s, the accelerations were in most cases too large, and the variations across countries too great, to be attributable solely to these. Furthermore, in all cases except Japan in 1979, accelerations in inflation were under way *before* the oil shock, usually by a year or more. Past experience, therefore, serves as a warning that the favourable performance with respect to inflation that currently prevails in many countries is not a signal that the problem of inflation can be ignored. The hard-won gains of recent years can easily be dissipated if policies are inappropriate.

3. IMPLICATIONS FOR THE ROLE OF MONETARY POLICY IN THE PRESENT RECOVERY

While comparisons of the present recovery with the past should not be pushed too far - comparability is difficult because the above comparison does not extend to other factors such as fiscal policy, oil prices, and the international debt situation - some parallels with earlier cycles, particularly that beginning in 1975, are evident. As in 1969-70 and 1974, the monetary authorities in many countries adopted a tough anti-inflationary stance between 1979 and mid-1982. The result, as in previous periods of restriction, was success in reducing inflation at the

Past Cyclical Behaviour of Inflation [1]

	Late 1960s upswing			Early 1970s upswing			Mid-1970s upswing		
	Recovery begins	Month in which inflation associated with previous recession was a minimum	Acceleration of inflation during expansion (percentage points)	Recovery begins	Month in which inflation associated with previous recession was a minimum	Acceleration of inflation during expansion (percentage points)	Recovery begins	Month in which inflation associated with previous recession was a minimum	Acceleration of inflation during expansion (percentage points)
United States	July 67	April 67	3.9	Nov. 70	Jun. 72	9.3	Mar. 75	Dec. 76	9.9
Japan	Sept. 68	Feb. 69	6.1	Jan. 72	Jan. 72	22.5	Mar. 75	Mar. 79	6.7
Germany	May 67	Dec. 67	3.4	Dec. 71	April 72	2.9	Jul. 75	Oct. 78	3.7
France	Oct. 67	Jul. 67	4.1	May 71	June 71	10.5	May 75	Jan. 77	5.3
United Kingdom	Aug. 67	Aug. 67	4.9	Feb. 72	Jul. 72	21.1	Aug. 75	Jun. 78	14.5
Italy	Mar. 68	Sept. 68	4.7	April 72	Dec. 71	21.6	May 75	Jan. 76	12.1
Canada	Feb. 68	Aug. 68	2.0	Oct. 70	Dec. 70	11.1	Oct. 75	Nov. 76	7.3
Belgium	April 67	June 67	2.6	May 71	Dec. 70	13.2	Aug. 75	June 78	6.2
Denmark	n.a.	n.a.	n.a.	Q2.71	July 71	11.6	Mar. 75	Dec. 75	10.0
Netherlands	May 67	June 67	5.9	Dec. 71	July 72	3.8	Aug. 75	June 78	3.7
Switzerland	Q1.68	Aug. 68	5.8	Q2.72	May 72	5.6	Q1.75	Jan. 77	4.3

1) See notes for table 1.

cost of substantial falls in output and rises in unemployment. The fall in inflation and the severity of the recession both exceeded expectations, which gave rise to pressures on policy makers to attach greater priority to supporting activity and less to inflation control. Without a change in attitudes toward the rôle of monetary policy, and a recognition of the limits to what monetary policy can achieve on its own, the stage would have been set for a repeat of the mistakes of the past.

The present recovery had its origins in the United States where the previous tight stance of monetary policy was reversed in mid-1982. Monetary growth accelerated very sharply in North America. While to some extent this has been explained in terms of distortions associated with financial deregulation and innovations, it should be recalled that at this time U.S. short-term interest rates fell by almost half. This pattern is not very different from that associated with earlier cycles. However, given the increased recognition of the dangers of providing too much stimulus, U.S. monetary policy has subsequently moved back towards a more restrictive stance. Similarly, in Germany, persistent overshooting of target growth of central bank money was permitted in 1983, but a decision was made to reduce, and to adhere more closely to, the target for 1984. It is to be hoped that the authorities in these countries succeeded in their efforts to withdraw their early support in a sufficiently timely fashion, so that a reacceleration of inflation is not already in the pipeline.

However, I want to stress that such discretionary monetary policy is difficult to implement in practice. Shifting monetary policy in an expansionary direction and withdrawing support just at the right moment require both a well calibrated assessment of potential inflationary consequences and the nature of the changes being offset. For my own part I am sceptical of the ability of policymakers to adopt this sort of "fine tuning" approach to monetary policy successfully.

Despite past experience, there are pressures both within the United States and abroad to relax U.S. monetary policy to some extent. The reasons for such pressures are well known. The shift to a more cautious monetary policy stance in the United States during 1983 came at a time when large U.S. budget deficits put pressure on U.S. capital markets - pressures which will continue. These large public sector credit demands compete with private sector needs which also are large because of the sheer buoyancy of the recovery. These credit demands have contributed to very high real interest rates in the United States, to which I have referred to above. Furthermore, the combination of high real interest rates and the apparent greater profitability of investment opportunity in the private sector in the United States than elsewhere have led to huge capital flows into the United States, and these have put upward pressure on the dollar. These high real interest rates and the persistent strength of the dollar have led to several concerns:

- that high real interest rates, both in the United States and elsewhere, discourage productive private investment, which endangers the long-term sustainability of the recovery.
- that the depreciation of other currencies against the U.S. dollar gives rise to inflationary pressures in the rest of the world, again endangering the sustainability of their recoveries.
- that high U.S. interest rates and a high dollar worsen the international debt situation and threaten to disrupt the international financial system.

What can monetary policy contribute to mitigating these problems? I will examine each issue in turn.

3.1. Should monetary policy be eased to encourage private investment?

One development which would enhance the likelihood of a sustainable recovery would be that a greater share of increases in output be directed towards productive investment. This would help in two ways. First, by ensuring that recent improvements in productivity growth, which have been greater in some countries than would normally be expected on cyclical grounds alone, are sustained, high investment would make it easier for the economic system to provide higher real wages. Second, it would accelerate the incorporation of new technologies in the capital stock. Third, it would effectively increase overall capacity in the economy by reducing the likelihood of widespread supply bottlenecks emerging as demand expands.

One argument that is often heard is that monetary policy could directly favour investment by holding down interest rates through deliberate expansionary monetary policy action. However, we should recognize that an important factor contributing to the prevailing high level of real interest rates is the failure of expectations about inflation in the future to respond fully to recent successes in reducing it. This, in turn, reflects a continuing need for monetary authorities to reinforce their credibility with respect to non-accommodation of inflation. A strong possibility exists that markets would perceive such expansionary policies, which would involve extra money creation, as inflationary so that interest rates might even rise rather than fall. Even if this did not occur the beneficial effects would be transitory as inflation would tend to reaccelerate later in the cycle. Even though inflation is low at the present economic situation, I have noted that this has often been the case at similar stages in previous cycles. Provision of extra support through monetary measures on a temporary basis clearly courts the risk of a recurrence of these past experiences. At some stage a reduction in the rate of monetary expansion would be needed if the temporary support monetary growth rate was not to become a medium-term trend with inflationary consequences. The resulting credit squeeze would serve only to bring the recovery to an end.

A major stimulus to higher investment would be a restoration of adequate industrial profitability, as it would provide both the incentive and much of the financing. In addition, if the relative costs of labour are not too high, it would improve the outlook for employment. During 1983 there has been a widespread improvement in profitability compared to the depressed situation prevailing in 1982, but such improvements are normal in the early phase of recovery. What is required is that this improvement be durable. The question therefore arises as to what extent monetary policy can influence the distribution of income between wages and profits.

One way monetary policy influences profitability and, hence investment, is via its overall impact on demand and activity. To the extent that it can contribute to a high level of capacity utilisation, it can enhance profitability. However, since the scope for expanding demand is constrained by the need to prevent a reacceleration of inflation if the recovery is to be durable, little can be done in this area. A second, indirect, way in which monetary policy can influence profitability is by influencing the exchange rate. A strong real exchange rate may have a powerful and immediate adverse effect on profitability in those industries most exposed to international competition, while favouring real wages generally. Conversely, a low real exchange rate favours profits at the expense of real wages. This suggests that a monetary policy which would favour a low real exchange rate might enhance the prospects for a sustainable recovery via its effects on profitability.

There are, however, two major difficulties with this argument. First, depreciation of a currency implies appreciation of other currencies in terms of it. Thus, while this option is open to individual countries, it is not possible for all countries simultaneously to pursue this strategy. Second, an artificially low exchange rate would lead import prices and import-competing prices to be higher and would be likely to generate wage responses to compensate for the effect on real incomes. Furthermore, if the policy shows signs of being succesful, wages in the industries most favourably affected are likely to respond, eroding many of the gains. Given the overall accommodating monetary environment, this would also risk generating a wage/price spiral. In consequence, it will be necessary to look to *non-monetary* measures to assure sustained improvement in profitability and to encourage a high level of investment.

There is a wide range of non-monetary measures that would make a contribution. Some should be directed at enhancing the ability of economies to adapt to innovation and change, thereby making use of the opportunities that are offered by technical progress and changing international specialisation. These measures extend to taxation and public expenditure; the operation of product, labour and capital markets; and industrial, regional and competition policies. Easing the burden of payroll taxes and improving the flexibility of labour markets, for example, would contribute greatly to improved profitability, and hence investment. Perhaps most significant, from an international perspective, would be a rollback of protectionism, both in industrial countries and in the developing world. Other measures should be directed at generating a flow of savings to the credit markets sufficient to put sustainable downward pressure on interest rates and available to finance private investment. The recovery itself, by leading to higher incomes, will make some contribution by generating greater savings and lower marginal tax rates in some countries, notably the United States and the United Kingdom, may also be of assistance. The most important contribution in this regard, however, would be a reduction in structural budget deficits during the upswing, as these represent claims on the flow of financial resources to the credit markets.

This, however, lies beyond the main scope of my subject. It is not through the fine tuning of monetary policy that greater efficiency can be encouraged. The distinctive contribution that monetary policy can make is to contribute to improving expectations with respect to price and wage formation in general, which would help to provide a stable environment to allow these structural improvements to benefit OECD economies in the medium term. It should act as a restraint on any tendency for inflation to reaccelerate while providing "growing room" for real growth of output in circumstances where cost and price developments are favourable.

3.2. Should monetary policies be altered to stabilize world exchange rates?

High real interest rates in the United States, together with the sheer dynamism displayed by the U.S. economy, have led in recent years to persistant upward pressure on the dollar. To date, policy responses elsewhere have differed from country to country. In Europe, even though the precise timing of interest rate changes may have been affected by developments in the United States, policies do not broadly appear to have been tightened due to the dollar's strength: monetary growth in major countries has shown little tendency to undershoot targets or to be particularly slow; real interest rates, as noted earlier, are not far out of line with past behaviour in the early stages of recovery; and exchange rates have depreciated in real terms against the dollar (see table 3), by amounts ranging from 18 per cent (Switzerland) to more than 50 per cent (Belgium) since 1980. Canada, on the other hand, has adjusted interest rates to prevent major downward movements of its nominal exchange rate against the US currency. The result has been that real interest rates there, if not far out of line with those in the early stages of past recoveries, are quite high, particularly at the long end, while the real exchange rate against the United States has actually appreciated. Japan, which since 1973 has shown considerable willingness to let the exchange rate bear much of the burden of adjustment to external disturbances, has been particularly concerned that a weak yen would exacerbate protectionism in trading partners. Consequently, it has endeavoured to moderate any tendency toward weakness of the yen by keeping interest rates higher than might have been desirable on domestic grounds. As a result monetary growth has decelerated since 1981 while the real depreciation of the exchange rate against the dollar, about 15 per cent since 1980, has been considerably less than experiences by most European currencies.

Many economists have argued that the dollar has become seriously overvalued and that it is becoming more so, and that steps should be taken to correct the situation. Two adverse consequences of an excessively strong dollar are often stressed:

- internationally traded commodities, notably oil, are denominated in dollars, so a persistently rising dollar will have direct inflationary consequences elsewhere via its effect on the terms of trade and import prices. A related concern is that weak exchange rates and rising import prices will have adverse expectational effects.
- misaligned exchange rates discourage investment, distort industrial structure and, perhaps most importantly, encourage protectionism.

In my view, the first of these concerns should not be given too much weight provided that the situation is one in which there is upward pressure on the dollar alone, so that when it rises other countries' effective exchange rates are only marginally affected, and the authorities adhere to their main, domestic, objectives. Just as monetary policy should not accommodate inflation, it should not be tightened excessively to achieve a particular exchange rate objective vis-à-vis the dollar, as this would act to forestall recovery unnecessarily. Even though a traded commodity may be dollar denominated, the price, in dollar terms, is adjustable. Food, raw materials and energy prices normally respond, though possibly with a lag, to market forces regardless of the currency in which prices are set, while prices of manufactured goods depend mainly on exporters' costs and competitive conditions in the importers' markets. Thus a rising dollar is likely to result in dollar prices of most

TABLE 3

Real Exchange Rates, vis-à-vis US Dollar[a] (indices: 1980=100)

	1981.I	1981.II	1982.I	1982.II	1983.I	1983.II	1984.I [*]
Japan	102.9	91.8	82.1	77.3	85.5	84.5	84.5
Germany	83.8	76.1	72.8	70.9	70.3	66.1	64.4
France	88.2	78.7	75.3	67.9	69.0	64.1	63.0
United Kingdom	99.1	81.6	78.7	74.0	68.4	68.4	66.1
Italy	87.7	80.7	76.6	76.5	82.7	79.1	78.1
Canada	101.9	104.1	106.9	108.4	108.8	109.9	105.0
Belgium	82.2	71.6	61.5	55.0	54.9	49.4	48.6
Denmark	81.4	73.2	69.6	64.1	66.1	62.9	61.4
Netherlands	80.9	73.4	70.5	67.7	66.0	59.3	57.0
Switzerland	85.3	84.9	87.8	81.4	83.5	84.9	82.2

(a) Nominal exchange rates versus the dollar adjusted for differential movements in unit labour costs.
* Secretariat estimates.

internationally traded commodities which are, if not falling, rising more slowly than would otherwise be the case. The problem, then, is largely limited to trade in manufactured goods with the United States, which is not large enough to have an important inflationary impact in most OECD countries apart from Canada and perhaps Japan (almost entirely on the export side).

While countries other than the United States would undoubtedly be somewhat better off if the dollar had not risen so sharply since late 1980, it is difficult to establish, empirically, a large inflationary impact of the dollar's rise, even in Europe. Tables 4 and 5 show the behaviour of the terms of trade and import prices (relative to domestic prices) in recent years. While the United States has experienced a favourable movement in the terms of trade since the dollar began rising in 1980, in other countries they have rarely deviated by more than 5 per cent from what they were in 1980. Given the very divergent movement of real exchange rates against the dollar (table 3) the stability and similarity of behaviour of the terms of trade on major countries would be surprising if the dollar was the major influence. In particular, there is no apparent difference between the experiences of Canada and Japan, where substantial depreciation against the dollar has been resisted, and most European countries, where real depreciation against the dollar has been large. Import prices had some tendency to rise faster than domestic prices in Europe during early 1981, reflecting small adverse terms of trade movements at that time. Since then they have acted in many countries as a *restraining* factor on inflation, as reflected in the persistent fall in their price relative to domestic prices. While the expectational aspect of the problem remains, it is unlikely to be damaging for long in the absence of an observed inflationary stimulus from abroad.

The second concern about the structural distortions associated with misalignments is more worrying. Clearly, greater stability of exchange rates would contribute to a more generally stable environment, in which private sectors can respond flexibly to new technologies, changing market conditions and shifts in international competitiveness. But how far can monetary policy help to establish this greater stability?

It has long been recognized, as in the IMF Articles of Agreement, that exchange rate stability cannot be imposed from without by relying solely on such devices as trade restrictions, capital controls or exchange market intervention. If it is to occur, it must arise as a *consequence* of "convergence" of the economies in major countries. This convergence must be interpreted broadly in terms of performance, not only with respect to inflation but also in terms of profitability, labour market flexibility and the overall dynamism of private sectors; and likewise in terms of economic policies, in particular the compatibility of the mix of fiscal and monetary policies in major countries. Furthermore, given the importance of expectations in financial markets generally and exchange markets in particular, this convergence must be seen to be durable so that it becomes reflected in market assessments of likely future developments.

The contribution monetary policies can make is clear. They must be directed toward achieving a common low rate of inflation everywhere. What should that rate be? The answer is that countries should aim to

TABLE 4

Terms of Trade[a] (indices: 1980=100)

	1981.I	1981.II	1982.I	1982.II	1983.I	1983.II	1984.I
United States	104.4	109.5	115.6	114.5	121.2	121.2	125.5
Japan	100.0	100.6	101.9	99.3	100.1	98.9	100.3
Germany	97.1	95.9	98.0	98.6	100.4	100.1	99.6
France	97.5	98.6	103.8	101.0	104.2	105.5	105.0
UK	103.1	100.2	99.9	101.0	99.7	101.4	100.4
Italy	95.8	93.7	98.2	98.2	99.8	102.1	102.1
Canada	97.0	96.1	94.9	94.7	96.5	95.4	95.3
Belgium	96.6	95.5	95.6	95.9	95.8	95.6	95.3
Denmark	97.4	96.6	96.9	97.0	97.4	98.1	97.8
Netherlands	98.9	99.0	100.8	101.7	100.5	99.8	99.8
Switzerland	100.0	101.5	104.5	106.0	107.9	108.9	108.5

(a) Ratio of price deflators for exports to imports of goods and services.

TABLE 5

Relative Import Prices[a] (indices: 1980=100)

	1981.I	1981.II	1982.I	1982.II	1983.I	1983.II	1984.I
United States	96.2	89.3	83.5	82.6	77.3	77.7	75.1
Japan	97.2	98.8	97.3	100.1	92.9	92.0	88.3
Germany	104.4	106.3	103.7	102.1	99.4	99.0	99.6
France	103.4	103.2	98.9	102.3	96.7	97.3	96.7
United Kingdom	94.0	98.6	97.3	96.7	100.0	98.5	98.5
Italy	105.4	110.3	101.9	100.7	92.4	91.8	92.4
Canada	101.2	99.4	96.2	93.9	89.0	88.8	89.9
Belgium	106.7	108.9	112.6	113.0	113.9	113.9	114.6
Denmark	105.9	107.1	106.4	106.0	˙103.8	102.4	103.0
Netherlands	108.7	110.1	106.4	104.6	105.0	105.7	105.8
Switzerland	99.5	96.4	91.7	89.4	87.4	86.6	86.6

(a) Ratio of price deflator for imports of goods and services to the GDP deflator.

converge at a rate not very different from zero, even though where inflation remains relatively high further adjustment efforts will at times be painful. There are several reasons for this. First, and as I have argued already, high inflation is inconsistent with the kind of stable economic environment that is necessary if industrial countries are again to enjoy the high growth and employment that prevailed during the 1950s and 1960s. Thus longer term output and employment performance is likely to be improved by achieving low rates of inflation. Second, any indication that the monetary authorities are prepared to accommodate high rates of inflation would influence expectations and adversely affect the formation of wages and prices. Third, several countries, notably Japan, have already reduced inflation to very low rates. To aim for a significantly higher common inflation rate would require these countries to sacrifice the gains they have already made.

The convergence of inflation to a common, low rate, however, might in itself be insufficient to stabilize exchange rates unless convergence of policy mixes and performance were more general. As long as this wider convergence is not fully achieved it would be a mistake to adjust monetary policies, particularly in Europe, to the fortunes of the dollar. It would be better to allow exchange rates to take most of the adjustment while monetary policy is oriented to domestic inflation control, particularly since, as I have argued above, dollar exchange rate-inflation links are difficult to identify.

3.3 Should OECD monetary policies be eased to help the international debt situation?

The threat of severe disruption to the international financial system which came to light in 1982, with a number of countries encountering severe liquidity problems, has been contained. However, it remains a source of concern. A case by case approach has been adopted up to now, and adjustment programmes under IMF auspices have been put in place in a number of countries. Their ultimate success in some cases remains uncertain, and a number of problems are yet to be dealt with. Industrial countries have a vital interest in the success of these adjustment efforts.

The loss of creditworthiness in many countries and their inability to service their debt undoubtedly owed much to their inflationary policies, and successful corrections in these policies must continue to form the basis for a solution to the problem. However, a fundamental development that set the stage for the debt crisis was the sharp increase in ratios of debt to exports and interest obligations to exports in a large number of countries during the early 1980s. The future resolution of the present problems will depend on the evolution of these variables, which in part lie outside developing countries' control. Action by OECD countries to assist developing countries' exports or to reduce their interest burden could in principle be helpful. What rôle can monetary policy play here?

It has sometimes been suggested that more accommodating monetary policies in the OECD area, particularly in the United States, would contribute to a resolution of the debt problem. This is linked with the view that an artificial lowering of interest rates might ease the immediate problem, both by reducing the burden of interest payments and by stimulating, for a time, OECD demand and hence developing countries' exports. However, this would be at the risk of allowing the expansion in the OECD to proceed too rapidly, generating a reacceleration of inflation and necessitating a recurrence of restrictive policies. This, in the end, would result in a worsening, rather than an improvement, of the situation.

Here again, the most appropriate course for monetary policy remains one formulated in a longer term perspective, aimed at ensuring the sustainability of the present recovery. A successful and durable recovery in the OECD would assist export revenues, and possibly the terms of trade, of developing countries for a long period. This would make their debt servicing burden increasingly less onerous and the gains would persist. It would also serve to make investment in primary industries more attractive, encouraging private capital flows in the form of direct investment and ensuring adequate supplies of commodities in the future when demand has fully recovered.

The most important supplementary policy measures which would contribute in a sound and sustainable way to easing the burden on developing countries would be a forceful rollback of protectionist measures. As I have stressed earlier, it is in the interests of all countries to move in this direction. The rollback should apply to all countries generally, rather than offering special concessions to large debtors only. This would strengthen market forces in debtor countries, encouraging more efficient use of resources, as well as encouraging exports by opening markets abroad. However strongly debtor countries implement domestic adjustment programmes, they will require export earnings to service their debt successfully. If they are to achieve their goals, markets in industrial countries must be open to their products.

A second set of measures which would assist developing countries' efforts to adjust would be a substantial reduction in OECD budget deficits as the recovery proceeds, reductions to which OECD governments are already committed for various domestic reasons. Since most of the external debt of developing countries is either short term or carries a floating interest rate, the tendency for budget deficits to make interest rates higher than they would otherwise be exacerbates developing countries' debt servicing burden. As a large share of the external debt in question is denominated in dollars, particularly for some of the countries whose situation is most difficult, a reduction in the budget deficit in the United States, if this led to a decline of the dollar's exchange rate as well as in interest rates, would be particularly helpful. More generally, reductions in public sector borrowing would lead to a more appropriate volume of capital exports in accordance with the OECD's traditional rôle.

4.   CONCLUDING REMARKS

The economic recovery which is now under way in a number of countries, and is proceeding particularly rapidly in the United States, is the fourth widespread upswing in the OECD area since the late 1960s. Over the period spanned by the three previous cycles there has been a general deterioration in performance with respect to employment, growth and inflation, compared to the broadly satisfactory record which was achieved until the late 1960s. Inflation has tended to accelerate, sometimes alarmingly, as cyclical peaks have been approached. By the second half of the 1970s its reduction had become an overriding objective. In many countries policies of steadily decelerating monetary growth were pursued in order to achieve this aim. Inflation has come down almost everywhere, although the cost in terms of output and employment have been high.

Looking forward, we must avoid the mistakes of the past. The rôle of monetary policy is a limited but important one. If it is directed steadily toward maintaining momentum in the fight against inflation, extending the gains of recent years, it will contribute to the creation of conditions which will allow the present recovery to proceed sustainably. However, monetary policy alone cannot solve all the problems currently facing OECD economies; in particular it cannot by itself guarantee durable economic growth.

Monetary policies, directed toward inflation control must be supported by complementary adjustments in other macroeconomic policy instruments. Structural budget deficits must be reduced in those countries where they remain excessive in order to ensure an adequate flow of finance for productive investment and to ease strains in capital and exchange markets. Measures should be implemented to roll back protectionism and strenghten the international trading system. In addition, policies to promote a more diversified pattern of capital flows to developing countries, including official flows through the multilateral institutions and direct foreign investment, should be put in place.

If the recovery is to be sustainable however, and we are to enjoy a return to the more prosperous environment that characterized most of the 1950s and 1960s, it will be necessary to do more than simply redress the main macroeconomic imbalances. High levels of new investment are required in order to make the best use of advances in technology. The restoration of industrial profitability which is now under way must continue if this is to occur. Structural policies, based more consistently and effectively than is now the case on the use of markets, are essential, particularly in regard to labour markets, financial markets and trade policies. The recovery now under way provides an environment conducive to implementing policies which will strenghten the market mechanism and enhance the resilience and flexibility of OECD economies: the challenge now is to make full use of this opportunity.

CHART A

CYCLICAL BEHAVIOUR OF MONETARY INDICATORS

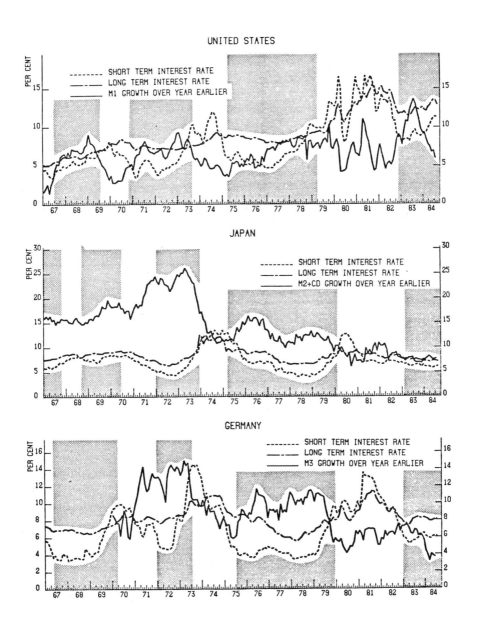

334

FRANCE

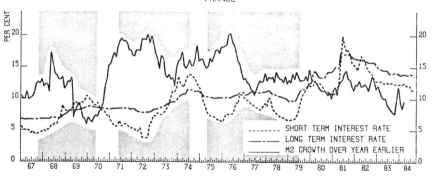

UNITED KINGDOM

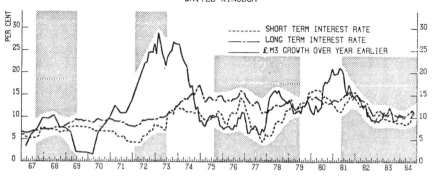

ITALY

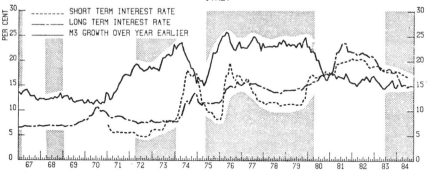

CANADA

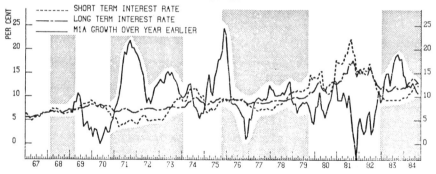

CHART A (continued)

BELGIUM

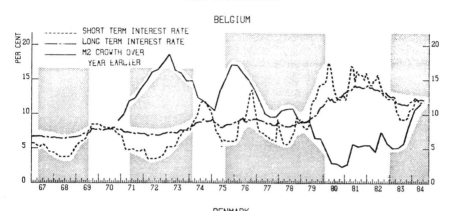

DENMARK

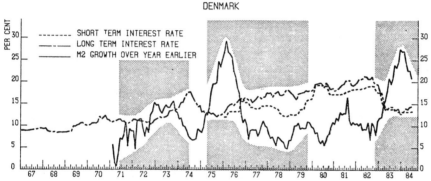

NETHERLANDS

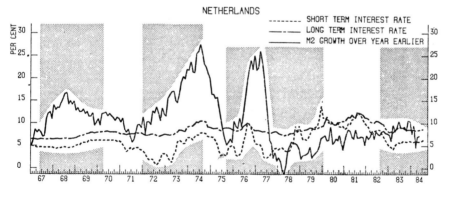

SWITZERLAND

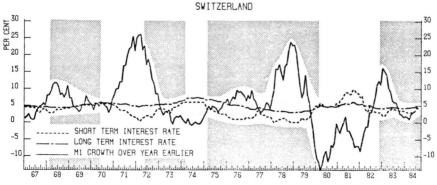

CHART B

CYCLICAL BEHAVIOUR OF REAL INTEREST RATES

[Real interest rates correspond to the nominal interest rates
shown in Chart A adjusted for changes in consumer prices over a year earlier.]

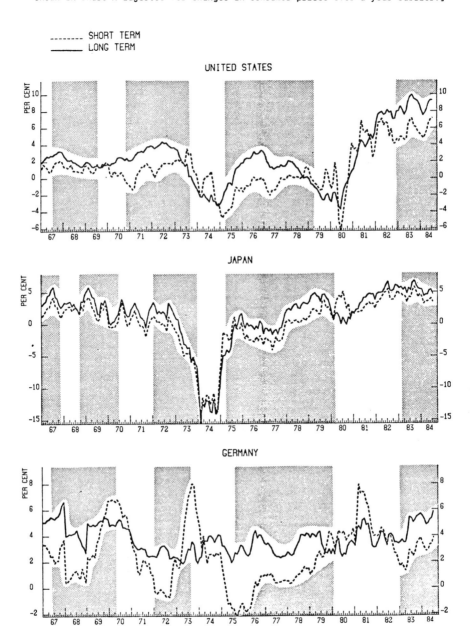

CHART B (continued)

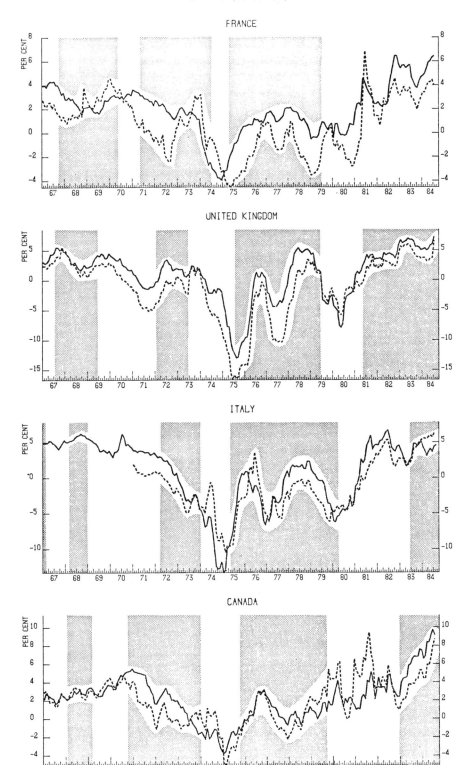

338

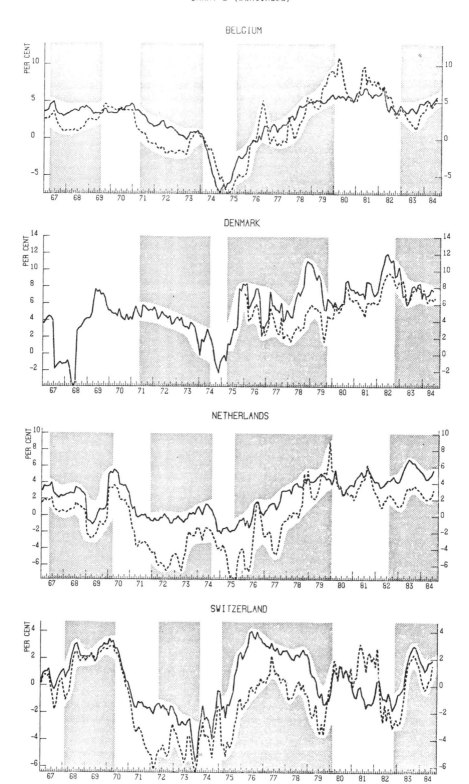

FINANCIAL AND MONETARY POLICY STUDIES

1. Multinational Enterprises – Financial and Monetary Aspects.
   Editors: J.S.G. Wilson and C.F. Scheffer, with 16 contributors.
   1974. ISBN 90-286-0124-4
   (SUERF Colloquium Nottingham University, England, April 1973)
2. Floating Exchange Rates – The Lessons of Recent Experience.
   Editors: H. Fournier and J.E. Wadsworth, with 14 contributors.
   1976. ISBN 90-286-0565-7
   (SUERF Colloquium Venice, October 1974)
3. The Development of Financial Institutions in Europe, 1956–76.
   Editors: J.E. Wadsworth, J.S.G. Wilson and F. Fournier, with 26 contributors.
   1977. ISBN 90-286-0337-9
   (SUERF Colloquium Brussels, April 1976)
4. New Approaches in Monetary Policy.
   Editors: J.E. Wadsworth and F. Léonard de Juvigny, with 29 contributors.
   1979. ISBN 90-286-0848-6
   (SUERF Colloquium Wiesbaden, September 1977)
5. Europe and the Dollar in the World-wide Disequilibrium.
   Editor: J.R. Sargent, with 17 contributors.
   1981. ISBN 90-286-0700-5
   (SUERF Colloquium Basel, Switzerland, May 1979)
6. Bank Management in a Changing Domestic and International Environment: The Challenges of the Eighties.
   Editors: Donald E. Fair and F. Léonard de Juvigny, with 25 contributors.
   1982. ISBN 90-247-2606-9
   (SUERF Colloquium Helsingør, Denmark, October 1980)
7. International Lending in a Fragile World Economy.
   Editors: Donald E. Fair in co-operation with Raymond Bertrand, with 25 contributors.
   1983. ISBN 90-247-2809-6
   (SUERF Colloquium Vienna, April 1982)
8. Currency Competition and Monetary Union.
   Editor: Pascal Salin.
   1984. ISBN 90-247-2817-7
9. Government Policies and the Working of Financial Systems in Industrialized Countries.
   Editors: Donald E. Fair in co-operation with F. Léonard de Juvigny, with 24 contributors.
   1984. ISBN 90-247-3076-7
10. Jelle Zijlstra, A Central Banker's View.
    Editors: C. Goedhart, G.A. Kessler, J. Kymmell and F. de Roos.
    1985. ISBN 90-247-3184-4
11. Monetary Conditions for Economic Recovery.
    Editors: C. van Ewijk and J.J. Klant.
    1985. ISBN 90-247-3219-0